Date: 1/27/22

**363.68 DRA
Drabelle, Dennis,
The power of scenery :
Frederick Law Olmsted and**

publication supported by a grant from
The Community Foundation for Greater New Haven
as part of the *Urban Haven Project*

The
POWER of
SCENERY

Frederick Law Olmsted and the
Origin of National Parks

DENNIS DRABELLE

University of Nebraska Press   Lincoln

Library of Congress Cataloging-in-Publication Data
Names: Drabelle, Dennis, author.
Title: The power of scenery: Frederick Law Olmsted
and the origin of national parks / Dennis Drabelle.
Description: Lincoln: University of Nebraska Press,
[2021] | Includes bibliographical references and index.
Identifiers: LCCN 2021015299
ISBN 9781496220776 (hardback)
ISBN 9781496230133 (epub)
ISBN 9781496230140 (pdf)
Subjects: LCSH: Olmsted, Frederick Law, 1822-1903. |
National parks and reserves—United States—History. |
Conservationists—United States—Biography. |
Yosemite National Park (Calif.)—History. | Yellowstone
National Park—History. | Niagara Falls State Park
(N.Y.)—History. | United States—Environmental
conditions—19th century. | BISAC: HISTORY / United
States / 19th Century | NATURE / Environmental
Conservation & Protection
Classification: LCC SB482.A4 D73 2021 |
DDC 363.6/80973—dc23
LC record available at https://lccn.loc.gov/2021015299

Set in Fournier MT Pro by Laura Buis.
Designed by L. Auten.

In memory of my grandmothers,
Claudia Franklin Drabelle
and Mabel Boyer

CONTENTS

List of Photographs   xi

Preface   xiii

Acknowledgments   xv

Introduction   xvii

1. You Can Have the Arno   1

2. Land of the Free and
   Home of the Sublime   13

3. The Counterexample   19

4. An Idea in Embryo   27

5. The Landscape Reader   39

6. How to Sell a Park Bill   61

7. In Praise of
   Diligent Indolence   75

8. The Nervous Promoter   91

9. Contested Ground   101

10. Whiffs of Sulfur   115

11. The Man Who Picked
    Up Stones Running   135

12. Saving Gravel   151

13. A Shaky Start   165

14. Cleaning Men   179

15. Going Out with
    Two Bangs   189

16. The Olmsteds   199

Notes   217

Index   237

PHOTOGRAPHS

Following page 90

1. At or near Yale College, ca. 1847
2. Olmsted as a cape-wearing young dandy
3. Carleton Watkins's 1861 photo of Cathedral Rock
4. California senator John Conness
5. Massachusetts newspaper editor Samuel Bowles
6. Geologist Ferdinand Hayden
7. Old Faithful by William Henry Jackson
8. Olmsted in his later years
9. Horace Albright with Charlie Cook in 1922
10. Mammoth Hot Springs by William Henry Jackson
11. Nathaniel Langford

PREFACE

Parks are so widespread today—as green spaces designed and maintained in cities or as wild tracts preserved in a more or less natural state by governments all over the world—that they seem to be an age-old feature of civilized life. In fact, before the nineteenth century, urban parks open to all were rarities, and public wilderness parks did not exist. The first example of the latter, Yosemite state park in California, wasn't established until 1864; America's and the world's first national park, Yellowstone, followed eight years later.

This book is an attempt to explain where the idea for national parks came from. The answer given by the great American landscape architect Frederick Law Olmsted was "the Genius of Civilization." But this particular manifestation of civilization's genius can be traced to multiple sources: shifts in how humans looked at and spoke of the natural world; the determination of the young United States to shake off its dependence on European culture and monuments; human cravings for outdoor rest and recreation; halfway measures to satisfy those appetites, sometimes taken without official sanction; impatience with these demotic and imperfect solutions; and a growing sense that Americans—and, after them, people everywhere—were standing idly by as too much of nature's bounty was tamed or ruined with little regard for the future.

The park movement had its standard-bearers, of course. The British philosopher Edmund Burke codified the use of the word *sublime* as a descriptor of nature's scary side. The American artist George Catlin's fascination with Indians inspired him to call for the founding of a "nation's park" in which they could maintain their traditional ways of life. The Irish immigrant John Conness, in his single term as a U.S. senator, sold his colleagues on an innovative bill to preserve Yosemite, which became the prototype for national parks. The geologist Ferdinand Hayden explored Yellowstone country with a scientist's attentiveness and a booster's gusto, then took the lead in persuading Congress to set it aside as a national park. A slew of painters and photographers—especially Frederic Church, Albert Bierstadt, Carleton E. Watkins, and William H. Jackson—helped make spectacular American natural features the glory of the nation and the envy of the world.

As this book's subtitle suggests, however, one of those men stood out from the others as a shaper of national parks. In 1865 Olmsted wrote a primer for managing Yosemite, which contributed to the intellectual climate that made establishing Yellowstone as the first national park feasible. Later Olmsted was in the forefront of the campaign to right a binational wrong he had first noticed as a child: the sad state of North America's first stellar tourist attraction, Niagara Falls.

Olmsted's reputation rests largely on his long and distinguished career as an analyst, remodeler, and groomer of landscapes. He had the good fortune to flourish at a time when much of America was still empty canvas, and he made the most of his chances to paint on it. From Boston to Asheville, from Atlanta to Buffalo, from Chicago to Berkeley, and from the U.S. Capitol Grounds to the Stanford University campus, Olmsted put his stamp on his homeland more widely and lastingly than anyone after him—and before him perhaps only Thomas Jefferson, in making the Louisiana Purchase, had a greater influence on the American scene. "Of all American artists," said nineteenth-century critic Charles Eliot Norton, Olmsted "stands first in the production of great works which answer the needs and give expression to the life of our immense and miscellaneous democracy."[1]

As a rule, Olmsted worked by manipulating nature, a prime example being his colossal makeover of the site for Central Park in midtown Manhattan. Yet when confronted with mesmerizing expanses of raw nature in the California backcountry, he had the sense to lay down his tools and urge a hands-off policy, which ultimately became the norm—perhaps the ideal is a better term—for American national parks. For four decades in the latter part of the nineteenth century, Frederick Law Olmsted and the Genius of Civilization were one, and national parks were their legacy.

ACKNOWLEDGMENTS

This book flows from three sources in my writing past. First came a chapter on the movement to restore Frederick Law Olmsted's urban parks as closely as possible to his original designs, in *The Art of Landscape Design* (1990), a book I wrote for the National Endowment for the Arts. The assigning editor was the endowment's Marcia Sartwell, to whom I owe my interest in all things Olmsted. The second source is my article "The Most Beautiful Street in Berkeley," about the few blocks surviving from Olmsted's first tryout of his parkway idea. The piece appeared that same year in an issue of the *East Bay Express*, whose editor, John Raeside, gave writers the rare luxury of (almost) more column inches than they knew what to do with.

Source number three is a 2016 article on Ferdinand Hayden for the *Pennsylvania Gazette*, the magazine of my alma mater the University of Pennsylvania. By then I had published dozens of pieces in the *Gazette* (there have been several more since), and I am grateful to its longtime editor, John Prendergast, for letting me pursue just about any Penn-related subject that strikes my fancy.

As always, my spouse, Michael Bell, was my in-house editor. This book has benefited greatly from his attentiveness to narrative structure, historical accuracy, and geography. The best advice I can give young writers is this: see if you can find a partner or faithful friend who will save you from literary missteps as tough-lovingly as Mike does for me.

I am much indebted to Douglas P. Wheeler, who hired me to work at the U.S. Department of the Interior in 1971 and took me along a couple of years later when he moved from the department's office of legislation to the domain ruled by the electrifying Nathaniel Reed, assistant secretary for fish and wildlife and parks. It was while working for Nat and Doug that I first encountered the rich history of the national parks, edited the department's 1977 "Preliminary Urban Parks Study," and drafted replies to peppery letters from Horace Albright, who in his retirement was happy to share his thoughts on how to run the national parks. Doug also vetted portions of the manuscript for this book, and I thank him for his suggestions.

My passion for wilderness parks predates my years at Interior. The fire was originally lit by James L. Murphy, whose contagious interest in camping and hiking crystallized into a five-week trip from our hometown, St. Louis, to the Canadian Rockies, which he led in 1962. I was lucky enough to take part in that glorious adventure.

Judy Carter kindly put me up at her house in Alexandria, Virginia, while I commuted to the Library of Congress; Kathy Woodrell of the LOC staff graciously helped me with my research there. I'm also grateful to two former colleagues at the *Washington Post*, Robert Mitchell and Frances Stead Sellers; Dede Petri and Lucy Howliss at the National Association for Olmsted Parks; architectural historian Katie Eggers Comeau; Professor Cheryl Foster at the University of Rhode Island; Professor Brian C. Kalt at Michigan State University College of Law; and Sue Jorgensen, Constance Casey, Konrad Kestering, and Brad Pomeroy. Thanks also to the folks at the North Carolina Arboretum in Asheville (which occupies land that once belonged to the Biltmore estate), who suffered my presence in their library day after day as I consulted their set of the Johns Hopkins edition of Olmsted's papers.

My editor at Bison Books, Bridget Barry, has been a pleasure to work with from start to finish—and both stages will stick in my mind. Her enthusiastic reaction to the book proposal I sent her in the spring of 2019 gave me the kind of boost a writer needs. And when the completed manuscript arrived in Lincoln with some flab on it, Bridget skillfully and patiently helped me reduce the text to the fitter version you hold in your hand. Finally, I want to thank Joyce Bond for her painstaking and skillful copyedit of the manuscript—as a former editor myself, I know how much this book has benefited from her attentiveness.

INTRODUCTION

The setting is a smoke- and beard-filled room, probably in San Francisco. The time is November 1865. The occasion is a rump meeting of the Yosemite Park Commission, which owes its existence to the year-old law that transferred title to Yosemite Valley and the Mariposa Grove of sequoia trees from the federal government to the state of California. The state has agreed to manage the tracts as an awkwardly configured park—the grove stands fifteen miles south of the valley, and the land in between was left out of the transfer. Regardless of shape, there is no precedent for such an entity. Congress ordered the state's governor to appoint eight commissioners to take care of it, and three of them have gathered behind the others' backs.

The commission's great catch was Frederick Law Olmsted, whose fame as superintendent and co-designer of New York's Central Park had preceded him westward. He moved to California in 1863 to take charge of the Mariposa Estate (not to be confused with the Mariposa Grove), a cluster of gold mines on a large private tract in the Sierra Nevada foothills. The state's governor, Frederick Low, was ex officio the Yosemite Commission's ninth member and chairman, but Olmsted had become its de facto leader. Although Yosemite was his first stab at planning a nonurban park, Olmsted seemed to know just what should be done with it. He poured his thoughts—eight thousand words' worth—into what he called "a preliminary report" on how to manage the majestic valley, its supporting cast of streams and foliage, and the breathtaking big-tree grove.

A bully opportunity to air these thoughts soon presented itself. Touring the West and closing in on Yosemite was a party of politicians headed by the speaker of the U.S. House of Representatives, Indiana Republican Schuyler Colfax, and trailed by several journalists, some of them working for influential eastern papers. Olmsted arranged for the two groups—the barnstorming easterners and the California park commissioners—to converge in Yosemite Valley, where he could try out his report on them.

The document they listened to him read was strikingly novel, all the more so for coming from the pen of a man known as the director of a massive engineering project that had magicked a raw strip of Manhattan real estate into an urban oasis. Olmsted applied to Yosemite the first principle behind his great New York project: a park should belong to and be usable by everyone. Then came a recommendation tailored specifically to this, the first public park in the wilds: leave it in its natural state, permitting only such minor additions as a road or two for better access and a handful of rustic structures to accommodate visitors. The report was well received, and Olmsted's fellow commissioners seemed to be in accord on what to do next: forward it to the governor as written.

Now, a few months later in the smoky room, three sneaky commissioners—Josiah Whitney, William Ashburner, and Israel Ward Raymond—are having second thoughts. As director of the state's geological survey, Whitney has the governor's ear. Whitney has soured on Olmsted's report because it calls for appropriating $37,000 for the roads, cabins, and assorted other expenses—a sum the geologist fears will come from his agency's coffers. In the grip of NOOMB (not out of my budget) myopia, he brings his co-conspirators around to his point of view.

The three dissidents have no idea they are sidetracking a visionary blueprint for managing a national park seven years before the first official holder of that title, Yellowstone, will come into existence. But they can hardly have missed the part of Olmsted's document that teaches a stirring civics lesson: "It is the main duty of government, if it is not the sole duty of government, to provide means of protection for all its citizens in the pursuit of happiness against the obstacles, otherwise insurmountable, which the selfishness of individuals or combinations of individuals is liable to interpose to that pursuit."[1] As Olmsted sees it, Yosemite has the potential to close out the era in which the prize manifestations of nature's beauty have been reserved for the wealthy.

Nonetheless, Whitney, Ashburner, and Raymond advise the governor to quash the report. Not only does Low accede, he also lies to the legislature, telling them that no Yosemite report exists.

Afterward, Olmsted gets a consoling letter from Samuel Bowles, one of the newspapermen present at the gathering in Yosemite Valley, a fellow workaholic with whom Olmsted had already struck up a friendship: "That was shabby treatment of you by Whitney, & without explanation, too. I have done some profanity on the subject."[2] The record is silent as to whether Olmsted did any profanity of his own, but he did not retaliate as a twentieth- or twenty-first-century draftsman might, by leaking his report to a friendly legislator or scandal-mongering reporter. Olmsted may have considered such tactics beneath him, or maybe his mind simply was elsewhere. In the next few months, he quit his Mariposa Estate post, resigned from the Yosemite Commission, and prepared to return to the East. His splendid Yosemite analysis went into his files, where it stayed buried for almost a century.

Buried but influential all the same.

THE POWER OF SCENERY

You Can Have the Arno 1

Americans have been famous—or infamous, if you prefer—for their swaggering self-confidence for such a long time that it's easy to forget that we were once an envious people, painfully aware of how poorly our culture stacked up against that of almost any European country. The part played by this national inferiority complex in the development of national parks is the theme of this chapter, and the best person to introduce it may be Charles Dickens, who, for all his good intentions, joined the crowd of British travelers who wrote disparagingly about the American customs and achievements.

When the twenty-nine-year-old novelist set off on his first visit to the United States in January 1842, he had a crush on the place. As a confirmed democrat, Dickens anticipated reveling in the company of "the freest people on earth," who were also his "distant countrymen."[1] He had no intention of joining the legion of predecessors who had served up American foibles and faults as so much red meat.

Before the era of sports heroes and movie stars, the reigning celebrities tended to be generals, statesmen, concert pianists, or authors, and Dickens came to the United States as a literary titan. His first four novels, *The Pickwick Papers*, *Oliver Twist*, *Nicholas Nickleby*, and *The Old Curiosity Shop*, had all been best sellers, both at home and in the United States.

Dickens's next book, *Barnaby Rudge*, was a departure for him—a historical novel about the anti-Catholic Gordon Riots of 1780—and a letdown, selling only about half as many copies as *The Old Curiosity Shop*. Afterward Dickens talked his publisher into sending him on a jaunt to America, where his muse could rally while he gathered material for a travel book.

At first Dickens enjoyed one worshipful American reception after another. "I can give you no conception of my welcome here," he crowed in a letter to an English friend shortly after disembarking in Boston. "There never was a king or emperor upon the earth so cheered and followed by crowds and entertained in public at splendid balls and dinners, and waited on by public bodies and deputations of all kinds."[2]

The adulation lasted a bit longer, but Dickens's euphoria did not, especially when bumptious fans wouldn't let him alone. His pique ripened into outright hostility after a dinner honoring him in Boston. He took the occasion to speak out against the lack of U.S. copyright protection for foreign authors, and the next day's newspapers told him to mind his own business. When Dickens elaborated on his complaint in Hartford, the Connecticut papers came down on him even harder, and he received hate mail.

Dickens's copyright grievance was both legitimate—he was losing thousands of dollars in royalties to pirated editions of his works—and less self-serving than his detractors may have supposed. Not only were foreign authors' books being shamelessly reprinted without permission in the States, but American authors were getting the same shabby treatment in England.

Unaware of or indifferent to the effects of book piracy on their own authors, many Americans took Dickens's complaint for a national insult and the novelist himself for a crybaby. "The wonder is that a breathing man can be found with temerity enough to suggest to the Americans the possibility of their having done wrong," he groused in a letter to a friend. The copyright brouhaha overshadowed the rest of Dickens's six-month American stay.[3]

Back in England, Dickens published his scathing travelogue *American Notes* in late 1842. Among his numerous targets were the foliage (gaze out the window of an American train and you see "mile after mile of stunted trees"); steamboats ("the wonder is, not that there should be so many fatal accidents, but that any journey should be safely made"); corn bread ("almost as good for the digestion as a kneaded pincushion"); and table manners ("the gentlemen thrust the broad-bladed knives and the two pronged forks further down their throats than I ever saw the same weapons go before, except in the hands of a skilful juggler").[4] But Americans had the last laugh. The *New York Herald* helped itself to *American Notes*, reprinting the book in its entirety without permission less than twenty-four hours after the first English copies reached the States.

The *Herald* could get away with that sort of thing until 1891, when the United States finally enacted an international copyright law. In the interim, a mellowed Dickens had revisited the United States and noticed what he described as "amazing changes . . . around me on every side," including "changes in the graces and amenities of life, [and] changes in the Press, without whose advancement no advancement can take place anywhere."[5]

Aside from Dickens, the main foreign irritant to Americans' thin skin was a woman who had made her way down a New Orleans gangplank in 1827: Fanny Trollope, mother of future novelist Anthony. Before returning home almost four years later to write a peppery two-volume account of her travels called *Domestic Manners of the Americans* (1832), Fanny Trollope had roamed widely and trained her gimlet eye on American ways. Not only did she observe slavery's direct effects on its victims, but she also was among the first to notice a systemic ill that Frederick Law Olmsted was to harp on a generation later: the degrading effects of slavery on the whole society that sanctions and defends it.

Some of the lesser American faults noted by Fanny Trollope were immediately obvious, such as Manhattan's feral pigs, which acted as community garbage disposals, dining on slops dumped in the streets and alleys by residents with no better way to get rid of them; the widespread contempt for Indians; and the ubiquitous male habit of spitting, an output of tobacco chewing. Most telling for our purposes, however, was a national character trait that took a little time to manifest itself: the pervasive touchiness that Dickens later railed against, a sulky resistance to even the slightest criticism of American mores or institutions. As Fanny Trollope put it:

A single word indicative of doubt, that any thing, or every thing, in that country is not the very best in the world, produces an effect which must be seen and felt to be understood. If the citizens of the United States were indeed the devoted patriots they call themselves, they would surely not thus encrust themselves in the hard, dry stubborn persuasion, that they are the first and best of the human race, that nothing is to be learnt, but what they are able to teach, and that nothing is worth having, which they do not possess.[6]

In spite of the author's badmouthing—or maybe because of it—Americans queued up to buy *Domestic Manners*. During its first year alone, the book ran to four editions in the United States and the same number in England; it soon appeared in French, German, Spanish, and Dutch translations. Some critics dismissed its author as a biased Tory, and "trollopize" became a vogue verb for trashing the United States. After making his own American visit, Fanny's son Anthony weighed in on *Domestic Manners*: "My mother had thirty years previously written a very popular, but, as I had thought, a somewhat unjust book about our cousins over the water. She had seen what was distasteful in the manners of a young people, but had hardly recognized their energy."[7]

Another British writer had noticed and lauded that very quality. In 1839 Capt. Frederick Marryat, best known for his seafaring adventure novels—his big hit was *Mr. Midshipman Easy*—published *A Diary in America*, based on a two-year residence. "America is a wonderful country," Marryat declared, "endowed by the Omnipotent with natural advantages which no other can boast of. . . . At present all is energy and enterprise; every thing is in a state of transition, but of rapid improvement."[8] It was possible, though, to write off Marryat as an exception that proved the rule, for he had an American mother.

Mark Twain vouched for Fanny Trollope in marginal notes to his personal copy of *Domestic Manners*: "She knew her subject well, and she set it forth fairly and squarely, without any weak ifs and ands and buts. . . . She did not gild us; and neither did she whitewash us. . . . [S]he was merely telling the truth, and this indignant nation knew it."[9]

At least Dickens and Fanny Trollope had spent time in the States, which was more than could be said for the influential English art critic John Ruskin. "I have kind invitations to visit America," he sniffed, "[but] I could not even for a couple of months live in a country so miserable as to possess no castles."[10]

Early nineteenth-century Americans resented Dickens's and Fanny Trollope's critiques all the more because they joined an onslaught of volumes and articles written by disillusioned European visitors. The unkindest cut may have been made by the English wit Sydney Smith, who had called

You Can Have the Arno

attention to American failings by firing a series of rhetorical questions in an 1820 issue of the *Edinburgh Review*:

> In the four quarters of the globe, who reads an American book? or goes to an American play? or looks at an American picture or statue? What does the world yet owe to American physicians or surgeons? What new substances have their chemists discovered? or what old ones have they analyzed? What new constellations have been discovered by the telescopes of Americans—what have they done in the mathematics? Who drinks out of American glasses? or eats from American plates? or wears American coats or gowns? or sleeps in American blankets?—Finally, under which of the old tyrannical governments of Europe is every sixth man a slave, whom his fellow creatures may buy and sell and torture?[11]

Independence had come with a hidden cost: Americans had forfeited their membership in the European culture club, leaving themselves to make the best of their own derivative and second-rate art, music, architecture, and literature, along with their flawed, slavery-sanctioning constitution. So many other visitors from the Old World struck a note similar to Smith's that America's first professional man of letters, Washington Irving, played defense. "We attach too much consequence to these attacks," he wrote in his essay "English Writers on America," circa 1820. "They cannot do us any essential injury. . . . All the writers of England united . . . could not conceal our rapidly growing importance and matchless prosperity."[12] His contemporary James Fenimore Cooper took a different tack. A decade after Irving, by which time the tally of book-length American critiques by foreigners exceeded forty, Cooper published a mock travelogue called *Notions of the Americans: Picked Up by a Travelling Bachelor*. Spoofing the anti-American travel book became a subgenre of its own, with such entries as Royall Tyler's *Yankey in London*, Charles Jared Ingersoll's *Inchiquin, the Jesuit's Letters, during a Late Residence in the United States*, and James Kirke Paulding's *John Bull in America, or The New Munchausen*, the Baron Munchausen being a notorious German spinner of tall tales.

While those authors provided comic relief, one indigenous travel writer attacked the problem directly by shining light on some of America's little-known assets. After turning out a series of books on his wanderings in Europe, Africa, and Asia, Bayard Taylor explored his own backyard. In *At Home and Abroad* (1860), he asked about Mammoth Cave in Kentucky, "What are the galleries of the Vatican, the Louvre, Versailles, and the Crystal Palaces of London and Paris to this gigantic vault hewn in the living rock?"[13]

Some of Taylor's compatriots, however, tacitly acknowledged the superiority of European arts and sciences by using their passports. They sailed to Europe and studied there, particularly in Germany, where the modern research university was being invented. Among the traveling Germanophiles were future historian George Bancroft, future poets Henry Wadsworth Longfellow and James Russell Lowell, and three future scientists, geologist Josiah Whitney and paleontologists Othniel C. Marsh and Edward Drinker Cope. Even Cooper and Irving betook themselves to Europe for long periods, though as observers rather than formal students, Cooper staying for seven years, Irving for seventeen. (In self-defense, Cooper wrote that "if any man is excusable for deserting his country, it is the American artist.")[14] And in 1850 a young American farmer named Frederick Law Olmsted embarked on a six-month European tour to learn as much as he could about city parks.

Yet there was plenty of work to do at home, where among those rolling up their sleeves was Edgar Allan Poe. His versatile genius had already declared itself in three books of poetry and a prize-winning short story, "MS. Found in a Bottle," which had helped him land a job with the *Southern Literary Messenger*, the Richmond-based magazine that had published the story. After being fired for going on one bender too many, Poe had dried out and been rehired. Largely on the strength of his fiction and criticism, the *Messenger* was attracting national attention.

When not creating genres (the detective story, the horror story) or binge drinking, Poe practiced literary criticism at a high level. One of his most talked-about essays appeared in an 1836 issue of the *Messenger*, when he was all of twenty-five years old.

Under review in Poe's essay were two collections of American poetry, one by the late Joseph Rodman Drake, the other by Drake's still-living

You Can Have the Arno

friend Fitz-Greene Halleck. Drake's fame rested on "The Culprit Fay," a 640-line poem about fairies. Unlike Edmund Spenser's "Faerie Queene," an allegory, or Alexander Pope's "Rape of the Lock," a satire, "The Culprit Fay" served its fairies straight up. Chronicling the exploits of a thimble-sized hero who likes to "drink the dew from the buttercup" and sun himself in a human lady's "eye of blue," "The Culprit Fay" allowed Poe to solidify his status as "the tomahawk man" of American letters.

"It is impossible to read without laughing [about] a Fairy . . . half an inch high," Poe wrote, "dressed in an acorn helmet and butterfly-cloak, and sitting on the water in a muscle-shell [*sic*], with a 'brown-backed sturgeon' turning somersets over his head." After tomahawking Drake, Poe bludgeoned Halleck, pronouncing his "poetical powers . . . essentially inferior, upon the whole, to those of his friend Drake."[15]

Poe was not the first critic to make fun of "The Culprit Fay." James Kirke Paulding had already done so in *Salmagundi*, the satirical magazine he coedited with Washington Irving. "Fairies, giants and goblins are not indigenous here," Paulding had pointed out, "and with the exception of a few witches that were soon exterminated, our worthy ancestors brought over with them not a single specimen of Gothic or Greek mythology."[16]

Why, then, bother with poor Drake and Halleck at all, let alone pummel them at such great length? (The critique takes up thirty-four pages in the Library of America volume of Poe's essays and reviews.) The answer can be found in an observation Poe made early on: "Perhaps at this particular moment there are no American poems held in so high estimation by our countrymen, as the poems of Drake, and of Halleck." Their overblown reputations supported a larger point Poe wanted to make: that Americans tend to like "a stupid book better, because . . . its stupidity is American." This was in contrast—too sharp a contrast, Poe felt—to the old days, when Americans "cringed to foreign opinion."[17] Since then, it seemed, Americans' sensitivity to foreign slurs on their native artistry had evolved into a perverse fondness for domestic dross.

Drake's imported fairies and that protective tariff for homegrown stupidity illustrate a challenge facing writers of his day. The nation's much-desired cultural coming of age would be hard to achieve until its writers got rid of quaint Old World diction, poetic meters that strained to do justice to its citizens' earthy everyday lives, and legends, institutions, customs, and creatures having little or no relevance to the New World. Philip Freneau, a far better American poet than either Drake or Halleck, had summed up the predicament in a heroic couplet (itself a form imported from the old sod): "Can we ever be thought to have learning or grace, / Unless it be sent from that damnable place?"[18]

Time has not been kind to Joseph Rodman Drake, who is remembered today, if at all, chiefly for his evisceration by Poe. In hindsight we can see that the future belonged not to writers celebrating tininess, but to those working at the other end of the spectrum: Herman Melville packing into *Moby-Dick* everything from a cetology lesson and a meditation on whiteness to an extended portrait of obsessional revenge on the high seas, Walt Whitman bragging that he contained multitudes and working a good many of them into *Leaves of Grass*, Mark Twain committing to memory the whole lower half of the Father of Waters in *Life on the Mississippi*. In any case, it's hard to see why a people still finding their way both geographically and artistically should give a hoot for an imp wearing an acorn helmet.

Adding weight to the chip on nineteenth-century American shoulders was the paucity of attractions to put up against Europe's. American cities looked stubby and grimy, and some of the land beyond the hundredth meridian still appeared as empty spaces on maps. Let Bayard Taylor plug Mammoth Cave until he was hoarse, but the fact remained that America could offer nothing so imposing and venerable as the Cathedral of Notre Dame, the Palace of Versailles, the Pantheon, the Parthenon, the Sistine Chapel, or Castle Howard. In his Gothic novel *The Asylum, or Alonzo and Melissa* (1811), the American writer Isaac Mitchell had just gone ahead and given Connecticut a castle, in which the fair Melissa was held prisoner to keep her from marrying the penniless Alonzo. (Mitchell's architectural invention must have gone over well: *The Asylum* was reprinted ten times.) Nor, with the possible exception of Niagara Falls, could Americans point to natural spectacles as storied as the Blue Grotto, Fingal's Cave, the Rock of Gibraltar, or the Matterhorn. (True, Lewis, Clark, and other explorers were sending back word of eye-popping American wonders, but many of these accounts met with skepticism, if not outright disbelief.)

You Can Have the Arno

The Connecticut Wit Timothy Dwight suggested a way for the United States to carve out a national identity distinct from the European varieties. "*The conversion of a wilderness into a desirable residence for man,*" he wrote in *Travels in New England and New York* (1821–22), "at least . . . may compensate for the want of ancient castles, ruined abbeys, and fine pictures."[19] Dwight was on to something—if treated right, America's vast supply of virgin wilderness might attain cultural significance—but he came at it the wrong way round. Manhandling that supply until the New World was as domesticated as the Old would be playing the Europeans' game, which Americans couldn't win.

Dwight's suggestion harked back to the early New Englanders, who scorned wilderness as menacing, pitiful, or both until they had subdued it and made it fruitful. Cotton Mather had praised his Puritan forebears as "a people of God [who] settled in those parts which were once the devil's territorie."[20]

A century and a half and countless land conversions later, easterners had conquered so much of their native wilderness as almost to lose sight of what was left of it. The French visitor and commentator Alexis de Tocqueville observed that "in Europe people talk a great deal of the wilds of America, but the Americans themselves never think about them. . . . Their eyes are fixed upon another sight, the march . . . across these wilds, draining swamps, turning the course of rivers, peopling solitudes, and subduing nature."[21]

The saga of how the American wilds shook off their diabolic origin and qualified as a dwindling asset in need of preservation has been well told by Roderick Nash in his book *Wilderness and the American Mind.* Leading roles in the drama were played by deists, who regarded wild nature not as a source of satanic temptation or a challenge to beavering pioneers, but as a display of God's virtuosity and might; by travel writers of the Romantic persuasion; and by artists who saw beauty and majesty in what their predecessors had either ignored or dismissed as chaos.

Among the last was the English-born American painter Thomas Cole, leading light of the Hudson River School of painting. Short on history as the United States might be, Cole wrote in his "Essay on American Beauty" (1836), the country is endowed with "features, and glorious ones, unknown to Europe. The most distinctive, and perhaps the most impressive, characteristic of American scenery is its wildness," almost none of which had been captured on canvas. "All nature here is new to art," Cole enthused—and threw himself into painting it.[22]

In his travelogue *Lotus-Eating: A Summer-Book* (1852), the American writer George William Curtis conceded that there was "a positive want of the picturesque in American scenery and life." But picturesqueness, Curtis added, might not be the best quality to look for. In its place, he proposed "space and wildness [as] the proper praises of American scenery. . . . We have only vast and unimproved extent, and the interest with which the possible grandeur of a mysterious future may invest it."[23]

For a rough measure of Americans' progress in making a literature of their own, we might consult the venerable Boston publisher Samuel Goodrich. In 1820, by Goodrich's estimate, 70 percent of all books published in the States were by British authors and 30 percent by American ones; thirty years later, those percentages had switched places. Nor, to revive Poe's indictment, could anyone of sound mind dismiss every homegrown book as "stupid." By the same year (1850), Cooper had finished his five Leatherstocking Tales; Emerson had written some of his finest essays, including "The American Scholar," with its hopeful observation that "our day of dependence, our long apprenticeship to the learning of other lands, draws to a close"; Melville was about to cut loose *Moby-Dick*; and Whitman was hard at work on *Leaves of Grass*.[24]

A generation later another literary giant—Mark Twain, who in 1850 had been the teenage Samuel Langhorne Clemens—tolled the beginning of the end of Americans' intimidation by European culture in a passage from his first book, a travelogue called *The Innocents Abroad* (1869). Twain embarked on his Grand Tour at a time when he and his fellow Americans were starting to realize that tracts of wild, rugged nature could do more than just pose fetchingly for painters and photographers. Saved and taken proper care of, these wonders could also qualify as works of art themselves, inspiring awe and sublimity, lifting the human spirit, and making up for the dearth of traditional high culture in the United States.

Twain managed to convey the imposing power of New World nature without mentioning it directly. Between visits to Florence's churches and museums, he recalled, "we used to go and stand on the bridges and admire the Arno. It is popular to admire the Arno. It is a great historical creek with four feet in the channel and some scows floating around. It would be a very plausible river if they would pump some water into it. They call it a river, and they honestly think it *is* a river, do these dark and bloody Florentines. They even help out the delusion by building bridges over it. I do not see why they are too good to wade."[25] When that passage was written, a decade and a half had passed since Yosemite Valley in the Sierra Nevada range of California hosted its first tourists.

Land of the Free and Home of the Sublime

2

As Americans nursed their case of cultural inferiority, people on both sides of the Atlantic were overcoming their distaste for the jagged unruliness of raw natural scenery. In the process, they reinvigorated a term dating back to antiquity.

Sublime owed its traditional meaning of "exalted" to the first-century AD treatise *On the Sublime*, wrongly attributed to Longinus, a Greek literary critic born two centuries too late to have written it. Whoever the author was, he or she attached the label "sublime" to an edifying style of writing or speaking, the kind wielded by master rhetoricians like Cicero. Much later, "sublime" was applied to uplifting messages transmitted by tangible objects, including natural ones. The eighteenth-century botanist William Bartram may have been the first American to use the word in that sense.

Thomas Jefferson praised the Natural Bridge in Virginia as "the most sublime of Nature's works."[1] Since Jefferson owned the bridge at the time, he was committing puffery, but he understood that with custodianship of such a treasure came responsibilities. "I view it in some degree as a public trust," he wrote to a friend, "and would on no consideration permit the bridge to be injured, defaced, or masked from public view."[2] Several decades later, Herman Melville called on the formation for help in conveying the tremendousness of a rogue whale: "Moby Dick moved on, still withholding from sight the full terrors of his submerged trunk. . . . But soon the fore part of him slowly rose from the water; for an instant his whole marbleized body formed a high arch, like Virginia's Natural Bridge."[3]

Impressive as Natural Bridge was (and still is), by the time Jefferson bought it, a better North American candidate for "the most sublime of Nature's works" had made itself known: Niagara Falls in upstate New York and downprovince Ontario, heralded by the French immigrant Hector St. John de Crèvecoeur as "a more sublime and uncommon object than is to be found in any other part of the world." Seconding that motion was the Duc de La Rochefoucauld-Liancourt, who in 1799 declared of the falls that "no one [should] expect to find here something pleasing, wildly beautiful or romantic; all is wonderfully grand, awful, sublime."[4] As indicated by the first two modifiers after that ducal semicolon, *sublime* had expanded to mean "awe-inspiring."

Fanny Trollope's first sight of Niagara Falls had made her giddy. "I can only say that wonder, terror, and delight completely overwhelmed me," she confessed. "I wept with a strange mixture of pleasure and of pain." Somehow she pulled herself together and wrote several hundred more words about her Niagara stay, crediting "the American cataract" with "all the sublimity that height and width, and uproar can give," although it had "none of the magic of its [Canadian] rival about it."[5]

It's worth mentioning that Dickens was immune to Niagara Falls' sublimity quotient; rather, his visit brought "Peace. Peace of Mind, tranquility, calm recollections of the Dead, great thoughts of Eternal Rest and Happiness; nothing of gloom or terror." He added, "Niagara was at once stamped on my heart, an Image of Beauty."[6] This idiosyncratic response may have been a function of the writer's nerves. Throughout most of his adult life, they thrummed at such a pitch that the roaring, tumbling juggernaut of Niagara may paradoxically have steadied them. More in the mainstream, if you will, was the American literary critic and feminist Margaret Fuller, who wrote darkly of her visit to the falls, "Before coming away I think I really saw the full wonder of the scene. After a while it drew me into itself as to inspire an undefined dread, such as I never knew before, such as may be felt when death is about to usher us into a new existence."[7] Niagara Falls was well on its way to being what American studies professor Elizabeth McKinsey has called "*the* American icon of the sublime in the early nineteenth century"—an icon that gave many a visitor the fantods.[8]

In applying "sublimity" to the emotion aroused by scarily attractive natural objects, Fanny Trollope was joining a line of British writers whose theoretician was Edmund Burke. Why the future statesman and political philosopher chose to make his first book *A Philosophical Enquiry into the Origin of Our Ideas of the Sublime and Beautiful* is hard to say. His biographer Conor Cruise O'Brien labeled the period between Burke's graduation from Trinity College Dublin in 1748 and the book's publication in 1757 as "the missing years" because so few of the young man's papers from the period have survived. O'Brien guessed that *A Philosophical Enquiry* was "an implicit rejection of the limitations of Burke's Quaker education" by a schoolmaster who loathed "'those authors who recommend in seducing language the illusions of love and the abominable trade of war.' Burke found the origin of 'the beautiful' in love, and the origin of 'the sublime' in war."[9]

Whatever the impetus may have been, in his treatment of the sublime and the beautiful, Burke capitalized on a distinction previously made by the essayist Joseph Addison. For Addison, beautiful objects had a pleasing symmetry but lacked the immensity or oddity that might earn them a rating of "great." By contrast, larger, irregular objects could achieve a fear-instilling greatness.

For Burke, that fear-making capacity was best described as "sublime." "Whatever is fitted in any sort to excite the ideas of pain and danger," he wrote, "that is to say, whatever is in any sort terrible, or is conversant about terrible objects, or operates in a way analogous to terror, is a source of the *sublime*; that is, it is productive of the strongest emotion which the mind is capable of feeling." Mind you, Burke noted, not every menacing experience will generate sublimity. "When danger or pain press too nearly, they are incapable of giving any delight, and are simply terrible; but at certain distances, and with certain modifications, they may be, and they are, delightful, as we every day experience."[10]

As his book's title suggests, Burke distinguished the sublime from the beautiful, which merely induces an "agreeable relaxation." In today's idiom, we might say that Burke wanted to nudge his readers out of their comfort zones for an occasional invigorating brush with "terrible objects." Not very helpfully for eighteenth-century readers unable or unwilling to traipse off to

Africa or the Far East, he pointed toward "the gloomy forest [or] howling wilderness" where can be found "the lion, the tiger, the panther, or rhinoceros."[11] Burke does not seem to have regarded mountains or waterfalls as generators of sublimity—at the time he was writing, Niagara's mightiness was little more than an unverified colonial rumor. But by encouraging readers to submit to the startling or blood-curdling aspects of encounters with the wild, he made such experiences better known and more sought after.

A generation after the French duke's visit, Niagara Falls had evolved into a tourist mecca, so popular and monetized that some visitors were hard put to see it with fresh eyes. One of these was the Scotsman John Duncan, who in his *Travels through Part of the United States and Canada in 1818 and 1819* (1823) wrote off the cataracts as "so frequently described, and the whole vocabulary of sublimity so completely exhausted in the service," that he gave them a miss.[12]

That mountains can be sublimely frightful should have gone without saying, yet as Marjorie Hope Nicholson points out in her book *Mountain Gloom and Morning Glory*, it took humans a long time to be able to look at mountains without feeling disgust, even longer to examine them with care. The seasoned traveler Sir Walter Raleigh had eyed mountains so cursorily that he called Tenerife in the Canary Islands "the highest mountain of the world known."[13] In fact, at 12,198 feet high, Tenerife (better known today as Mount Teide) is shorter than more than a hundred peaks in the Alps alone.

Writing circa 1650, Andrew Marvell addressed mountains directly only to give them a curt poetic dismissal:

Here [at Bill-borrow] learn, ye Mountains more unjust,
Which to abrupter greatness thrust,
That do with your hook-shoulder'd height
The earth deform and Heaven fright,
For whose excrescence ill design'd,
Nature must a new Center find,
Learn here those humble steps to tread,
Which to securer Glory lead.[14]

In the Romantic era, English writers more than made up for their literature's past neglect of mountainous sublimity, but the example had been set by such predecessors as the eighteenth-century poet Richard Blackmore: "See how sublime th' uplifted Mountains rise, / And with their pointed Heads invade the Skies."[15]

The American historian Francis Parkman added a pinch of melancholy to the mix in his travelogue *The Oregon Trail.* "That morning's march was not one to be forgotten," he said of the approach to Laramie Creek in Wyoming in the year 1846. "It led us through a sublime waste, a wilderness of mountains and pine-forests, over which the spirit of loneliness and silence seemed brooding."[16]

When Parkman wrote that, "sublime" was becoming so domesticated as to be interchangeable with "heavenly" or "divine" in the secular sense, or even with "very impressive." That's how Longfellow had used the word in his much-anthologized poem "A Psalm of Life" (1838), which can stand for myriad other, similar examples: "Lives of great men all remind us / We can make our lives sublime."[17]

Shortly after the end of the Civil War, two new friends, the newspaperman Samuel Bowles and the landscape architect Frederick Law Olmsted, both used "sublimity" to characterize their response to Yosemite Valley. They did so at a time when so many accounts of fabulous natural phenomena sighted in the American Far West had appeared that the skeptics were wavering. Perhaps hot water really did spout up to scald the air above Wyoming Territory, perhaps stupendously tall trees really did grow in the mountains of California, perhaps a river really had cut a mile-deep, color-drenched canyon through the Southwest. As Mark Twain and other American writers forswore their allegiance to European lore, literary forms, and cultural standards; as sublimity chasing became a popular pastime; as explorers continued to discover eye-popping western landscapes, Americans were getting used to the idea that they might hold title to a greater variety of scary-sublime natural wonders than any other country in the world. This ripple in the zeitgeist suggested that Americans might want to go easy on Timothy Dwight's program of converting wilderness into "desirable residence[s] for man."

"It may be argued," Walt Whitman stated in his prose work *Democratic Vistas*, written in 1871, two years after completion of the transcontinental railroad, "that our republic is, in performance, really enacting today the grandest arts, poems, etc., by beating up the wilderness into fertile farms, and in her railroads, ships, machinery, etc. And it may be ask'd, Are these not better, indeed, for America, than any utterances even of greatest rhapsode, artist, or literatus?"[18]

By the end of the same book, though, Whitman appears to have changed his mind, calling nature itself "the only complete, actual poem."[19] If he was right about that, wouldn't it follow that instead of "beating up the wilderness" to a fare-thee-well, we should take care to leave some of it intact? What Wallace Stegner was to call America's "best idea"—national parks—was getting ready to be born, in part because Burke had preached the gospel of the sublime. As Marjorie Hope Nicholson has pointed out, "What men see in Nature is a result of what they have been taught to see—lessons they have learned in school, doctrines they have heard in church, books they have read."[20] Edmund Burke's book on the sublime taught men to see the beauty in nature with a sinister tinge.

The Counterexample 3

Ideas often come as reactions to precursors found wanting. The U.S. Constitution was, among other things, an answer to the unwritten British one, with its monarch and nobles and established church. And the national park idea was a repudiation of what had befallen North America's first world-famous natural extravaganza. Almost everyone taking part in the early movement to save great American natural wonders had a good idea of what they hoped to save those wonders from: the Niagara Falls treatment.

The falls' first publicist was Louis Hennepin, a Catholic priest from what is now Belgium who saw them in the late 1600s while accompanying the French explorer La Salle on his quest for the semilegendary Mississippi River. Collectively, the three Niagara Falls—Horseshoe (also known as the Canadian Falls), American, and Bridal Veil—outperform most other waterfalls in thrust and breadth, but Hennepin would have them be vertical prodigies too. In his account of his travels, *Description de la Louisiane* (1683), he gave the falls a height of 500 feet (the correct figure is roughly 170); in a later edition, he tacked on 100 feet more. When the truth came out, Hennepin became known as *un grand menteur*, a big liar. His exaggerations gave Europeans, as well as some Americans, reason to discount reports of other flabbergasting New World natural phenomena—a habit that was to persist for centuries.

Niagara Falls' first recreational users came from the ranks of the stout-hearted and well-heeled. Roads were so primitive, and inns so few, that to reach the site you practically had to mount an expedition, and you definitely had to beware of wolves. By the early nineteenth century, however, amenities had improved and hazards had diminished to the point that upstate New York was drawing vacationers "from outside the tiny sphere of American aristocrats." In 1818 the New York merchant John Pintard informed his daughter by letter that Niagara Falls qualified as "a fashionable place of resort."[1] The falls were taking their place in a fairly well-developed and accessible network of Northeast American tourist destinations.

The network centered on the Hudson Valley, its appeal enhanced by its proximity to the young nation's financial center and most populous city, by good transportation on the Hudson River, and by scenery so pleasing as to give rise to an artistic movement, the Hudson River School. Valetudinarians favored the region, especially the town of Saratoga Springs, where the sick in body and mind sought relief in spas. Not that every spa-goer showed up with a thermometer in his mouth. Pleasure seekers came, too, eager to kick off the traces, flirt, maybe even find a mate. It wasn't long before the social opportunities available at spas outshone such benefits to human health as mineral water can provide.

As spas proliferated in Saratoga, their owners vied for patrons by adding pleasure gardens, copied from prototypes such as England's Vauxhall Gardens. Winding through the greenery were promenades along which guests could strut their stuff before taking in a concert at a bandstand. Spa gardens were among the forerunners of the modern urban park.

With the publication of the first American travel guides, such as Gideon M. Davison's *The Fashionable Tour, or A Trip to the Springs, Niagara, Quebeck, and Boston in the Summer of 1821*, northeastern touring became more dependable. Upon completion of the Erie Canal in 1825 Niagara Falls was not only a must-see but also a can-do, as tourists could get there with ease from the canal's terminus at Buffalo, New York. With the coming of the railroad in the mid-1830s, the twentieth-century Canadian journalist Pierre Berton notes, "The Falls . . . was on the way to becoming a carnival for the masses."[2] Prominent among the carnival-goers were honeymooners, later the butts of a joke attributed to Oscar Wilde: "Every American bride is taken there, and the stupendous waterfall must be one of the earliest, if not the keenest, disappointments in American married life."

Land adjacent to the falls on either side of the U.S.-Canadian border had long attracted small-business men. At first they concentrated on importing and exporting, a harmless enough livelihood as a rule, although operating in the shadows was a cohort of smugglers trying to elude customs agents.

The Counterexample

As early as 1794 the visiting Duc de La Rochefoucauld-Liancourt took note of the offices and shops proliferating near the falls. In the North American travel book he produced four years later, his lordship became the first to propose the eventual remedy for this piecemeal and rivalrous exploitation: government ownership and management of the falls and their approaches. His foresight put him nearly a century ahead of what American and Canadian politicians could stomach—in 1805 the state of New York put its holdings alongside the falls up for sale, setting the stage for the unholy mess that ultimately had to be cleaned up at great cost.

Niagara Falls played host to the first in what became a long line of daredevils in 1829, when the twenty-three-year-old Sam Patch, also known as the Jersey Jumper, accepted an invitation from local hoteliers to wow their guests. Patch delivered as promised, executing a dive from Goat Island into the Niagara River above the American Falls. In the words of an excitable observer, "Sam Patch has immortalized himself—he has done what mortal never did before—he has precipitated himself eighty-five feet in one leap; that leap into the mighty cavern of Niagara's Cataract; and survived the romantic feat uninjured!!!"[3] Although Patch may have immortalized his name, he still had a mortal body to look after. Shortly after his Niagara jump, he pushed his luck too far, flinging himself over Genesee Falls in Rochester, New York, and drowning. Edgar Allan Poe so disliked a ballad written to lament Patch's death that he awarded the title "worst of all wretched poets" to its author, one Jack Downing.[4]

In *Domestic Manners*, Fanny Trollope gave an exaggerated account of a cheesy stunt: sending derelict boats over the falls to see how they would fare. She put the number of vessels sacrificed at three, but in fact there had been only one, the *Michigan*, cruelly loaded with circus animals. The *Michigan* disappointed an estimated ten thousand spectators by breaking up before it reached the falls, with some of the animals swimming safely to shore.

By then the local small-business men had been joined by ones with bigger britches. In the 1750s an entrepreneur had diverted water above the Upper Falls to turn the wheel of a sawmill; other industrial diversions followed. In 1831 Tocqueville told a friend to get a move on if he wanted to see the falls in anything like a natural state: "If you delay, your Niagara will have been spoiled for you. Already the forest round about is being cleared. . . . I don't give the Americans ten years to establish a saw or flour mill at the base of the cataract."[5] That didn't happen, but a generation later a railroad bridge constructed by John A. Roebling (future designer of the Brooklyn Bridge) linked the American and Canadian sides of the river. "By the late 1860s, spurred by demand during the Civil War," writes Francis R. Kowsky, "an assortment of mills turning out various products had grown up along the American shore above the falls." Flanking a canal dug parallel to the river stood a gaggle of enterprises, "including a laundry, a furniture factory, a paper mill, planing mills, and a foundry. All of these buildings received power from shafts or rope drives propelled by the age-old system of waterwheels."[6]

As time went on, the clutter multiplied. "The American side," Berton notes, "was disfigured by ugly stone dams, gristmills, outdoor clotheslines, heaps of sawdust, stables, advertising placards, shanties, lumberyards, a pulp mill, and a gas works."[7] In 1874, when William Cullen Bryant edited *Picturesque America*, a catalog with full-page engravings of top-notch American scenery, he called Niagara Falls "a superb diamond set in lead."[8]

By this time generations of tourists had run a gauntlet of sideshows and temptations having little to do with falling water. Here was the scene as captured by the British historian George Warburton after his 1847 visit: "Now the neighborhood of great wonder is overrun with every species of abominable fungus—the growth of rank bad taste, with equal luxuriance on the English and American sides—Chinese pagoda, menagerie, camera obscura, museum, watch tower, wooden monument, tea gardens and old curiosity shops."[9] That decade came to an end with the "abominable" fungi attracting forty thousand visitors a year.

"Everybody is Niagarized," lamented a visitor in 1851, "and flies to the centre as filings to a magnet."[10] En route, the human "filings" were sure to be pestered by hawkers competing to sell tickets to *their* employers' vantage points on the falls, *their* curiosities, *their* refreshments. The British visitor Sir Richard Bonnycastle excoriated these pests as "pedlars and thimble-riggers, barkers and the lowest rulls and vilest scum of society [who] congregate to disgust and annoy visitors from all parts of the

The Counterexample

world, plundering and pestering them without control."[11] Henry James complained that Niagara's environs were "choked in the horribly vulgar shops and booths and catchpenny artifices which have pushed and elbowed to within the very spray of the Falls. . . . The importunities one suffers here . . . from hackmen and photographers and vendors of gimcracks, are simply hideous and infamous."[12] The English designer William Morris complained more succinctly of being hassled by "the very pick of the touts and rascals of the world."[13]

High among the touts' and rascals' offenses was the peddling of irrelevant souvenirs and experiences. In 1856 the American periodical *Frank Leslie's Illustrated Newspaper* warned that "every place that is sacred [there] is invaded by a glaring hotel, an apple stand, a paper mill, or Lady-book and Hiawatha Indians. . . . Turn which way you will at Niagara, you find . . . the money-changers are indeed profaning the great temple."[14]

Not just elitists like Bonnycastle and James bewailed the falls' sorry state. That man of the people Mark Twain gave a low rating to his 1869 visit after overhearing one tour guide "tell the [same] story nine times in succession to different parties, and never miss a word or alter a sentence or a gesture."[15] When Twain asked an insider where the Indian moccasins and beadwork on sale in local shops came from, the answer was Limerick (in Ireland).

Berton offers an example of how the multiple charges levied on tourists could add up to a daunting sum. In 1877 a dismayed farmer kept track of all the entrance fees and expenses incurred by him, his wife, and their two daughters during their daylong visit to the falls:[16]

To Goat Island	$2.25
To Prospect Park	1.00
To Railway Suspension Bridge	1.00
To new Suspension Bridge	2.50
To Whirlpool Rapids, American Side	2.00
To Whirlpool Rapids, Canadian Side	2.00
To the Whirlpool	2.00
To the Burning Springs	1.60
To the Battle Ground	2.00

To under the Horseshoe Falls	4.00
To "Into the Shadow of the Rock"	4.00
To through the Cave of the Winds	6.00
To hack hire	7.00
To fee to driver	0.50

When Berton provided this table in 1997, the total of $37.85 was the equivalent of roughly $530 in that year's money.

The most unscrupulous gougers were barely a cut above kidnappers. They would reel in the unwary by promising them a free look at the falls, herd them into a room to don slickers for protection from the spray, and demand an exorbitant rental fee for the slickers. If the marks balked, they were held prisoner in the changing room until they paid up, sometimes as much as $12 a head.

Both sides of the falls were rank, but the Canadian Front may have been the ranker of the two. In Berton's words, "That notorious quarter-mile strip . . . provided a haven for half a century for every kind of huckster, gambler, barker, confidence man, and swindler. Here half a dozen hotels soon sprang up along with a hodge-podge of other shops, booths, and taverns. And here Thomas Barnett built his famous museum with its Egyptian mummies and Iroquois arrowheads."[17]

The stunts proliferated. The preeminent Niagara daredevil was the tightrope walker Jean François Gravelet, known as Blondin for the color of his hair. "I do not remember his face, which was no doubt as good or as bad a face as any mountebank's or monarch's," wrote editor and novelist William Dean Howells after watching a Blondin performance in 1860, "but his feet seemed to me the very most intelligent feet in the world, pliable, sinuous, clinging, educated in every fibre, and full of spiritual sentience."[18] The smart-footed Blondin became the Franz Liszt of tightrope walkers, and Niagara Falls his concert hall. (Not precisely the falls themselves; Blondin performed his stunts three-quarters of a mile downstream, though nobody seemed to mind.) Over the years, he worked variations on the basic crossing. He did it on stilts. He did it with a sack over his head. He did it pushing a wheelbarrow. He carried a stove out to midrope, set it up, cooked a meal, and lowered morsels down to passengers on the tour boat *Maid of*

The Counterexample

the Mist waiting below. By the time he hung up his pole for the last time in 1896, he is said to have made the crossing three hundred times. One can admire Blondin for his athleticism and steely nerves but still blame him for his role in cheapening the scene. Later, and outside the time frame of this book, came the foolhardiest stuntmen and women of all, those who went over the falls in a barrel, some of whom lived to tell the tale.

Blondin's act was not the only temptation to which Howells succumbed. Twenty-three years old at the time of his first visit, he was financing his travels with money earned from writing a campaign biography of Abraham Lincoln. Four decades later, in his contribution to *The Niagara Book*, an essay collection published in advance of the 1901 Pan-American Exposition in Buffalo, Howells recalled the seductiveness of the old, tawdry Niagara Falls: "If you find a marvel advertised, and you learn that you cannot see it without paying a quarter, every coin upon your person begins to burn in an intense sympathy with your curiosity, and you cannot be content till you have seen that marvel. This was the principle of human nature upon which private capital had counted."[19] On the Canadian side, the impressionable young visitor had stooped so low as to hand over a burning quarter for a look at a five-legged calf.

Not everything going on at the falls was exploitative or circuslike, however. The painter Frederic Church, a pupil of Thomas Cole's, won fame with a grand work called *Niagara, from the American Side*, which he finished in 1856 after sketching the falls from multiple vantage points. Now hanging in the National Gallery of Art in Washington DC, the painting is a sweeping, kinetic work that gives the illusion of having been done not by an artist with his feet on the ground, but by a birdman hovering in midair. Shortly after its completion, *Niagara* was sent to London, with *Frank Leslie's Illustrated* predicting it would "startle those 'croakers' across the water into a recognition of American genius."[20] *Niagara* did exactly that, prompting English art critics to wake up and declare that American painting had come of age. Church's masterpiece not only firmed up American egos but also spoke to the painters and photographers who were to figure in the saving of Yosemite and Yellowstone.

After the falls were finally cleaned up—thanks in large part to the efforts of Church and his distant cousin Frederick Law Olmsted—a New York state official put in perspective the region's near ruination by those who had "outraged public decency by their importunate demands, exorbitant actions and swindling deceits." Had it not been for the backlash generated by all that greedy and vulgar overreaching, the official explained, "the task of securing the public reservation [of the falls] would probably have been even greater than it was."[21]

At its nadir, Niagara Falls had served as a much-cited counterexample. Brave its crowds, endure its touts and shills, pay the outlandish fees charged for taking it in and you would have patronized North America's, and perhaps the world's, foremost example of how *not* to treat a great natural wonder.

In 1878, after Yosemite had been set aside as the first state park and Yellowstone as the first national park, an astute British traveler named Lady C. F. Gordon-Cumming summed up Niagara's tenure as a cautionary tale. "Happily," she wrote, "the United States Government (warned by the results of having allowed the Falls of Niagara to become private property) determined that certain districts, discovered in various parts of the States, and noted for their exceeding beauty, should, by Act of Congress, be appropriated for evermore 'for public use, resort, and recreation and be inalienable for all time.'"[22]

An Idea in Embryo   4

In later chapters of this book, we'll see Indians being crowded out of America's first wild parks, Yosemite and Yellowstone. It's good to remember, then, that we owe the first formulations of the national park idea to two men who favored allowing Indians to maintain their traditional ways of life in situ. They were the painter and writer George Catlin, whose passionate devotion to Indians residing on the Great Plains inspired him to urge setting aside part of that region for them, and Henry David Thoreau, who wanted to accommodate "the hunter race" in the national preserves he proposed as democratic American alternatives to European royal forests. A third writer, John Muir, emulated both Catlin and Thoreau in looking closely at the natural world around him and agitating to keep some of it intact, though not intact enough to include its original inhabitants.

Catlin's vision of a refuge for Indians and bison came to him in the early 1830s, when he was traveling in the Great Plains and sending back letters for publication to a newspaper called the *New York Commercial Advertiser*. In letter 31, which brings to a ringing close the first volume (of two) of those letters as later collected, Catlin asked his readers to use their imagination. Picture "a *magnificent park*, where the world could see for ages to come, the native Indian" as Catlin liked to paint him, "in his classic attire, galloping his wild horse, with sinewy bow, and shield and lance, amid the fleeting herds of elks and buffaloes. What a beautiful and thrilling specimen for America to preserve and hold up to the view of her refined citizens and the world, in future ages! A *nation's Park*, containing man and beast, in all the wild and freshness of their nature's beauty!"[1]

Catlin assured readers that his proposal would not stand in the way of American progress, "for the tracts of country on which the buffaloes have assembled, are universally sterile, and are of no available use to cultivating man."[2] This was an early statement of what became a leitmotif for a nation steeped in the Protestant ethic: it's all right to establish wild parks on land where no better uses—that is, extractive or consumptive ones—are likely to emerge.

It so happened that during the same year in which Catlin wrote the above, 1832, the U.S. government took over a popular natural attraction. Responding to a request from the Arkansas Territorial Legislature, Congress established the Hot Springs Reservation. Good idea, though not a fertile one. People came, poached themselves in the reservation's basins, and left without giving much thought to whether more federal playgrounds should be established elsewhere. And when more reservations did come, they served a quite different clientele: Indian tribes ousted from their homelands so that miners, loggers, and homesteaders could move in. In 1921 Hot Springs was elevated from a reservation to a park, but it remains one of a kind: our national hot tub.

In an 1858 issue of the *Atlantic Monthly*, Thoreau floated an idea similar to Catlin's. After noting that the kings of England had owned forests in which they razed villages to improve sport hunting, he asked, "Why should not we . . . have our national preserves, where no villages need be destroyed, in which the bear and panther, and even some of the hunter race, may still exist, and not be 'civilized off the face of the earth'?"[3] On another occasion, Thoreau wrote out a prescription for every American town to fill for its citizens: "a park, or rather a primitive forest, of five hundred or a thousand acres, where a stick should never be cut for fuel, a common possession forever, for instruction and re-creation."[4]

Neither Catlin nor Thoreau developed his recommendation in any detail. Catlin may have been too busy acting as a one-man conservator, putting down on canvas and paper the people he met and the practices he observed in Indian country. He left us a nation's park of the mind, along with an invaluable artistic and anthropological record of doomed cultures. Thoreau's real ardor was not for "the hunter race," but for wildness, in which, he proclaimed, "is the preservation of the world."[5] In any case, he had only a few more years of thinking and writing ahead of him before his death of tuberculosis in 1862, at age forty-four.

Yet a promising start had been made. Rough drafts of the national park idea had debuted in journals issuing from the nation's two most important cities: New York (the *Commercial Advertiser*) and Boston (the *Atlantic*).

A "park" was originally an outdoor enclosure, not necessarily fenced off. North, Middle, South, and San Luis Parks in central Colorado are flat-lands set apart by the mountains that cup them. In England, a park was a preserve in which royals and nobles could hunt deer and other game but from which commoners were excluded, or it was the grounds of a stately country house, off-limits to the uninvited. By custom, however, the public had been allowed to walk in the hunting parks of London since the days of the Plantagenets. "By the latter part of the eighteenth century in St. James's Park, Green Park, Hyde Park, and Kensington Gardens," writes Olmsted scholar Theodora Kimball, "this privilege had become practically a public right."[6]

In 1833 a select committee advised Parliament to think more highly of parks open to all. Especially in the kingdom's manufacturing towns, the committee observed, "the middle or humble classes" needed "means of exercise or amusement," and the "provision of public walks and open places would much conduce to the comfort, health and content of the classes in question."[7] A few years later an anonymous writer for *Blackwood's Edinburgh Magazine* emphasized the salubrious properties of city parks by titling an article he wrote on the topic "The Lungs of London." In 1840 the town of Birkenhead, on the other side of the Mersey River from Liverpool, commissioned a landscape architect to design a tract acquired specifically as the site for a public park.

Early in American history, the role of public park went by default to the village green, which was usually small, and to cemeteries, which people visited not only to honor their dearly departed but also to stroll and picnic in—or, increasingly, *just* to stroll and picnic in. This trend came to the attention of a man who saw its implications: Andrew Jackson Downing, America's first landscape architect and the editor of the *Horticulturist* mag-azine. "Judging from the crowds of people in carriages, and on foot, which I find constantly thronging Greenwood and Mount Auburn [cemeteries in Brooklyn, New York, and Cambridge, Massachusetts, respectively],"

Downing wrote in one of his *Horticulturist* editorials, "I think it is plain enough how much . . . our citizens, of all classes, would enjoy public parks on a similar scale."[8] Before Downing's death in 1852 at age thirty-sex, Olmsted got to know him, wrote articles for him at the *Horticulturist*, and examined European parks under his influence.

The first man to envisage a nation's park inhabited by Indians came from a family that knew Indians better than most. George Catlin's mother, Polly Sutton, had grown up in Pennsylvania's Wyoming Valley, where, at the age of seven, she and her mother were taken captive by Indians. They were freed unharmed after being treated with what went down in family lore as "the greatest kindness."[9]

George was born in Wilkes-Barre, Pennsylvania, in 1796. When he was eight, his father, Putnam Catlin, a lawyer, relocated the family to a farm near Windsor, New York, where Oneida Indians had once lived. The following year George came upon an Indian who, with his wife and young daughter, had returned to hunt on ancestral ground. Though wary, the boy stood his ground. "For here was before me," he recalled, "for the first time in my life, the living figure of a *Red Indian*!"[10] Man and boy hit it off so well that George fetched his father, who invited the family back to the house. The Indian husband and father, whose name George heard as "On-o-gong way," made a bonnet for the boy, and George's mother gave the wayfarers provisions for their return trip. The heartwarming episode came to a grim end, however. A few days later On-o-gong-way's body was found. He had been shot dead. There was no sign of his wife or daughter.

At age twenty-one, Catlin went off to study law in Litchfield, Connecticut, where portraits hanging on the walls of local houses (Litchfield was a fancier town than Windsor) stimulated his aptitude for drawing. After three years of practicing law in Luzerne County, Pennsylvania, he gave it up, moved to Philadelphia, and eked out a living as a painter of miniatures. He painted his first Indian portrait (not a miniature) without a live model, making do with the Indian artifacts on display in what was then the pride of Philadelphia: the eclectic museum owned by Charles Willson Peale.

Catlin moved on to New York City and found a patron for his art in Gov. DeWitt Clinton, whom he painted several times. Also dating from this period is Catlin's striking *Niagara Falls, View of Table Rock and Horseshoe Falls, from Below*. The painting shows the cascades as advertised, from below, but also from just outside the curtain of water. The artist, who made five more Niagara paintings, could hardly have missed the crowds tramping all over the riverbanks and the scramble for tourist dollars that was reducing the site to a shoddy fairground.

Catlin married Clarissa Gregory in 1828 but didn't let that detail keep him from taking off for St. Louis without her a couple of years later. There he presented a letter of introduction to Gen. William Clark (of Lewis and Clark), superintendent of Indian affairs for the western tribes. In St. Louis, Catlin encountered more Indians, including two visitors from the Northwest whom he painted. With a recommendation from Clark, in 1832 Catlin latched on to an expedition going up the Missouri River on the steamboat *Yellow Stone*, owned and captained by the St. Louis fur trader Pierre Chouteau Jr.

Traveling as he was in a remote and raw part of the country, Catlin had to let his letters to the *Commercial Advertiser* pile up until the *Yellow Stone* reached the next outpost on the river and he could mail them off in a batch. Even a decade later, when Catlin revised this material for book publication, his rapture practically leaped off the page: "One thousand miles or more of the upper part of the river, was, to my eyes, like fairy-land; and during our transit . . . I was most of the time rivetted to the deck of the boat, indulging my eyes in the boundless and tireless pleasure of roaming over the thousand hills, and bluffs, and dales, and ravines; where the astonished herds of buffaloes, of elks, and antelopes, and sneaking wolves, and mountain-goats, were to be seen."[11]

Catlin also indulged his eyes in Indian sightings and embarked on his prolific series of portraits, taken from life and memorializing men and women whose faces and forms, dress and customs might otherwise have left no trace. Among his eventual subjects were the two most famous sachems of the era, Black Hawk of the Sac and Fox and Osceola of the Seminoles.

To Indians, Catlin was a charming novelty who mingled with them, took notes on their activities, won their confidence, and re-created them on canvas. Well aware that he was acting as a kind of recording secretary, he became such a stickler for accuracy that before depicting a buffalo chase, he mounted a horse and kept up with the hunters. While living with the Mina-tarees, he stripped to the buff to participate in a horse race because that was how the thing was done. While recovering from the flu during a stay with the Riccarees (now known as the Arikaras), Catlin accepted a solicitous tribesman's offer to use his "bedaubed and bear-greased body for a pillow."[12]

In his ninth letter to the *Commercial Advertiser*, Catlin rated Indians by the wildness of their spirits, which was in direct proportion to the integrity of their tribal culture. He much preferred Indians who were "uncorrupted by the vices of civilized acquaintance, . . . well clad, in many instances cleanly, and in the full enjoyment of life and its luxuries. It is for the char-acter and preservation of these noble fellows that I am an enthusiast; and it is for these uncontaminated people that I would be willing to devote the energies of my life."[13]

Catlin took more such trips, sometimes with Clarissa but more often without, earning such a reputation for artistic sensitivity and accuracy that Indians sought him out to paint them. As he recalled with pride, "They pronounced me the greatest *medicine-man* in the world; for they said I had made *living beings.*"[14]

At the end of his travels in Indian country, Catlin tallied up the numbers: forty-eight tribes visited, four hundred thousand souls encountered, and over five hundred paintings made, three-fifths of them portraits and the rest scenes of tribal activities such as sham fights (training exercises for boys), religious ceremonies, dances, and games. Of all the tribes he visited, he lost his heart to one in particular: the Mandans, who lived along the Upper Missouri in what is now North Dakota and with whom he spent a short but eventful period in that glorious summer of 1832. It was then that he captured, in both words and images, O-kee-pa, an annual four-day ordeal in which young men proved their mettle by dangling from ropes attached to skewers driven into their bare chests and shoulders.

The paintings Catlin made from his O-kee-pa sketches are vital to our understanding of the ritual; with them and the fourteen letters he devoted to the Mandans, he achieved anthropological greatness—and not a moment too soon. In one of his letters, he lamented that "[their] fate, like that of all their race is sealed;—[their] doom is fixed, to live just long enough to be imperfectly known, and then to fall before the fell disease or sword of

An Idea in Embryo

civilizing devastation." In an appendix to volume 2 of the book he compiled from the letters, Catlin told how that prediction had panned out. In the summer of 1838 the "fell disease," known as smallpox, "was accidentally introduced amongst the Mandans by the Fur Traders; and . . . in the course of two months they all perished except some thirty or forty."[15] Because of Catlin's fascination with them, however, we know the Mandans and their traditions far better than "imperfectly."

In 1837 Catlin took his collection to New York, where he dubbed it Catlin's Indian Gallery, displayed it in Clinton Hall, and lectured on it. He then shipped everything to Washington DC for the launch of a one-man campaign to sell it to the federal government, which he hoped would build a museum specially to house it. He won over such congressional power brokers as Daniel Webster and Henry Clay, and you might think that acquiring and displaying this peerless historical record was the least the United States could do to atone for its seizures of aboriginal land and near obliteration of one tribal culture after another. But other, less visionary politicians balked at spending federal money to commemorate "savages." The Catlin Indian Gallery bill died in the Senate.

Catlin moved his paintings, along with two live grizzly bears, to London. There he revived his show to good effect, although high costs kept profits low. He and his traveling gallery toured England, Scotland, and Ireland, and a group of Ojibwa Indians crossed the Atlantic to join the cast. The grizzlies, however, proved too hard to handle; Catlin foisted them off on the London Zoo, where they soon died.

While in London, Catlin revised and gathered his *Commercial Advertiser* dispatches into the two-volume *Letters and Notes on the Manners, Customs, and Condition of the North American Indians: Written during Eight Years' Travel amongst the Wildest Tribes of Indians in North America*, which he published in 1842. "The work was enthusiastically reviewed in America and abroad," writes the ethnologist John C. Ewers, "and was reprinted five times in as many years."[16] Dickens met Catlin and became a fan of both the man and his writing. "He is an honest, hearty, famous fellow," the novelist declared, "and I shake hands with him at every page."[17]

Catlin and his show went to Paris and stayed on the Continent for three years, until the Revolutions of 1848 drove him back to London. Always on the lookout for opportunities, he built life-size wooden models of Indians and displayed them at the first-ever world's fair, the 1851 Crystal Palace Exhibition in London. After a partnership with America's leading impresario of titillation, P. T. Barnum, ended badly, Catlin fell on hard times—ironically so.

Once while chatting with a worldly Sioux chief on the Upper Missouri, Catlin had championed the Anglo-American system of justice over Indians' ad hoc style. Hold on, the chief objected. Don't forget your prisons, in which you confine men for "a great part of their lives *because they can't pay money*."[18] Catlin had conceded the point. Now, decades later, he was thrown into Queen's Bench prison for nonpayment of his own debts. His release was effected by Joseph Harrison, an American tycoon who happened to be in London; Harrison assumed Catlin's liabilities and shipped his collection to Philadelphia for safekeeping.

In 1870 Catlin ended his long exile from the States by moving to Washington DC. Two years later, at age seventy-six, he died of kidney failure at his brother-in-law's house in Jersey City, leaving his Indian Gallery in the possession of his creditor, Harrison. A few years later, Harrison's widow donated the gallery to the Smithsonian Institution—certainly a good place for it, though not the all-Catlin, all-the-time venue of the artist's dreams. (The place to visit if you want to see his paintings is the Smithsonian American Art Museum in Washington DC.)

A passage from his letter 31 indicates that Catlin's nation's park idea may have mattered even more to him than his art: "I would ask no other monument to my memory, nor any other enrolment of my name amongst the famous dead, than the reputation of having been the founder of such an institution."[19] Yet he was more of an artist than a thinker, and his "institution" stayed tantalizingly vague.

Catlin wanted to protect the Plains Indians as they were. To do that, he would have to save the bison too. As he entertained those two impulses, they fused—perhaps at the very moment he was putting pen to paper for his newspaper readers—into a vision of a nation's park. He could imagine it and rhapsodize about it but couldn't work it up into the nineteenth-century equivalent of a PowerPoint presentation.

But Catlin should be remembered for what he could and did do. As a passenger on the first steamboat to go up the Missouri beyond Council

Bluffs, Iowa, he took advantage of an unparalleled opportunity to serve his fellow Americans, giving them dispatches to read and paintings to view, rousing more interest in and sympathy for Indians than anyone else of his time. Though rudimentary and quixotic, his nation's park idea was doubly generous: to Indians, whose way of life it was meant to perpetuate, and to outsiders, who could enjoy vicariously the same experience that had thrilled him to the core—getting acquainted with "man and beast, in all the wild and freshness of their nature's beauty!"

Americans couldn't do very well at saving and protecting any of their natural heritage without taking a good look at it—not so simple a matter as it might sound. The first known account of anyone climbing a hill just to take in the view from the top was written by Petrarch in the 1300s. "If it was done before him," writes historian Jacques Barzun, "it wasn't recorded. Nature had been endlessly discussed, but as a generality, not as *this* landscape."[20] Five centuries later, Henry Thoreau, a Harvard graduate, sometime pencilmaker, and protégé of Emerson made a habit of scrutinizing landscapes with Petrarchan intensity.

Thoreau's complete works run to twenty volumes in the 1906 Walden Edition, but he published only two books during his lifetime. The second of these was *Walden* in 1854, so eagerly anticipated by the poet and abolitionist Thomas Wentworth Higginson that he managed to get hold of the proof pages ahead of publication. Higginson left an account of their effect on him: "Thoreau camps down by Walden Pond and shows us that absolutely nothing in Nature has ever yet been described—not a bird nor a berry of the woods, nor a drop of water, nor a spicula of ice, nor summer, nor winter, nor sun, nor star."[21]

Thoreau's first book, the one that had whetted Higginson's appetite for more, was *A Week on the Concord and Merrimack Rivers* (1849). Early on, the author makes the customary obeisance to the Old World. "The murmurs of many a famous river on the other side of the globe reach even to us here . . . and I trust that I may be allowed to associate our muddy but much abused Concord River with the most famous in history."[22] Once Thoreau hits his stride, however, he forgets Europe and scraps the prevailing American dollars-and-cents approach to a slice of raw nature—grading it by its suitability for farming or mining or some other profit-making scheme—to concentrate on the impression it makes on the senses, the wildlife it supports, how its constituent parts combine to make it what is.

A fine example of Thoreau's acuity comes in a passage about a phenomenon to which perhaps no American before him except a hydrologist had given a second thought: natural potholes in riverbeds. "Their origin is apparent to the most careless observer. A stone which the current has washed down, meeting with obstacles, revolves as on a pivot where it lies, gradually sinking in the course of centuries, deeper and deeper into the rock."[23] There is so much more to Thoreau's explanation of the potholes that his claim that it would occur "to the most careless observer" reads like an early example of the humblebrag. At the time, paying such close attention to the dynamics of a natural phenomenon was almost unheard of in American letters.

Thoreau's most influential disciple was a man who never met him: John Muir. When that multivolume set of Thoreau's writings came out in 1906, Muir acquired it for his library. Long before that, however, he had read and marked up *Walden* and the Thoreau essays that were gathered posthumously into a book called *Excursions*. In a journal entry, Muir challenged himself in a way that harked back to Higginson as stimulated by Thoreau's writings: "I have yet to see the man who has caught the rhythm of the big slow pulse beats of Nature."[24]

Among Muir's many attempts to capture that rhythm, here is one about the Merced River as it flows through Yosemite Valley: "How beautiful a rock is made by leaf shadows! Those of the live oak are particularly clear and distinct, and beyond all art in grace and delicacy, now still as if painted on stone, now gliding softly as if afraid of noise, now dancing, waltzing in swift, merry swirls, or jumping on and off sunny rocks in quick dashes like wave embroidery on seashore cliffs."[25]

Muir's powers of observation and deduction helped him get the better of no less a pooh-bah than Josiah Whitney, the director of California's Geological Survey, who had led the charge to scuttle Olmsted's Yosemite report. The topic under debate had to do with Muir's beloved Yosemite: How did the valley and its granite sentinels come to look the way they do?

An Idea in Embryo

Glaciers scraped against them over the eons, said Muir, grinding and sculpting them into the muscular forms they have today. Poppycock, replied Whitney in his 1869 Yosemite guidebook. "A more absurd theory was never advanced than that by which it was sought to ascribe to glaciers the sawing out of those vertical walls and the rounding of the domes."[26] The true cause, Whitney believed, was a sudden collapse of the material holding up what is now the valley.

Muir stood by his unorthodox conclusion—which he had reached while tramping all over Yosemite and trying to make sense of what he saw—but Whitney was adamant too. Calling Muir an "ignoramus," the geologist never recanted his curt dismissal of the glaciation hypothesis, which has since been shown to be the correct one. Muir was advancing the same cause as Thoreau before him: we can all profit from opening our eyes wider and studying nature with care. Muir went on to play a leading role in the second phase of what Olmsted called the "park movement": the proliferation of parks and the resistance of attempts to compromise their integrity for the sake of mammon or expediency. In light of the recent revelation that Muir accused Indians of leading a "dirty and irregular life," it's worth repeating that he did not share Catlin and Thoreau's willingness to accept Indians as charter inhabitants of national parks.[27]

In 1880 Olmsted used the occasion of a speech he gave to the American Social Science Association to reflect on the park movement's origins. He had city parks in mind, but his words applied equally to Yellowstone, the wild park shaped in part by his ideas. While giving some credit to his mentor Andrew Jackson Downing, Olmsted concluded that the park phenomenon was just one of those things that come along when conditions are right. "Parks have plainly not come as the direct result of any of the great inventions or discoveries of the country," he declared. "They are not, with us, simply an improvement on what we had before, growing out of a general advance of the arts applicable to them. It is not evident that the movement was taken up in any country from any other, however it may have been influenced or accelerated. It did not run like a fashion. It would seem rather to have been a common spontaneous movement of that sort which we conveniently refer to the 'Genius of Civilization.'"[28]

"Genius of Civilization" is a synonym for what we might call the spirit of the age or zeitgeist. But Olmsted's personification of the movement works well, for in this case the Genius of Civilization must have bent the ears of George Catlin, Henry Thoreau, John Muir, and Olmsted himself.

The Landscape Reader 5

The nineteenth century saw the introduction of one new form of mechanized transportation after another—the railroad, the streetcar, the bicycle, the automobile—yet it was also an era of indefatigable walkers. Baudelaire prowling the streets of Paris to soak up material for his poems. Dickens doing the same in London on behalf of his novels. Rimbaud roaming all over France to get away from his mother, or away from his lover Paul Verlaine, or away from himself. Young Abe Lincoln trudging for miles to borrow books from a friend who had what the boy's parents lacked: a decent private library. Whitman chanting "The Song of the Open Road," with "the long brown path before me leading me wherever I choose."[1]

As an adult, this book's central figure, Frederick Law Olmsted, liked to reminiscence about the many walks he took as a boy, the pièce de résistance being a sixteen-mile trek he and his brother, John Hull Olmsted, made to an aunt's house when they were nine and six years old, respectively. "We were two days on the road," Fred recalled, "spent the night at a rural inn which I saw still standing a few years ago, and were so tired when we arrived that, after sitting before that great fireplace and being feasted, we found that our legs would not support us and were carried off to bed."[2] Mostly, though, Fred rambled all over creation for the same reason as Whitman—the joy of it—and often went solo.

Born in Hartford in 1822 to an old Connecticut family, Fred had a patchy childhood. His mother died when he was three—"so young," he said, "that I have but a tradition of memory rather than the faintest recollection of her. When I was a small schoolboy if I was asked if I remembered her I could say 'Yes; I remember playing on the grass and looking up at her while she sat sewing under a tree.' . . . [I]t has always been a delight to me to see a woman sitting under a tree, sewing and minding a child."[3]

The "troublesome" Fred (his adjective) was handed off to one relative—and one tutor or school—after another. Yet through it all he could count on the love of his adoring father, John Olmsted, the prosperous owner of a Hartford dry-goods store, who took the boy on his first walks and instilled in him a love of nature. In "Passages in the Life of an Unpractical Man," the same autobiographical fragment that contains that tribute to his mother, Olmsted extolled his father as a man whose "sensitiveness to the beauty of nature was indeed extraordinary, judging from the degree in which his habits were affected by it; for he gave more time and thought to the pursuit of this means of enjoyment than to all other luxuries."[4] This sensitiveness was transmitted to the boy, who recalled taking pleasure in scenery at a very young age.

He also took pleasure in his reading, especially of books that few other boys would have cracked, such as William Gilpin's *Remarks on Forest Scenery* and Uvedale Price's *Essay on the Picturesque*, both borrowed from the Hartford Public Library. But a mysterious illness left Fred's eyesight so impaired that he had to forgo a college education. When his vision cleared up, he attended some lectures at Yale while his brother was there. Considering himself an honorary member of the class of 1847, Fred became best friends with John's classmate Charles Loring Brace, around whose shoulder Fred has his arm draped in a group photo taken in New Haven.

By then Fred was a man of the world. In 1840, at the age of eighteen, he'd left Hartford for New York, where thanks to connections a job awaited him: clerk in the office of a firm that imported dry goods from France. The young man commuted to his Manhattan workplace from Brooklyn, where he grew fond of Greenwood, the cemetery doubling as a park. On the job he picked up the skills of bookkeeping and office management, but the routine grated on him; after a year and a half, he quit and returned to Hartford. In 1843 he was back in New York long enough to ship out as an apprentice seaman on the bark *Ronaldson*. His itch to travel, however, was not well scratched. During much of the yearlong voyage, he suffered from seasickness, malaria, or scurvy, and he saw little of the place he'd most looked forward to: Canton, China.

Back in the States, with financial backing from his dad, Olmsted tried his hand at farming in Connecticut and on Staten Island, New York. His pears took a prize at an agricultural fair, but he didn't make much money at farming. His most promising venture was a nursery, though he didn't expect it to turn a profit until five years went by and the trees had matured. This was also the period in which he was hanging around Yale and contributing articles to the *Horticulturist*, the magazine edited by Andrew Jackson Downing. But Downing's profession, landscape design, had little appeal for Olmsted because most people lumped its practitioners in with gardeners.

With his brother and Charley Brace, Fred traveled to Great Britain, France, and Belgium in 1850. John interrupted his medical studies in New York to make the trip; Brace took a leave of absence from Union Theological Seminary because of doubts about his vocation. (Fred summed up his own religious beliefs as "a vague blundering indefensible rationalism.")[5] Brace took the opportunity to write travel articles for newspapers in Boston, New York, and Philadelphia, and Fred's account of a parliamentary debate appeared in the *Hartford Courant*, which was edited by Brace's father.

Fred was pleased to find that most English men and women treated Americans with respect and kindness, but the same could not be said of upper-class Britons' dealings with their own inferiors. In the book Fred wrote about his travels, *Walks and Talks of an American Farmer in England* (1852), he vented his disgust: "We hold that party in England, which regard their labouring class as a permanent providential *institution*, not to be improved in every way, educated, fitted to take an equal share with all Englishmen in the government of the commonwealth of England, to be blasphemers, tyrants, and insolent rebels to humanity."[6]

He found another English feature far more to his liking: its winsome countryside. And it was on this trip that he first encountered public city parks, including the one at Birkenhead, laid out by Joseph Paxton, the same architect who had designed the Crystal Palace in London. Birkenhead embodied the democratic ethos that Fred looked for in a park: "All this magnificent pleasure ground is entirely, unreservedly, and forever the People's own," he wrote in a piece for the *Horticulturist*. "The poorest British peasant is as free to enjoy it in all its parts, as the British Queen."[7]

Another park, a private one on the estate of the marquess of Westminster, coaxed a prescient exclamation out of Fred: "What artist, so noble, has often been my thought, as he who, with far-reaching conception of beauty and designing power, sketches the outline, writes the colors, and directs the shadows of a picture so great that Nature shall be employed upon it for generations, before the work he has arranged for her shall realize his intentions."[8] As a landscape architect, he was to see and feel the great disadvantage to such long-gestating artistry: the tendency of politicians to authorize deviations from his designs before they could ripen.

While in England, Fred demonstrated that he was one of those on whom nothing is lost—or at least nothing pertaining to landscapes. This receptiveness, along with a hint of the direction his life ultimately took, can be found in a letter he sent home to his father. Rural England owed its singular beauty to "the frequent long, graceful lines of deep green hedges and hedge-row timber, crossing hill, valley, and plain, in every direction, and in the occasional large trees, dotting the broad fields, either singly or in small groups, left to their natural open growth." The result, he added, was trees that branched low and wide, becoming "much more beautiful, than we often allow our trees to make themselves."[9]

That passage brings to mind the classic *Peanuts* Sunday strip in which Lucy, Linus, and Charlie Brown stretch out on a hilltop and put into words what they make of the clouds overhead. The precocious Linus tosses off one erudite association after another: this cloud resembles a map of British Honduras, that one the profile of the great American painter Thomas Eakins, and the formation over yonder is a vapory vision of Stonehenge. Now it's Charlie Brown's turn. "Well, I was going to say I saw a ducky and a horsie," he ruefully confesses, "but I changed my mind." So it must have been with John Olmsted and Charley Brace as they kept Fred company, their gazes glancing off this tree and that rock while his took in the big picture.

Fred was also constructing a personal philosophy. Well aware that he had benefited from his father's subsidies and the family's high standing in the world, he espoused a noblesse oblige precept: Americans like himself should mingle with the rest of the population so that the good qualities of the former could rub off on the latter, the end result being "a classless society of gentlemen."[10] In 1853 he elaborated on this vision in a letter to Brace, who was going for a master's in divinity at Union Theological Seminary and putting together a nongovernmental organization, the Children's Aid Society, in New York. (One of the society's projects was to establish boardinghouses for newsboys, an initiative that may have inspired Horatio Alger's tales of plucky lads lifted up from poverty by kindly philanthropists.) "The poor need an education to refinement and taste and the mental & moral capital of gentlemen," Olmsted told Brace. "'[Go] ahead with the Children's Aid and get up parks, gardens, music, dancing schools, reunions which will be so attractive as to force into contact the good & bad, the gentlemanly and the rowdy. And the state ought to assist these sort of things."[11]

Although Olmsted couldn't see it yet, a means of addressing both of his pet concerns at once—bringing out the best in landscapes and elevating the hearts and minds of ordinary Americans—lay almost within reach. He could devote himself to replicating the idyllic countryside that had meant so much to him as a vagabonding child. He could "get up" parks in cities, making natural beauty accessible to one and all.

The middling sales of *Walks and Talks of an American Farmer in England* didn't stop its author from copping a juicy assignment from a young newspaper called the *New-York Daily Times* (later simply the *New York Times*). Playing middleman was Brace, who, on hearing that the *Times* was in the market for a northerner who could report dispassionately on the American South, recommended his friend. In a letter to Frederick Kingsbury, another participant in the Yale group photo, Olmsted summed up what he hoped to make of these dispatches: "a valuable book of observations on Southern agriculture and general economy as affected by slavery . . . matter of fact to come after the deluge of spoony fancy pictures now at its height shall be spent."[12] Olmsted hit the road in late 1852, thinking of himself as thoroughly nonspoony but only moderately antislavery.

He ran headlong into southerners' suspicion of any northerner in their midst. "You can't imagine how hard it is to get hold of a conversable man," he wrote Brace, "—and when you find [one] he will talk about anything else but Slavery."[13] The prevailing silence on the topic seemed only to quicken Olmsted's analytical powers. By his reckoning, once you factored in the market price of slaves and their understandable habit of doing as little work as they could get away with, the institution did not make economic sense. "There is not room for the shadow of doubt across my mind," he wrote, "that slave labor makes the cost of cultivating such lands [as are found on Virginia plantations] greater, and the profits (!) less, than it would be under free labor."[14]

The few southerners who would talk to him about slavery did so in lyrical terms, a habit that provoked Olmsted to begin his forty-seventh letter, published in January 1854, on a Swiftian note: "Southerners often represent the condition of their slaves to be so happy and desirable that we might wonder that they do not sometimes take measures to be made slaves themselves, or at least occasionally offer their children for sale to the highest bidder."[15]

To refute the argument that slaves came from such inferior stock that they would be lost without their masters, in one of his letters Olmsted drew an analogy in the form of a question and answer. What would happen if you kept a man blindfolded throughout most of his life? Just as that man's eyesight would deteriorate, Olmsted argued, so do "the mind and soul" of human beings held in bondage. "Thus, it is a mistake to jump from the limitations exhibited by some freedmen and women in the North to the conclusion that slavery is justified in the South."[16]

In another of his letters to the *Times*, Olmsted had expanded on the tenet he'd tried out on Brace. Governments should do more than just protect private property, advance capitalism, and give "native genius" space in which to grow. Governments should also strive to "exert an elevating influence upon all people, [promoting] public parks and gardens, galleries of art and instruction in art, music, athletic sports and healthful recreations, and other means of cultivating taste and lessening the excessive materialism of purpose in which we are, as a people so cursedly absorbed."[17] The more Olmsted saw of the South, the surer he was of his opinions. In both quantity and quality, the region's cultural amenities fell far short of New England's, but enlightened lawmakers could close the gap. He was laying groundwork for what he later called "the park movement," as well as for, eventually, such agencies as the National Endowment for the Arts.

On his second journey to the South, starting in late 1853, Olmsted found a southerner who was conversable on at least one aspect of slavery: what a

The Landscape Reader

society based on it could show for itself. This was Samuel Perkins Allison, a Tennessean who had been a college classmate of John's. When Fred looked him up in Nashville, Allison boasted that slavery had enabled the South to produce a cohort of cultivated gentlemen without equal in the North. Writing to Brace, Fred made short work of the rest of the conversation: "I tried to show him that there were compensations in the *general* elevation of all classes at the North, but he did not seem to care for it."[18]

From Olmsted's two extended visits to the South for the *Times* emerged three books: *A Journey in the Seaboard Slave States* (1854), *A Journey through Texas* (1857), and *A Journey in the Back Country in the Winter of 1853–54* (1860). Accompanying him on the Texas swing had been his brother, who was suffering from tuberculosis and seeking relief from the wet, heavy northeastern air; John cobbled together the second of those volumes from Fred's *Times* articles and raw notes. In 1861 Fred condensed the trilogy into one volume, *Journeys and Explorations in the Cotton Kingdom*, adding a preface, "The Present Crisis," to cover the recent outbreak of the Civil War.

In the German-American enclaves of Texas, Olmsted had found confirmation for his thesis that slavery was holding the South back. Flush with shops and skilled workmen, newspapers, free schools, private academies, and civic and cultural institutions, the German towns were regional standouts. "That such a community," he wrote for the *Times*, "—generally industrious, active-minded, and progressively intelligent—can never exist in intimate connection with enslaved labor, I am well convinced."[19]

The extent to which Olmsted's travels had deepened his once-moderate opposition to slavery can be gauged by two prefaces he wrote in 1857. In the first, "Letter to a Southern Friend," which introduces *A Journey through Texas*, he argued that in the South, "slavery educates, or draws out, and strengthens, by example and exercise, to an inordinate degree, the natural lust of authority, common as an element of character to all mankind." He contributed the second preface to *The Englishman in Kansas, or Squatter Life and Border Warfare*, a book by a *Times of London* correspondent named Thomas H. Gladstone. Olmsted had come to believe that the slaveowner's whip lashed back at its wielder, inculcating in southern gentlemen habits that, in the North, "belong only to bullies and ruffians."[20] (In Russia at about the same time, Leo Tolstoy reached the same conclusion with regard to masters and their serfs. In *War and Peace*, Tolstoy's character Prince Andrey Bolkonsky laments how callous and miserable landowners become "just from having the ability to inflict punishment on all sides. These are the people I feel sorry for. They're the ones who make me want to see the serfs liberated.")[21]

The art historian and social reformer Charles Eliot Norton, who later became a friend of Olmsted's, judged his books on the South "the most important contributions to an exact acquaintance with the conditions and result of slavery in this country that have ever been published."[22] Other reviewers were less enthusiastic, however, and on his return to New York, Olmsted sold his farm to his brother and reentered journalism through another door, that of the publishing house Dix, Edwards and Company, which had recently bought *Putnam's Monthly Magazine*. As managing editor, Olmsted returned to England to see about signing up writers for the firm's booklist, but owing to the continuing lack of an international copyright law, he got nowhere. During his tenure at *Putnam's*, the magazine ran Melville's story "Benito Cereno" and some of Thoreau's Cape Cod writings, but the firm struggled financially. Although Olmsted bailed out shortly before Dix, Edwards and Company folded, taking the magazine down with it, he felt honor bound to help pay off the firm's debts.

In August 1857, when Olmsted was in his mid-thirties, a chance encounter changed his life. While holed up at a Connecticut inn to work on volume three of his southern travels, he ran into Charles Wyllys Elliott, a New Yorker whom he had met through Charley Brace. At the time, the Republican-majority state legislature was stripping New York City's Democratic mayor, Fernando Wood, of regulatory powers and handing them over to independent commissions. One such commission was now in charge of New York's nascent Central Park, Elliott was one of the commissioners, and Olmsted was a Republican. At Elliott's urging, Olmsted applied for the job of park superintendent. He went all out to get it, rounding up almost two hundred endorsements from eminent men, among them the poet and journalist William Cullen Bryant, the painter Albert Bierstadt, and the man of letters Washington Irving. During Olmsted's interview, the park's engineer, Egbert Viele, wondered aloud whether the post shouldn't go to "a practical man." "This objection would have defeated me," Olmsted later admitted, "had it not been for the autograph of Washington Irving on my papers. That turned the balance."[23] Olmsted was hired, but the gap between his annual salary of $1,500 and Viele's $3,000 reflects the initial pecking order.

As Laura Wood Roper observes, when Olmsted took the reins, "Nothing in his record—a farmer who had not made his farms pay, a writer who had made nothing but reputation, a publisher who had gone bankrupt— suggested his capacities."[24] Yet he had a good feeling about the new post. For, as he explained half a dozen years later in a letter to his partner, Calvert Vaux, it answered to "a special instinctive passion of my nature." "While others gravitated to pictures, architecture, Alps, libraries, high life and low life when travelling, I had gravitated to parks."[25] A photograph of Olmsted taken around this time shows a young dandy whose curling locks and smart cape seem at odds with his clenched fists. (Later, when his hairline had receded and his face was still thin and beardless, Olmsted looked decidedly eggheaded.)

New York had set aside a small public park at the Battery as early as 1826, but as the city grew, the need for more of the same became a crying one. There were a few privately owned parks, such as Gramercy, but these were not open to the public. In the 1840s Bryant had called for more open-to-all parks in an editorial for the *New York Evening Post*. Downing had returned from a visit to England impressed by "the great parks of London" and scornful of the situation in America's most populous city. "What are called parks in New-York," he needled the city fathers from his editorial pulpit in the *Horticulturist*, "are not even apologies for the thing; they are only squares or paddocks. . . . [T]he question may well be asked, is New-York really not rich enough, or is there absolutely not land enough in America, to give our citizens public parks of more than ten acres?"[26]

In 1851 the newly elected mayor, Ambrose C. Kingsland, had sent the city council a message calling attention to the flow of New York's population northward, away from what few parks the city had. Moreover, his honor had continued, "There is no park on the island deserving the name."[27] The council had agreed, and the state legislature had passed a law authorizing acquisition of a tract along the East River. When that choice didn't pan out, the city fathers turned to a larger, more conveniently located site: the midtown acreage that became Central Park.

The *New York Herald* greeted the incoming superintendent with a haughty prediction: "It is all folly to expect in this country to have parks like those in old aristocratic countries. . . . Is it not obvious that . . . the great Central Park will be nothing but a great beer-garden for the lowest denizens of the city?"[28] How badly and lastingly this editorial stung can be gauged from the fact that Olmsted quoted the above passage thirteen years later in a paper he read before the American Social Science Association.

Superintendent Olmsted's main responsibility was to direct the draining of swamps and the clearing of hovels, sheds, trees, and rocks from the long, slender plot of land (two and a half miles long and half a mile wide) acquired for the park. It was a prodigious task—Olmsted estimated that by the time it was over, nearly five million cubic yards of soil and rock had either been removed entirely or shifted from one spot to another, enough to form a single-file parade of one-horse cartloads thirty thousand miles long—and at first the workmen doubted the boss's ability to pull it off. They hazed him, taking him on long, muddy walks up and down the property and rattling off facts and figures in an effort to demoralize him.

Olmsted recalled an irksome experience with a foreman who was showing him around on a sultry summer afternoon. When Olmsted stopped to scrape mud off his clothing, the foreman made a comment suggesting that the boss was out of his depth. Olmsted was pretty sure he had "been through fifty miles of swamp to his [guide's] one" and that there "was not one operation in progress in the park in which [he] had not considerable personal experience." But Olmsted confined himself to remarking how nasty the place was—and in fact, he recalled, "the low grounds were steeped in the overflow and mush of pig-sties, slaughter-houses, and bone-boiling works, and the stench was sickening." A few days later, another foreman greeted the super with cheeky familiarity: "Hello, Fred; get round pretty often, don't you?"[29]

Yet Fred was savvier and tougher than he looked. As Norton put it after getting to know him, "All the lines of his face imply refinement and sensibility to such a degree that it is not till one has looked through them to what is underneath, that the force of his will and the reserved power of his character become evident."[30] It didn't take subordinates long to realize that in addition to being a literary type with connections in high places, Olmsted was a leader with unflagging energy, prodigious organizing powers, an eye for detail, and a firm resolve.

His diligence and quick mastery of the job were all the more remarkable in light of what was going on in his private life at the time: his brother was losing his battle with tuberculosis. On November 24, 1857, John died, leaving behind a wife, Mary Perkins Olmsted, and three children. In a letter to Fred, his father summed up their grief: "In his death I have lost not only a son but a very dear friend. You almost your only friend."[31] Fred took his duties as surviving brother so much to heart that nineteen months later he ended his bachelorhood by marrying Mary, becoming stepfather to her three children. (The couple eventually had two children of their own who survived infancy, and their marriage was a long success.) Also in the eventful year 1857 Olmsted was presented with another big opportunity: a contest for best Central Park plan, which Calvert Vaux proposed they enter as a team.

In the course of writing *Walks and Talks*, Olmsted had paid a call on Andrew Jackson Downing at the latter's home in upstate New York. While there Olmsted had met Downing's assistant, Vaux, the bricks-and-mortar architect destined to be the other half of a most fruitful partnership.

Unlike Olmsted's, Vaux's path to his calling had been straightforward. Born in London to a surgeon and his wife in 1824, Vaux apprenticed with an architectural firm in his hometown. But faced with limited opportunities in England, he jumped at an offer from Downing, who, while on a visit, admired some drawings of Vaux's at an exhibition. Downing proposed that they work together, with Vaux's designs for houses complementing Downing's landscape plans for private estates.

Vaux hadn't been in America long when a civic project came his and Downing's way. At the urging of President Millard Fillmore, the new partners were asked to design a park to fill the space between the White House and the Capitol. Congress gave its approval in 1851, and work began later that year. It was going well until two blows fell. En route to Washington to check on progress, Downing was killed in a steamboat explosion on the Hudson River, and Fillmore, who had not been nominated by his Whig Party for a second term, left office. The project was canceled.

Had Downing lived, he would have been the odds-on favorite to design Central Park, probably with Vaux's help. With Downing gone, it occurred to Vaux that Olmsted, who as park superintendent had come to know every square foot of the fledgling park, would be a good replacement. The idea of holding a competition for the park's design had originated with Vaux himself, and Olmsted must have been flattered when the architect asked him to collaborate on an entry. Olmsted felt he had to decline, though, in deference to his colleague Viele, who was preparing an entry of his own. But when the cocky Viele said he didn't give a damn whether Olmsted competed against him, Olmsted changed his mind and threw in his lot with the Englishman.

The contest rules made certain elements de rigueur for each entry, among them a parade ground, some playgrounds, a site for an exhibition hall, and a skating pond. At first Olmsted and Vaux chafed under these constraints—rather than check off items on an outdoor-activity wish list, they wanted to create "a single work of art . . . framed upon a single, noble motive, to which the design of all its parts, in some more or less subtle way, shall be confluent and helpful."[32] But they put their heads together and met the specs by repurposing existing features of the site. The meadows could serve as the parade ground and playgrounds, an existing arsenal could become the exhibition hall, and the lakes could be skating ponds.

Olmsted and Vaux's entry, which they dubbed the Greensward Plan, took the form of a pamphlet. As explained by the Olmsted scholar Charles E. Beveridge, they supplemented the pamphlet with "a large map (ink on paper, 43" high x 132" wide) of the design they proposed, and eleven smaller presentation boards featuring before and after views and other details."[33] When Greensward came out on top, the thirty-odd losers had reason to cry foul: What chance had they stood against two such well-placed insiders? But the judges had chosen well. Among Greensward's distinguishing features was an ingenious response to another specification: given its location astride midtown Manhattan, the park would have to accommodate through traffic. Olmsted and Vaux proposed constructing four sunken roads, allowing vehicles to cross the park's width without disturbing activities on the surface above.

Olmsted and Vaux had anticipated possible objections to what Greensward did *not* include. "Buildings are scarcely a necessary part of a park," they asserted; "neither are flower gardens, architectural terraces or fountains."[34] They justified another omission in a section summarizing the plan: "It will be perceived that no long straight drive has been provided on the plan: this feature has been studiously avoided, because it would offer opportunities for trotting matches. The popular idea of the park is a beautiful open green space, in which quiet drives, rides, and strolls may be had. This cannot be preserved if a race-course . . . is made one of its leading attractions."[35]

Witold Rybczynski, himself an architect, has made an educated guess as to how the partners divvied up work on their entry. Vaux's skills as a draftsman would have made him responsible for "the 'before and after' sketches that were an effective feature of their submission." Olmsted probably took the lead in writing the text and drawing up the budgets. "He also compiled the planting lists, which . . . were explicit and detailed. Both men probably collaborated on the site plan; Vaux's son later recalled that family and friends were enlisted in drawing the thousands of trees and dotting the grass pattern on the ten-foot-long drawing." "Many of the key ideas in the plan," Rybczynski adds, "have no precedent in either Vaux's or Downing's work"—which suggests that Olmsted was at least the catalyst for those ideas, if not their sole source.[36] Begrudging of structures, hostile to trotting matches, but rich in pictorial and verbal detail, the Greensward Plan garnered seven of the eleven commissioners' votes.

In his dual role as superintendent and co-designer, Olmsted kept in mind the democratic principles he had been expounding. While wealthy New Yorkers could betake themselves to rural open spaces that promised relief from the pressures of urban life, less well-off city dwellers could not. The park would correct this imbalance by making a sizable "specimen of God's handiwork" accessible to "hundreds of thousands of tired workers."[37] The idea, in its simplest form, was that if city dwellers could not give themselves a change of scenery, the city would bring a change of scenery to them.

To evoke spaciousness, Olmsted was not above resorting to artifice— building hillocks to obtain a rolling effect, planting trees alongside a pond where their reflections would give an illusion of depth, lending perspective by planting dark foliage in the foreground seen from a given viewpoint and lighter foliage in the distance. Later, in the paper he read to the American Social Science Association, Olmsted used prose that rings with the cadences of Whitman to express how he'd wanted visitors to behave in this blend of the natural and the contrived: "coming together . . . , with a common purpose, not at all intellectual, competitive with none, disposing to jealousy and spiritual or intellectual pride toward none, each individual adding by his mere presence to the pleasure of all others, all helping to the greater happiness of each." By then (1880) that part of Olmsted's agenda had been realized. "I have seen a hundred thousand [people] thus congregated," he said, and although some seemed "a little dazed" by their surroundings, "I have looked studiously but vainly among them for a single face completely unsympathetic with the prevailing expression of good nature and lightheartedness."[38]

Olmsted's mission to alleviate metropolitan angst had a personal dimension; he was prone to overwork, insomnia, depression, and nervous collapse. In the mid-1860s, while living in California, he acknowledged this syndrome as intrinsic to his personality. "I am liable to break down entirely and suddenly," he wrote to a friend, "—and I see that it's the worst feature in my life."[39] His Central Park workforce had multiplied from five hundred men on his arrival to twenty-five hundred by the end of 1858. He drove them and himself so hard and achieved such pleasing results that the park commissioners abolished Viele's job and in effect made Olmsted CEO, with the title of architect in chief and a salary of $2,500. Vaux, who unlike Olmsted was a trained architect, could swallow his annoyance at being named Olmsted's assistant because he had little interest in, or aptitude for, managing a workforce. He concentrated on making sure that his structural designs, notably for graceful bridges over waterways, were faithfully carried out.

Although Central Park officially opened on December 11, 1858, Olmsted and Vaux regarded it as a work in progress that would not fully ripen until at least a generation had passed. For one thing, trees by the thousands had yet to be planted, after which they would take years, if not decades, to mature. (Later in his career, Olmsted called park making an exercise in forecasting.)

The park got rave reviews. "Vast and beautiful . . . majestic," crowed the *Times*. "A royal work . . . the beau-ideal of a people's pleasure ground," trilled the *Atlantic*.[40] But by the fall of 1859 the unrelenting pressure had worn Olmsted out. The park commissioners, fearing for his health and wanting to deviate from the Greensward Plan in ways he would be sure to resent, sent him off on a six-week holiday to Europe with a $500 expense account. Before leaving, he received a chaffing note from Vaux: "I will not forgive you if you do not make a better show. Who will be tempted to a study of nature and the polite arts if the best paid and most popularly appreciated professors cut such a lugubrious, sallow, bloodless figure as you insist on doing?"[41] The letter's gloomy recipient all but ignored this scolding; rather than rest up, he devoted his holiday to visiting and studying parks in England, Ireland, France, and Germany.

He returned to pick up where he'd left off, only to meet with scrutiny of the park by the state legislature in Albany, requests that he hire this or that man as a favor to this or that park commissioner, and micromanaging by Andrew Haswell Green, a commissioner who doubled as the park's comptroller. Olmsted complained of the parsimonious Green that "not a dollar, not a cent, is got out from under his paw that it is not wet with his blood and sweat."[42] In a classic example of cheese-paring oversight, Green choked off the supply of pencils, which he thought were being wasted; to keep up with their work, Olmsted's draftsmen had to spring for their own number twos. On August 6, 1860, Olmsted was in an accident that added to his frustrations. As he drove a buggy in Manhattan with his wife and infant son as passengers, the horse bolted. One of the buggy's wheels struck a lamp post. Olmsted went flying and broke his left thighbone so severely that a portion of it was sticking out of his trousers. There was talk of amputation; ultimately, the leg was saved, but Olmsted walked with a limp for the rest of his life.

Green consolidated his power until he was, in Roper's phrase, "absolute czar of the park," lording it over not just Olmsted and Vaux but also his fellow commissioners.[43] When at Green's request the board ordered Olmsted to keep closer track of expenditures, he found himself in such a bind—denied the manpower he would need to comply—that he tendered his resignation. The board's president wouldn't accept it: pending before the state legislature was a bill to extend the park's northern boundary from 106th Street to 110th, and this was no time for a shakeup. Mollified by a concession—he could approve expenditures of up to $100 without obtaining Green's approval—Olmsted withdrew his resignation.

When the Civil War broke out in April 1861, Olmsted's bad leg ruled out the possibility of enlisting as a soldier. Casting about for an opportunity to serve—and to submit a resignation the park board could not in good conscience reject—he imagined himself as commissioner of "contrabands," the term given to liberated slaves by Union general Benjamin Butler as a dig at southerners' insistence that they were property. In a letter to one of his high-placed friends, the Boston Unitarian minister Henry Whitney Bellows, Olmsted made the case for himself: "I have, I suppose, given more thought to the special question of the proper management of negroes in a state of limbo between slavery & freedom than any one else in the country. I think, in fact, that I should find here my 'mission,' which is really something I am pining to find, in this war."[44]

Bellows had a better idea for how his friend might contribute to the war effort. He happened to be president of the U.S. Sanitary Commission, and with his endorsement, Olmsted was appointed its executive secretary—in effect, its CEO. Patterned after the British Sanitary Commission, which had acquitted itself so well and made Florence Nightingale so famous during the Crimean War, and chartered by an executive order from President Lincoln, the U.S. Sanitary Commission pooled the efforts of thousands of volunteers, most of them women. As its name suggests, the organization's primordial mission was to ensure a basic level of cleanliness and health for Union soldiers—something that the army's antiquated Medical Bureau had been making a poor job of. On reporting for duty that summer, Olmsted visited camps on the outskirts of Washington and came away appalled: the men were lousy in the original sense of lice ridden, the absence of fresh vegetables from their diet left them prone to scurvy, and for latrines they typically made do with open trenches.

Nor could Olmsted see the commission getting much done; at least on paper, its power was advisory only—it could make recommendations to the Medical Bureau and to commanding officers in the field but could not enforce compliance. He was also discouraged by the confusion and demoralization exhibited by Union soldiers after their defeat in the July 21 Battle of Bull Run. In a letter to his wife, who was still in New York with the children, Olmsted groused, "There is but one Sanitary measure to be thought of now & that is discipline."[45] His spirits were buoyed, though, by a declaration of support from the Union Army's commander, Gen. George McClellan.

With the army taking on volunteers at a dizzying rate, the Medical Bureau's performance grew worse. Under Olmsted's direction, the Sanitary Commission began operating as a kind of shadow bureau, then as an all-purpose dispensary, supplying the men with bandages, blankets, food, drink, even tents and horses. Doctors and nurses who got nowhere with the Medical Bureau would turn to the Sanitary Commission for help, as they did after a smallpox epidemic broke out in a Washington hospital; when the bureau ran out of vaccines, the commission scrounged up enough to inoculate twenty thousand men. Also gratifying to Olmsted was the audience he had with Lincoln on October 11. Olmsted showed up with a low opinion of the president, so low, in fact, that in another letter to his wife, he had said he would just as soon have Andrew Green in the White House. Olmsted came away from his meeting with Lincoln critical of the president's inelegant diction but allowing that "his frankness & courageous directness overcame all critical disposition."[46]

Olmsted's allusion to Lincoln's lack of polish can serve as a reminder that the Sanitary Commission, like Central Park, was run by elitists. The commission's treasurer, Wall Street lawyer George Templeton Strong, confided to his diary that the commission's work was vital because "neither the blind masses, the swinish multitudes, that rule us under our accursed system of universal suffrage, nor the case of typhoid can be expected to exercise self-control."[47] The elitist but not haughty Olmsted transformed the commission into a model of efficiency. Impressive figures can be cited to demonstrate its ability to give aid and comfort quickly—the twelve hundred pairs of crutches it sped to soldiers wounded at Gettysburg, for example. Over time the commission expanded its purview beyond life's necessities to address almost any shortage felt by the men in the field, books and brandy included.

Strong fretted, however, about how often Olmsted and the commission's board were at loggerheads. A pattern had taken hold—Olmsted was happy to give orders, loath to take them. But with the relocation of Olmsted's family to Washington, it became clear that the executive secretary had settled in and committed himself to the work.

He was committed to the soldiers too. Time permitting, Olmsted would visit the sick wards in Washington. Roper tells of how, late one night, a female nurse "surprised him seated on the floor by a dying man's pallet, his arm around his pillow, speaking gently to him. Olmsted came in only when the wards were quiet, [the nurse] noticed, and he thought there was no one around to observe him."[48]

Walt Whitman, by the way, had little use for the Sanitary Commission, perhaps because he fancied himself a one-man band playing a similar tune. His stint as a nurse without portfolio dated from December 1862, when he picked up a copy of the *New York Tribune* and saw his brother George's name on the casualty list for the Fredericksburg Campaign. Walt went south and found George, who had been wounded but not gravely. But Walt was so moved by the plight of the wounded generally that he settled in Washington to do his part. At the end of his workday as a clerk in the army Paymaster's Office, he would make the rounds in military hospitals, giving comfort to ailing Union soldiers by chatting with them, bringing them treats (which he paid for himself), writing letters for them, and in some cases keeping vigil as they died.

What galled Whitman was the icy demeanor of the Sanitary Commission's nurses, who performed their duties with machinelike indifference, although this was probably because they had so many patients to take care of that maintaining a stone face helped them stay sane. He sweepingly claimed that the commission's "hirelings . . . get well-paid & are always incompetent & disagreeable." One of those hirelings, a pious woman from Connecticut, returned the favor by writing to her husband, "There comes the odious Walt Whitman to talk evil and unbelief to my boys. I think I would rather see the Evil One himself. . . . I shall get him out as soon as possible."[49] Whitman might have thought better of the commission if, while making his rounds, he had walked in on Secretary Olmsted taking time out to comfort a dying soldier.

Not least among Olmsted's responsibilities were fundraising for the commission and collecting supplies for the boys. He inveigled dignitaries into spreading the word. One of these was Horace Howard Furness, a well-known compiler of variorums for Shakespeare's plays, who represented the commission in New York and Connecticut. "I have addressed large bodies and little bodies, and nobodies and somebodies," Furness reported to Olmsted. "I have spoken in Town Halls, in Concert Halls, and in Court Rooms, in Presbyterian, Methodist, Baptist, Lutheran and Episcopalian Churches, from pulpits and from judicial benches, before communion tables and baptismal fonts. I have seen before me eyes glistening with interest and eyes drowsy with sleep."[50]

Speaking of sleep, Olmsted's tenure at the commission only accentuated his workaholism; in a May 1862 letter to Bellows, Olmsted confessed to having nodded off several times while writing it. (Late in his life, Olmsted told psychology professor William James of several occasions when he'd slept and dreamed with his eyes open.) There was no end to the work for him or for his employees. Writing to his wife from a floating hospital, Olmsted called the horror of war on the field "beyond, far beyond all imagination. One of our most efficient men, who worked through all with untiring nonchalance, today, being the first day of rest, broke out in hysterics."[51] Strong, in another diary entry, can almost be seen shaking his head in dismay as he portrays the feverishly busy Olmsted on the job: "He works like a dog all day and sits up nearly all night, doesn't go home to his family (now established in Washington) for five days and nights altogether, works with steady, feverish intensity till four in the morning, sleeps on a sofa in his clothes, and breakfasts on *strong coffee and pickles*!!!!"[52]

In March 1862 New York City mayor George Opdyke had sounded Olmsted out on the possibility of becoming the city's street commissioner. Olmsted was willing to change jobs again—indeed, at the time he was angling to become a commissioner of Port Royal, the collective name for the South Carolina sea islands captured by Union forces the previous November and put to use as a kind of refuge for liberated slaves. But it soon became clear that a majority of New York's aldermen weren't going to vote him in as street commissioner, and the Port Royal job eluded him too. In August the exhausted Olmsted shuffled off to Saratoga Springs for a rest.

On his return, he found himself vexed by a problem that had been brewing for some time: the tendency of the Sanitary Commission's state and city branches to favor their own boys with the money they raised and the supplies they collected. Olmsted fulminated about this parochial tendency in a long letter to the secretary of the Iowa affiliate. The commission and its subdivisions should adhere to the principle of all for one and one for all. A state or city that deviates from that rule, Olmsted charged, takes on "a stain of the very soil, out of which the monster Secession has grown."[53] On top of everything else, Olmsted was having a rare quarrel with his father, who was disappointed to hear that once again, Fred was looking to change jobs.

Early in his time at the commission, Olmsted had periodically darted back to Central Park, where Vaux was doing his best to keep the grand project on track and Czar Green at bay. (To reflect their respective contributions, the conscientious Olmsted had gotten his salary reduced to $2,000 and Vaux's raised to $2,500. As the amount of time Olmsted could spare for the park dwindled, his pay went down to $100 a month.) But with Green pinching pennies harder than ever, Vaux gave Olmsted a warning: the day was coming when Vaux would have to resign on behalf of them both. In May 1863 Vaux made good on that threat. As Olmsted put it in a letter to his father, "Vaux has finally been badgered off the park and my relations with it are finally closed. We couldn't bear it even as consulting architects. They wound it up with a very innocent complimentary resolution."[54]

In Washington, Olmsted was becoming more enmeshed in the coils of the federal bureaucracy. To cite just one case, his attempt to get some medical monographs into print was stymied by the secretary of war, Edwin Stanton, who denied having any authority over the Government Printing Office. Olmsted was gratified by Ulysses Grant's praise of the Sanitary Commission's work when he paid the general a visit during the Siege of Vicksburg, and the commission's stellar performance at Gettysburg became another source of pride. Yet Olmsted complained of being "oppressed beyond endurance."[55] Compounding his troubles was his reluctance to take orders. As Bellows pointed out in a letter, "You ought not to work under

The Landscape Reader

anybody. . . . With subordinates you have, and would have, no difficulties. It is only with peers or superiors (official) that you cannot serve."[56]

The next prospect to tempt Olmsted was helping found a new kind of journal in New York—hardly an endeavor likely to alleviate fatigue and feelings of oppression, but that's Olmsted for you. The idea came from his friend Edwin Lawrence Godkin, an Irish immigrant who had studied Olmsted's dispatches for the *Times* before undertaking his own reporting on the South for the *London Daily News*. Now, six decades ahead of the birth of *Time*, Godkin wanted to create and edit a weekly magazine that would put the news in perspective, and he invited Olmsted to be its publisher.

But raising the capital needed to start a magazine proved to be a time-consuming job: the *Nation*, as the weekly was called, didn't publish its first issue until 1865. In the interim, another opportunity—rather different from anything he'd done before—fell Olmsted's way.

How to Sell a Park Bill   6

When California entered the Union in 1850, San Francisco's population stood at twenty-five thousand, the Sierra Nevada foothills crawled with gold seekers, but the rest of the state was lightly populated and little known. The first whites to see Yosemite had been a party of mountain men led by Joseph Walker in 1833; while scouting an overland route to California, the roughneck explorers got a glimpse of the valley from what was probably its north rim. Many a Forty-Niner must have paused to gawk at the valley while rushing toward gold country, but the first real invasion came in 1851.

Invasion is *le mot juste* because the valley had long been occupied by the Ahwahneechees, an Indian tribe who took their name from a word meaning "place of a gaping mouth," which nicely captures one aspect of the scenery. The Ahwahneechees had recently been accused of raiding trading posts along the Merced River, and a band of vigilantes styling themselves the Mariposa Battalion rode in to teach the Indians a lesson. They failed—the Ahwahneechees caught wind of them and melted away—but did have a look around. A year later the Ahwahneechees attacked some prospectors, who may or may not have provoked the incident, and killed two of them. The U.S. Army retaliated by killing five Indians, and the Ahwahneechees abandoned the valley.

They left something behind, however: the name Yosemite, about which a misconception arose. According to the diary of a Mariposa Battalion member, the Ahwahneechees applied "Yo Semite" or some approximation thereof to him and his fellow vigilantes, and it meant "grizzly bear"; in this reading, the Indians had conferred a fearsome honorific on their pursuers. More likely, though, the term meant "some among them are killers," and the Ahwahneechees intended it as a warning that the white invaders were not to be trusted.

Over the next decade or so, Yosemite's image was shaped by a number of less pernicious white men: Thomas Starr King, James M. Hutchings, Horace Greeley, Carleton E. Watkins, and Albert Bierstadt. King, a Unitarian minister, had attracted a large following in Boston but nevertheless felt snubbed by the city's establishment. The early death of his father, also a minister, had left the family too strapped to send Thomas to Harvard; instead, he'd seen to his own education by reading widely and paying for private tutoring in divinity. On the strength of his charisma, he was invited to preach at the college he'd been too poor to attend; in 1860, when he was thirty-five, he agreed to move to San Francisco and take over a Unitarian church there.

King went west with a sense of clerical duty toward an underserved population and high hopes for his own advancement, but when he and his wife stepped ashore, he wondered why they'd come. San Franciscans rose to the occasion. Flattered by King's willingness to trade the hallowed precincts of Boston for their rough-hewn town, they gave the couple an effusive welcome. Even better, they helped the Kings become financially secure by steering them toward good investments: stock in gold and silver mines on the Comstock Lode in Nevada Territory, which was riding high on a streak of bonanzas. King remembered why he'd come—to become a great man, a label he might never have qualified for in the snooty East. When not preaching the gospel in San Francisco, he toured the state, as well as Oregon and British Columbia.

King was so moved by his first sighting of the Sierra Nevada, from a steamboat on the Sacramento River, that he compared it to "a vision from another world, like the street and wall of the new Jerusalem."[1] Already the author of *The White Hills*, a guidebook to the White Mountains of New Hampshire, he became an emissary for the West by publishing a series of letters about it in the *Boston Evening Transcript*.

King campaigned for Lincoln in 1860. After the Civil War broke out, Californians found the minister's pro-Union oratory so stirring that they led the nation in contributions to the U. S. Sanitary Commission. But the book King hoped to write about Yosemite never materialized; stricken with diphtheria and pneumonia, he died on March 4, 1864. What he had done for California was summed up by his friend and fellow clergyman Henry

Bellows, after he came west to take over King's orphaned congregation. "No one had really seen the Sierra Nevada, Mount Shasta, the Yosemite Valley," Bellows declared, "until [King's] fine eye saw and his cunning brain and hand depicted them." New Englanders kept the newspapers in which King's dispatches had appeared, Bellows noted, "as permanent sources of delight."[2]

At the time of King's death, Yosemite was on its way to becoming a park, with strong support from another, more self-serving admirer. This was the English immigrant James M. Hutchings, who could have held his own at Niagara Falls when entrepreneurs were vying for lucrative vantage points on the riverbanks. After being lured to California by the gold rush, Hutchings calculated that an illustrated magazine ballyhooing the young state's incomparable scenery would be a better bet for him than prospecting. At the time, members of the Mariposa Battalion were still buzzing about what sounded like the finest spectacle of all—Yosemite Valley, which Hutchings was determined to see for himself. Unable to find any white men to guide him, in June 1855 he and three companions gave the job to a pair of Indians. Hutchings was so astounded by what they showed him that he published a florid article about it in a local newspaper, the *Mariposa Gazette*. In it he quoted one of his fellow travelers exclaiming about the valley, "What! have we come to the end of all things?" and another asking, "Can this be the opening of the Seventh Seal?"[3] A year later Hutchings launched the journal he'd been dreaming of, *Hutchings' Illustrated California Magazine*, with a mission to publicize what lay beneath seal number seven.

In 1856 Hutchings returned to the valley with an artist, Thomas A. Ayres, whose drawings were converted into lithographs and printed in the *Illustrated*. Ayres also made freelance sketches, some of which he sold to *Harper's Magazine* in New York, giving easterners a look at Yosemite's vaunted grandeur. As the season opened that year, tourists could reach the valley on a newly blazed rough trail, and a hotel was under construction. Three years later Hutchings settled in the valley to make his living as a tour guide and innkeeper. On behalf of his magazine and his new onsite enterprises, he commissioned the photographer Charles Leander Weed to take pictures there. A San Francisco gallery owner marketed the resulting stereoscopic images as samples of the delights in store for adventurous travelers. In 1860 Hutchings self-published a book, *Scenes of Wonder and Curiosity in California*, which laid out an eight-day Yosemite excursion. A year later he bought a failing hotel in the valley.

By 1864 Hutchings was not only the valley's leading interpreter and publicist but also the proprietor of its best lodgings, the refurbished Upper Hotel. Yet because the federal government had never surveyed Yosemite country, not an acre of it had been legally claimed or occupied. Hutchings, in short, was a squatter.

In 1859 the New York newspaper editor Horace Greeley had toured the Far West, Yosemite included. It was during this trip that the white-knuckled Greeley implored his coach driver to take it easy on a rough road. "Keep your seat, Horace," the driver replied in words made famous by Mark Twain in his second book, *Roughing It*. In Twain's telling, Californians were so proud of the driver's put-down of this eastern swell that they couldn't repeat it too often.

Greeley recovered enough of his dignity to write *An Overland Journey*, a book about what he'd seen and done out west. In it he called Yosemite Valley the "greatest marvel of the continent" and urged the state of California to get busy saving the nearby big trees from the ax.[4] For all of Twain's derision (see also the Hawaiian section of *Roughing It*), Greeley was a big shot who later became a major-party candidate for president of the United States, and his excitement about Yosemite proved contagious.

Charles Leader Weed's stereoscopic photographs may have been the talk of San Francisco, but an upstart named Carleton E. Watkins was sure he could do better. In 1861 he went out to the valley and proved it.

Originally from upstate New York, Watkins had migrated to California ten years earlier with his friend Collis P. Huntington to prospect for gold. Neither man struck it minerally rich, but Huntington went on to attain robber baron status as one of the Big Four, the other three being Leland Stanford, Charles Crocker, and Mark Hopkins. The quartet made colossal and malodorous fortunes from building the Central Pacific, the western leg of the transcontinental railroad. Watkins settled in San Francisco knowing almost nothing about photography but willing to give it a go. He found the relatively new medium so much to his liking that he took lessons from the city's leading practitioners.

Watkins brought two cameras with him to Yosemite, a portable stereoscopic model for small-scale subjects like trees and boulders, and a mammoth-plate affair to capture the granite spires and plummeting waterfalls. The big camera was housed in a custom-built cabinet with an opening in the front for the lens and a slot in the back to hold a ground-glass plate—a package so cumbersome that it had to be lugged in by mule. About seventy-five of Watkins's 1861 stereo plates have survived, along with a third that many of the mammoth kind. "Watkins took great pride in the work," writes art historian Weston J. Naef, "captioning the stereos by hand on the mounts and carefully printing the mammoth negatives on albumen paper, which he then mounted on large cards and framed behind glass." These, Naef adds, are "not the first landscape photographs, but they are the first to present nature from a deliberately assumed artistic posture."[5]

As Watkins assumed that posture in 1861, he was still mastering the big camera and coming to terms with the play of sunlight on glacier-polished granite. In his photo of El Capitan, the peak almost fades out behind the inkblot solidity of trees along the Merced River in the foreground. Viewers were dazzled anyway. In the July 1863 issue of the *Atlantic Monthly*, America's premier photography critic, Oliver Wendell Holmes, credited Watkins with "a perfection of art which compares with the finest European work."[6] California senator John Conness got hold of some of Watkins's Yosemite photos and used them in making his case for the Yosemite Park bill (more on this episode is coming up).

Also in 1863 the German-born painter Albert Bierstadt visited Yosemite, which he depicted in two of his typically grandiose and liberty-taking works, *Domes of the Yosemite* and *Valley of the Yosemite*. Not everyone was enamored of Bierstadt's fast-and-loose treatments. Mark Twain teased him in a critique published by the San Francisco *Alta California*: "Some of Mr. Bierstadt's mountains swim in a lustrous, pearly mist, which is so enchantingly beautiful that I am sorry that the Creator hadn't made it instead of him, so that it would always remain there."[7] But Bierstadt's visual hyperbole hardly damaged Yosemite's cause, nor did the prose poem about the valley written by his traveling companion, Fitz Hugh Ludlow, for the June 1864 issue of the *Atlantic*. Ludlow's tribute to Bierstadt's precursor in another medium set a new standard for effusiveness: "We were going into the vale whose giant domes and battlements had months before thrown their photographic shadow through Watkins's camera across the mysterious wide continent, causing . . . ecstasy in Dr. Holmes's study."[8]

In addition to the publicity conferred by writers, photographers, and painters, Yosemite benefited from the symbiotic relationship between American nature and transportation modes. A notable early instance had occurred in 1857, when the Baltimore and Ohio Railroad treated a number of painters and photographers to an all-expenses-paid excursion in what is now West Virginia. Although the train was outfitted with a special dining saloon and a piano, the guests had little time to quaff, nibble, or sing along. They were too busy capturing the scenery outside—the Potomac and Monongahela Rivers—in sketches and photos that might tempt others to make the same trip as paying customers.

Before completion of the transcontinental railroad in 1869, travel by sea—interrupted by a dry-land crossing of the isthmus of Panama—was the safest and surest way for easterners to reach the Far West; among many others, Watkins and Huntington had come that way. Accordingly, Israel Ward Raymond, California agent of the Central American Steamship Transit Company of New York, may have regarded Yosemite as a potential drawing card for his firm's customers. On February 20, 1864, possibly after discussing the matter with a newcomer to the state named Frederick Law Olmsted, Raymond wrote a letter to California's junior senator, John Conness. With support from a photo taken at what is now known as Inspiration Point, Raymond raved about Yosemite's scenic values and sounded a note, first struck by Catlin, that became a constant in early campaigns to carve parks out of federal land: "The summits are mostly bare Granite Rocks and in some parts the surface is covered only by pine trees *and can never be of much value*."[9] The only thing Yosemite was good for, in other words, was enthralling tourists.

Raymond not only urged the introduction of a bill to preserve the valley and, for good measure, the Mariposa Grove of sequoia trees; he also tried his hand at drafting the legislative language, to wit: "The above [tracts] are granted for public use, resort, and recreation and are inalienable forever but leases may be granted for portions not to exceed ten years."[10] Raymond's bill proposed the state of California as the tracts' owner and instructed it to delegate management of both properties to a board of commissioners. The helpful agent even recommended members for the board, among them himself and Olmsted. Although, if enacted, Raymond's proposal would likely increase ridership on the Central American's steamships, in other respects it was public-spirited, directing that profits from concessions be plowed back into the park and that the commissioners serve gratis.

In John Conness, Raymond had found the right drum major for the Yosemite band. Conness was born in County Galway, Ireland, in 1821, the last of fourteen children. The family immigrated to America in 1836, settling in New York City, where the boy apprenticed to a piano maker. Thirteen years later Conness answered the call of the gold rush. He did all right as a miner, better as a supplier of provisions to others. In 1852 he ran for the state assembly as a Democrat—half a century later he recalled being apolitical until "efforts to ally California with proslavery" got his dander up—and won the election.[11] In office, he opposed the importation of Chinese laborers to California as indentured servants but didn't see why they shouldn't be let in as free men and women.

Conness served four terms as an assemblyman, becoming so well thought of that in January 1861 he was nominated to be speaker; after ninety-three inconclusive ballots, however, he removed his name from consideration. Later that year, as a stalwart of the Democratic Party's pro-Union wing, he challenged the incumbent governor, John G. Downey, who was running for a second term. Conness got the nomination but lost the general election to the Republican candidate, future railroad magnate and U.S. senator Leland Stanford.

Two years later Conness became a U.S. senator himself almost by accident. Those were the days when senators were elected by state legislatures. As chronicled by Albert D. Richardson of the *New York Tribune* (Greeley's paper), California lawmakers caught a colleague taking a bribe for his vote. The legislature, disgusted at the corruption, "went outside of all the candidates and elected Conness, who was lying ill at the time."[12] The accidental senator later used his newfound clout to help foil Stanford's bid for a second term as governor. Victory in that race went to Frederick F. Low, who thus became the boss of state geologist Josiah Whitney, soon to be the squelcher in chief of Olmsted's Yosemite report.

Conness forwarded Israel Raymond's Yosemite letter to the commissioner of the U.S. General Land Office with a request to draw up a proper bill. In so doing, the senator seconded Raymond's recommendation that the grant be "inalienable." The General Land Office delivered a bill that Conness introduced on March 28, 1864. By the time a Senate committee reported it out favorably on May 17, Conness appears to have made a strategic decision: focus less on the majestic valley than on the gargantuan trees. Accordingly, the *Congressional Globe* printed the floor debate under the heading "Mariposa Big Tree Grove," relegating Yosemite Valley almost to an afterthought.[13]

When the bill reached the Senate floor, Conness walked his fellow senators through its provisions. He emphasized a point made by Raymond: the tracts to be conveyed to and protected by the state were "for all public purposes worthless, but . . . constitute, perhaps, some of the greatest wonders of the world." Worthlessness was becoming a prerequisite; later candidates for park status that did have potential for commercial exploitation, especially mining or timbering, would run into delays, be whittled down to little more than barren mountaintops, or be rejected in toto. But Conness knew his audience; after explaining his bill, he reiterated that "the property is of no value to the Government."

Senator Lafayette Sabine Foster from Connecticut piped up to ask what the state of California thought of all this. Conness assured his colleague that "the application [for a grant of the land] comes to us from various gentlemen in California, gentlemen of fortune, of taste, and of refinement, and the plan proposed in this bill has been suggested by them." Foster kept at it, calling the grant "a rather singular [one], unprecedented so far as my recollection goes," and speculating that "unless the State through her appropriate authorities signified some wish in the matter, it might be deemed by the State officious on our part to make a grant of this kind." To this objection Conness gave what, depending on his tone of voice, may have been a sarcastic reply: "Ordinarily I should hope I spoke for the State of California here. I feel authorized to do so under existing circumstances. There is no parallel, and can be no parallel for this measure, for there is not . . . on earth just such a condition of things. The Mariposa Big Tree Grove is really the wonder of the world, containing those magnificent monarchs of the forest that are from thirty to forty feet in diameter." Here Conness was probably going by hearsay; so far as we know, he had not yet laid eyes on either the valley or the grove.

Senator Garrett Davis, a Union Democrat from Kentucky, asked how old the trees were, a question that allowed Conness to administer his coup de grace. After giving a number—"estimated to reach an age of three thousand years"—he claimed that at stake here was nothing less than American credibility. From another grove of sequoias, the Calaveras, "some sections of a fallen tree were cut during and pending the great World's Fair that was held in London some years since. One joint of the tree was sectioned and transported to that country in sections, and then set up there. The English who saw it declared it to be a Yankee invention, made [up] from beginning to end; that it was an utter untruth that such trees grew in the country; that it could not be." Not even the disclosure that transporting the sections to England had cost "several thousand dollars [could] convince them that it was a specimen of American growth," Conness added. "They would not believe us. The purpose of this bill is to preserve one of these groves from devastation and injury. The necessity of taking early possession and care of these great wonders can easily be seen and understood."

By now it had dawned on the gentleman from Connecticut that his demand for the state of California's opinion on the bill could be taken as a breach of senatorial courtesy. Foster backtracked, disingenuously professing not to understand how he could have given the impression that Conness did not possess "the most perfect and entire right to speak for his State." With that the world's greatest deliberative body prepared to vote. Probably because senators had so much else on their minds—waging a war to preserve the Union, for example—the bill seems to have passed without further debate or challenge.

The House followed suit and, complete with a reminder that the tracts were being ceded to the state "upon the express conditions that these premises shall be held for public use, resort and recreation, [and] shall be held inalienable for all time," the enrolled bill was signed into law by President Lincoln on June 30, 1864. By casting the British as a bête noir, by reducing the issue before the Senate to the sloganlike sentence "They would not believe us," Conness had succeeded in framing an innovative measure in a patriotically appealing way.

It didn't hurt that this was a period when one could hardly go wrong by playing to anti-British animus. The outbreak of the Civil War had prompted Sir John Ramsden to rise in the House of Commons to mark the bursting of "the great republican bubble."[14] The *New York Times* had reported that on the 1862 Commemoration Day at Oxford University, the mention of Jefferson Davis's name had brought "tumultuous and unanimous applause," whereas Lincoln's name "was greeted with hisses and groans."[15] In his *Memoirs*, Grant recalled thinking that "our republican institutions were regarded as experiments up to the breaking out of the rebellion, and monarchical Europe generally believed that our republic was a rope of sand that would part the moment the slightest strain was brought upon it."[16] The saving of Yosemite and the big trees taught England and other monarchical countries that Americans were telling the truth about their fabulous geographic blessings and willing to back up their words with action. Presented as a thumbing of the nose at John Bull, the Yosemite Park bill had ended up being an easy yes vote.

But Senator Conness's memory had played him false. The world's fair he cited, popularly known as the Crystal Palace Exhibition, began and ended in the year 1851, but the big-tree sections from California didn't reach England until 1857, when they scored an unequivocal triumph. What happened in between was a far cry from Conness's accusations.

In the summer of 1852 a handful of miners had taken time out to make a quick financial killing by cutting down a Calaveras Grove sequoia, putting cross sections of it on display, and charging a fee for the privilege of viewing them. The miners had felled their victim not with saws but with tools of their trade: pump augers, which the historian Joseph H. Engbeck

How to Sell a Park Bill

Jr. describes as "approximately three-inch diameter drills used for making hollow, wooden pipes or flumes."[17] As one might imagine, augering the giant tree down was deuced hard work, and the miners' doggedness became a feature of their tale, as recounted in newspapers across the country. After making a brief appearance in San Francisco, the tree sections were shipped to New York via Cape Horn in the care of one Capt. W. H. Hanford.

In New York, Hanford ran afoul of a formidable adversary, the shameless impresario Phineas T. Barnum. The city had built a copycat Crystal Palace, which had become a white elephant. Barnum had publicly vowed to put on a show at the palace good enough to turn its fortunes around. Hanford was sure that his tree sections would make a superb addition to that spectacle, but Barnum told him to get lost. Undaunted, Hanford went off and rented space for exhibiting the sequoia sections on his own. On hearing of this, Barnum planted stories in New York newspapers calling Hanford's exhibit a fake. Most people believed Barnum—if the country's huckster without peer said something was phony, then by God it must be—and skipped Hanford's exhibition. The few who did attend came out muttering "that it was impossible, that such a thing never grew, and that they were being humbugged" (fairly close to the words Senator Conness was to attribute to skeptical English men and women in 1864).[18] Not ready to give up yet, Hanford readied his tree parts for shipment to Paris, but the disaster became utter when they burned up in a New York fire.

Back in California, another gang of vandals was chipping away at a second sequoia, the pride of the Calaveras North Grove, where its magnificence had earned it the sobriquet Mother of the Forest. As explained by Engbeck, it took the work crew about ninety days in the summer of 1854 to accumulate "some sixty tons of bark lying on the ground in carefully numbered eight-foot-long plates that were from one to nearly two feet in thickness."[19]

On being shipped to New York in 1855 by an entrepreneur named George D. Trask, these items got a much better reception than Hanford's had. In the meantime, the American Crystal Palace had changed hands; it was now managed and about to be reopened by none other than Horace Greeley. Working out a deal with Trask, Greeley renamed the tree the Mastodon, rounded up testimonies to its authenticity from experts, and took out a newspaper ad calling the Hanford exhibit of three years earlier "almost a pygmy compared with this mastodon."[20] On reopening day, July 4, 1855, Greeley succeeded where Barnum had failed. "For the first time, and at least for one season," Engbeck writes, "the [New York] Crystal Palace was solvent and successful."[21]

How would the Mastodon fare at the real Crystal Palace? Trask meant to find out. On April 10, 1857, the tree bark made its English debut in the original glass structure, which had recently been moved from its first location in Hyde Park to another part of London. The imported American spectacle did boffo business. "Twenty-seven thousand people were able to get in that first day," Engbeck states, "and it was estimated that an equal number were turned away for lack of room."[22] The display stayed in place, presenting legions of visitors with an example of America's natural prodigiousness until 1866, when the Crystal Palace was destroyed in a fire.

In sum, the truth was almost the opposite of what Conness had said to sway his fellow senators. The discrediting of the original sequoia exhibit was engineered by Barnum and ratified by American visitors who fell for his allegation that the tree sections were phony. It was a cynical New York episode, which the English had nothing to do with. What's more, when the Brits finally did have a sequoia exhibit in their midst—starring the integument of the Mother who became a Mastodon—they flocked to it and loved what they saw. This is not to accuse the senator of knowingly misleading his colleagues. With its two violated trees, two Crystal Palaces, and four exhibitors, the story was an easy one to get wrong. Conness may well have believed every syllable of his spiel about the big trees' English reception, although when he added the fillip that transporting the sequoia sections to England had cost "thousands of dollars," he was surely winging it. In any case, nobody fact-checked his story, then or later.

Nor did Conness mention the effects on the trees themselves. In 1853 the Boston-based magazine *Gleason's Pictorial Drawing-Room Companion* had published a screed about the damage done to Hanford's auger-drilled, fallen giant. The author was a Californian who thought it "a cruel idea, a perfect desecration, to cut down such a splendid tree," saying, "We hope that no one will conceive the idea of purchasing Niagara Falls for the same purpose."[23] The twentieth-century historian Francis P. Farquhar tallies up further indignities suffered by what was left of that tree. "The stump . . . was smoothed off, and on it thirty-two persons were able to dance a cotillion. . . . Soon a pavilion was erected over the stump; theatricals were performed; and for a short time in 1858 a newspaper was published there."[24] Also in 1858 *Harper's Weekly* ran "The Big Trees of California," an investigative piece on the fate of the still-standing Mother of the Forest. She had been stripped of her bark, the writer charged, "with as much neatness and industry as a troupe of jackals would display in cleaning the bones of a dead lion."[25]

Yosemite was soon being referred to as a national park, never mind that the nation had donated the property to California and the word *park* appeared nowhere in the law. The term's most influential popularizer was Josiah Whitney, who in his Yosemite guidebook characterized the valley as "an exceptional creation . . . exceptionally provided for both by the Nation and the State—it has been made a National public park and placed under the charge of the State of California."[26] Once again he was in error, at least technically. But courtesy of Whitney and of Yosemite's pedigree as a tract originating in the public domain, the park wore a federal halo during the period between its inauguration in 1864 and its designation as a thoroughgoing national park in 1906.

The most important thing about Yosemite, however, was not the accuracy of the remarks that led to the park's establishment or which level of government owned and took care of it, but the example it set. As the historian Hans Huth observed, the 1864 law marked the first time that federal land had been set aside for "a strictly nonutilitarian purpose. It is necessary to stress this point in view of the claims that Yellowstone set this precedent."[27] The historian Alfred Runte supports Huth's thesis: "The park act of 1864 was the first instance of scenic preservation in the United States and thus represented the conceptualization of the national park idea."[28] That this conceptualization emerged from a politician's garbled chronicle of Anglo-American relations hardly detracts from Yosemite's luster as a world premiere.

On the evening of April 14, 1865, Conness was at home in Washington, entertaining two colleagues, Senators Charles Sumner of Massachusetts and William Stewart of Nevada, when word came that Secretary of State William Seward had been shot. The three senators rushed to Seward's lodgings, where they were told that the president, too, had been wounded—perhaps mortally. Jumping to the conclusion that this was "a conspiracy to murder the entire cabinet," Conness sent soldiers off to protect Secretary of War Edwin Stanton.[29] The senators then hurried to Ford's Theatre, where they learned that Lincoln was not expected to live. Five days later Conness was one of the pallbearers at Lincoln's funeral.

In a case of odd political bedfellowship, toward the end of his Senate term Conness became an ally of the Big Four—his former political enemy Leland Stanford included—as they built their segment of the transcontinental railroad. Conness's sympathy for immigrants, you see, dovetailed nicely with the railroad's interests: as white workers drifted away to try their luck at prospecting on the Comstock Lode, the Big Four recruited Chinese replacements, going so far as to take out ads in newspapers published in the old country. Many Chinese men responded, and not only did they pick up the slack but, as usual, they worked hard for less pay. Conness was an honored spectator on May 10, 1869, when Stanford linked the line's eastern and western segments by driving a gold spike into the roadbed at Promontory Point, Utah Territory.

By then Conness was an ex-senator, having lost his bid for a second term because his pro-Chinese policies sat poorly with the California legislature. He withdrew from politics and moved to Boston, where he lived quietly until his death in 1909. But his role in establishing Yosemite Park was not forgotten: Mount Conness and Conness Creek in the Sierra Nevada pay homage to his finest achievement.

In Praise of Diligent Indolence   7

We left Frederick Law Olmsted pondering whether to quit the Sanitary Commission and go to work for the new magazine being launched by his friend Edwin Godkin. Olmsted ran the idea by another friend, Charles A. Dana, a former colleague at the defunct *Putnam's Monthly* who was now serving as both a Central Park commissioner and U.S. assistant secretary of war. Don't do it, Dana advised; too risky a venture in wartime.

Dana promised to keep Olmsted in mind, though, and a few months later had surprising news for him. Olmsted was being considered for a job thousands of miles away and unrelated to journalism: manager of the Mariposa Estate, a cluster of gold mines on forty-four thousand acres of private land in California from which the peaks rising above Yosemite Valley could be seen in the southeast. Dana had been offered the job himself but had declined it and recommended Olmsted instead.

The estate's previous owner—the explorer, erstwhile U.S. senator from California, failed presidential candidate, Union Army general, and tireless self-promoter John Charles Frémont—summed up his own mining career by quipping, "Why, when I came to California I was worth nothing, and now I owe two millions of dollars!"[1] Olmsted was probably unaware of that sally, or that the Mariposa was one more example of the messes Frémont was so good at leaving for others to clean up. Two years earlier, for example, President Lincoln had removed General Frémont from his command after he took it upon himself to issue a proclamation freeing the slaves in the state of Missouri at a time when neither Lincoln nor, in the president's estimation, the Union itself was ready for such a step. After unloading the Mariposa Estate, Frémont had stayed involved as a member of its board of directors, which was stacked with New York City grandees, Mayor George Opdyke among them. It took Olmsted only a few months in California to make up his mind about Frémont, whom he excoriated in a letter to a German-American friend as "a selfish, treacherous, unmitigated scoundrel."[2]

Yet no less a figure than Josiah Whitney, director of the state's geological survey, was bullish on the Mariposa—and the world had not yet caught on that regardless of subject matter, you could pretty well count on Whitney to be wrong. Olmsted was leery of mining's grubby side, but he had a wife and children to support, and the $10,000-a-year salary—quadruple his peak at Central Park—was too good to pass up. He wasn't just looking out for himself and his dependents either. The late publishing firm's debts still weighed on his conscience.

Olmsted's friend Henry Bellows, the Boston clergyman, lodged a highly flattering protest: "At this special juncture in our National life, I have the gravest objections to your taking yourself out of the centre of affairs, & giving to Mariposa, what belongs to your Country & mankind."[3] Olmsted fended Bellows off with an in-joke: "As the clergymen say when a rich parish bids for them against a poorer, I think the call to California is a *clear* one if not as loud as [the call] to the battle here."[4]

Olmsted resigned from the Sanitary Commission and set out for California, again leaving his family behind for the nonce. The mine's owners must have rejoiced. They could now boast that in charge of their enterprise was the illustrious co-creator of Central Park and the mighty molder of the U.S. Sanitary Commission rolled up into one.

For all his sophistication, Olmsted arrived at the company's headquarters in the village of Bear Valley with no idea what he was getting into. The Mariposa Estate contained appreciable amounts of gold but, like all nineteenth-century American mining ventures, was lightly regulated, both in the field and on stock exchanges, and thus susceptible to all sorts of fiddling, such as cooking the books, watering the stock, and inflating the stock's price. Looking back on Olmsted's tenure, his friend Samuel Bowles had this to say: "Much more money has been made on Mariposa stock and bonds in Wall Street than from Mariposa gold in California. Indeed, the only great capacity there ever seemed to be in the property . . . was in carrying an immense, a magnificent, indebtedness."[5]

In Praise of Diligent Indolence

The Mariposa gave its new leader a Wild West baptism worthy of a dime novel. "A store has been robbed," Olmsted wrote a friend; "two men have been killed with knives; another severely wounded in a fight; another has been stoned; and a plot of murder and highway robbery is reported to have been detected—all in the three days I have been on the estate."[6] What's more, Olmsted found the place woefully short of an ingredient essential to mining—water. "One becomes strongly inclined to think," he complained, "that half the gold on the estate might well be exchanged for a very small stream." In November 1863 he went looking for that stream; on the way, he took time out to visit another Mariposa, as a locally famous grove of giant sequoia trees was named (how often that musical Spanish word for "butterfly" tripped off early Californians' tongues). "They don't strike you as monsters at all," he wrote to his wife, Mary, "but simply as the grandest tall trees you ever saw." He described the nearby mountain scenery to her as "at some points grand-terrible. One or two annual trips into it are the highest gratifications peculiar to the country that you have to look forward to."[7]

That compound adjective "grand-terrible" is about as close as Olmsted ever came to voicing the Burkean concept of the sublime. In that way, he was being true to the profession he eventually settled into. Any good landscape architect can arrange a picturesque effect, whereas a sublime one is all but out of reach. To put it another way, there is a landscape architectural feature called a "ha-ha"; there is not one called a "whoa."

Olmsted pored over the estate's books, which belied the owners' public optimism. "Things are worse here than I dare say to anybody but you—and to you with a caution," he confided to Mary. "There is not a mine on the Estate that is honestly paying expenses."[8] But by emphasizing the boom expected to be set off by completion of the transcontinental railroad (after more than a decade of wheel-spinning, Congress had authorized construction a year earlier) and by assuming he would eventually tap into a reliable water supply, Olmsted talked himself into believing he could turn the business around. He translated his gameness into action by summoning Mary and the kids to join him in California.

The Mariposa crime wave ended, and Olmsted tried to raise the level of refinement by setting aside a reading room for public use; back east, Godkin pitched in by subscribing on the miners' behalf to selected American and British periodicals. Olmsted kept in touch with Central Park affairs as best he could at a three-thousand-mile remove and placated Vaux, who had asked him to state for the record that their respective contributions to the park had been equal. In a private note to Vaux, Olmsted reiterated his contempt for Green, who had been "slow murder" to work with.[9]

To cut costs, Olmsted hired Chinese workers, who would accept less pay than white men. Just before his wife and children arrived, he reduced white miners' daily wages from $3.50 to $3.15. The men walked out. Olmsted hired scabs and prepared to use force if necessary, but after five days the strikers capitulated. For all his urge to provide parks for the common folk, Olmsted reflected the establishment's attitude toward laborers: their interests were decidedly subordinate to those of a business's owners and managers.

With the strike settled and his family on hand, a period of relative tranquility set in. The dreamland that is California cast its spell on Olmsted, who wrote to Godkin that he'd never been happier. Bellows, who came to San Francisco to fill in for the late Rev. Thomas Starr King until a permanent replacement could be found, paid Mariposa a visit in June 1864. "He is a kind of little monarch here," Bellows averred of Olmsted, "has his own horses & servants at command, is universally well-spoken of & respected—conquered in that strike business, has reduced wages, improved comfort among the men, retains the best workmen . . . & on the whole is much better situated than I feared to find him."[10]

A couple of weeks after Senator Conness's park bill became law, with much of the state baking in a protracted drought-cum-heat-wave, Olmsted left the Mariposa Estate to its own devices and took Mary and the kids on a camping trip to those two exceptional parcels of no-longer-federal land, Yosemite Valley and the Mariposa Grove. He described the valley in a letter to his father as "awfully grand, but . . . not frightful or fearful. . . . The valley is as sweet & peaceful as the meadows of the Avon, and the sides are in many parts lovely with foliage and color. There is little water in the cascades at this season, but that is but a trifling circumstance. We

In Praise of Diligent Indolence

have what is infinitely more valuable—a full moon & a soft hazy smokey atmosphere with rolling towering & white fleecy clouds."[11]

That delicately detailed approach was typical of Olmsted when facing awesomeness in nature: he saw Yosemite Valley not as "frightful or fearful" but as "sweet & peaceful." While saying nothing specifically about Half Dome or El Capitan or Yosemite Falls, he compared the Merced River to the bucolic Avon and preferred ferns and rushes to chasms. When it came to nature's extravagances, Olmsted had a blind spot. Toward the end of his career, in 1893, he admitted as much, mentioning his susceptibility to natural beauty but adding a qualification. "Not so much grand or sensational scenery as scenery of a more domestic order. Scenery to be looked upon contemplatively and which is provocative of musing moods." It all went back, he thought, to "the enjoyment which my father and mother (step-mother) took in loitering journeys; in afternoon drives on the Connecticut meadows."[12] As for all things craggy, they struck him as anything but tranquilizing. "Mountains," he said, "suggest effort."[13]

On his return to Bear Valley, he was surprised—pleasantly, no doubt—to learn of his appointment to the state commission charged with administering the very properties he'd just delighted in. And the glow from that summer getaway lingered because the Mariposa Estate seemed to be turning the corner, as was Olmsted himself. He had invested a portion of his salary wisely—not in mines but in other, steadier enterprises: a steamship company, a telegraph company, a water company. To his great relief, he finally paid off the debts left from the failure of *Putnam's Monthly*.

In January 1865 the idyll came to an abrupt end when representatives from the Bank of California showed up with a sheriff in tow. Their message was blunt: start reducing the estate's magnificent indebtedness—or else. The dumbfounded Olmsted wired his board of directors in New York for an explanation. Their reply dripped with double-talk. The facts, when he managed to piece them together, were these: A New York newspaper had accused Opdyke, no longer the city's mayor but still on the Mariposa Estate's board of directors, of diverting public funds to his private use while in office. Opdyke had sued the paper for libel; not only had the verdict gone against him, but also during the trial the egregious Frémont had confessed to having misstated the estate's indebtedness—on the low side, naturally—when he sold it. The Mariposa's reputation took such a hit that between the end of December and the middle of January, the company's stock lost more than half its value.

From San Francisco, where he had moved temporarily to mount a salvage campaign, Olmsted sent Mary a comforting letter: "We have lived so very happily of late, & you & the children are doing so well, I shall be disposed to stay as long as possible" as manager of the estate.[14] Nevertheless, with the board's approval, he struck a deal with one group of creditors, the owners of a general store. After a suitable transition period, he would resign; they would take over the mine and try to restore its reputation and worth. When not worrying about the estate, he freelanced as a landscape designer and gathered his thoughts on how to manage the new park in his preliminary report on Yosemite.

As mentioned in the introduction to this book, Olmsted tried out the report on two powerful groups at once: a few of his fellow commissioners and a larger group of eastern junketeers. It's time for a closer look at that document, followed by an account of how, despite being sidelined, it had an influence.

The presiding dignitary in Yosemite Valley on August 9, 1865, was the speaker of the U.S. House of Representatives, Schuyler Colfax, whose affability had earned him the nickname Schuyler the Smiler. What was understood to be Colfax's remit for this western junket couldn't have made a better fit with his talents. He was to reassure westerners that the previous four years of federal neglect were an unfortunate by-product of the overriding need to save the union and should not be construed as indifference to their bright future or current needs. For help in getting this message across, Schuyler allowed a clutch of newspapermen to tag along as his unofficial publicists.

One such tagger-along was Samuel Bowles, who sang Colfax's praises in an "introductory letter" to *Across the Continent*, the book Bowles compiled from his dispatches about the trip for his paper, the *Springfield Republican*. How "pleasant and profitable" it was, the editor-publisher apostrophized Colfax, to travel with a dignitary whose "amiability and . . . popularity so

In Praise of Diligent Indolence

readily unlocked all mysteries and made all paths so straight [that] even Nature gave kinder welcome to your progress than [is] her wont."[15]

If anything, that western welcome may have been *too* kind. Two decades later Bowles's biographer, George S. Merriam, described a numbing succession of fetes and baby kissing: "[The Colfax party] were treated everywhere as public guests; . . . at every town on the Pacific Coast they were met by the inevitable brass band; . . . Mr. Colfax averaged a speech a day; . . . receptions, dinners, balls were unintermitted."[16] At last in August the Colfax gang fled the madding crowd to hole up in the new quasi-national park 170 miles east of San Francisco, where they treated themselves to an interlude of what the poet Keats had called "diligent indolence."[17]

On August 9 Olmsted took the floor in Yosemite Valley to present his report with every confidence that it would be well received. For in addition to the eastern bigwigs, many of them already fans of his and Vaux's masterly Central Park, the audience included four of Olmsted's fellow Yosemite commissioners, among them William Ashburner, a mining engineer who served with Whitney on the California Geological Survey.

Olmsted began by recalling the late war, though not in the martial style his listeners might have expected. "It is a fact of much significance with reference to the temper and spirit which ruled the loyal people of the United States during the war of the great rebellion that a livelier susceptibility to the influence of art was apparent, and greater progress in the manifestations of artistic talent was made, than in any similar period before in the history of our country."[18] He was off to a lapel-grabbing start. The tumultuous years 1861–65 as a period of artistic renaissance—what a novel insight!

Olmsted developed that insight by citing such examples as the Capitol dome, "the noble front of the Treasury building with its long colonnade of massive monoliths," and his own Central Park. He did not include Yosemite itself—it would take a visionary like Walt Whitman to go all the way and classify nature as a work of art—but the Far West was represented by "the paintings of Bierstadt and the photographs of Watkins, both productions of the War time, [which] had given to the people on the Atlantic some idea of the sublimity of the Yo Semite, and of the stateliness of the neighboring Sequoia grove." That mention of Yosemite brought

Olmsted to the business at hand: airing his thoughts about the new park before this informal gathering of its commissioners, who were duty bound to provide the state legislature with what he called "a sufficient description of the property, and well considered advice as to its future management."[19]

Let's pass over Olmsted's "description of the property" for now and go straight to his "advice as to its future management." Keep in mind, he told his listeners, how much a region's economy can gain from the presence of accessible natural scenery and built attractions. Or as he rather clunkily phrased it, "Direct and obvious pecuniary advantage . . . comes to a commonwealth from the fact that it possesses objects which cannot be taken out of its domain that are attractive to travellers and the enjoyment of which is open to all."[20] (Bowles's verdict on another example of Olmsted's prose applies equally well to the foregoing: "He writes hard and it reads hard, but there is meat in his thought.")[21] As examples, Olmsted cited the confederation of Switzerland, which was raking in revenues from Alpine tourism, and the kingdom of Bavaria, which attracted visitors by building museums and planting gardens. Laura Wood Roper believed that Olmsted had a particular Bavarian site in mind: "the six-hundred-acre *Englischer Garten* laid out by Count Rumford northeast of Munich under Maximilian I."[22] There can be no doubt, Olmsted went on, "that when it shall have become more accessible the Yosemite will prove an attraction of a similar character, and a similar source of wealth to the whole community, not only of California but of the United States."[23]

But the prospect of financial gain was not Congress's only motive for making a present of Yosemite to the state. As Olmsted saw it, the lawmakers had also hearkened to a bedrock political principle: "It is the main duty of government, if it is not the sole duty of government, to provide means of protection for all its citizens in the pursuit of happiness against the obstacles, otherwise insurmountable, which the selfishness of individuals or combinations of individuals is liable to interpose to that pursuit." The specific "pursuit of happiness" Olmsted had in mind was the enjoyment of secluded fresh-air retreats, and by borrowing that phrase from the Declaration of Independence, he was in effect taking the Declaration out for a hike in the wilds. He viewed parks and the recreation to which they lend themselves as de rigueur for a thoughtful and inclusive democracy. To

In Praise of Diligent Indolence

underscore the point, Olmsted cited the British upper classes, especially its statesmen, who gave themselves annual respites in "their parks and shooting grounds, or in travelling among the Alps or other mountain regions." As a result, these wise men tended to stay in harness longer than their counterparts in other nations, "where the same practice is not equally well established."[24]

As examples of English statesmen still plying their trade despite being long in the tooth, Olmsted cited Lord Brougham, "an active legislator" at age eighty-eight; Lord Palmerston, the eighty-two-year-old incumbent prime minister; and Lord Russell, the seventy-four-year-old foreign secretary. These and other peers of the realm were enjoying such productive old ages because there were "in the islands of Great Britain and Ireland more than one thousand private parks and notable grounds devoted to luxury and recreation." The total annual cost of maintaining these estates was greater than the budget for "the national schools," and yet, he pointed out, "[their] owners with their families number less than one in six thousand of the whole population."[25]

Surely we don't want to emulate England, Olmsted was arguing, in standing by while a minority of toffs enjoys a near monopoly on parks, mountain scenery, vigorous outdoor recreation, and the concomitant benefits of improved physical and mental health that undergird a long and energetic life, even as members of the working class stagnate in cramped, sooty towns and cities. In America, it follows, "the establishment by government of great public grounds for the free enjoyment of the people . . . is thus justified and enforced as a political duty."[26] Here Olmsted might have quoted to good effect an aphorism of Samuel Johnson's: "A decent provision for the poor is the true test of civilization."

Olmsted then segued to his guiding principle for taking care of Yosemite and, by extension, any other valuable natural site: "The first point to be kept in mind . . . is the preservation and maintenance as exactly as is possible of the natural scenery; the restriction . . . within the narrowest limits consistent with the necessary accommodation of visitors, of all artificial constructions and the prevention of all constructions markedly inharmonious with the scenery or which would unnecessarily obscure, distort or detract from the dignity of the scenery." Even with that rule in mind, however, he proposed that the state of California appropriate $37,000 to get the park up and running. This amount would pay for a few structures (he thought five cabins ought to do it), a circuit road around the valley, a road linking Yosemite with the Mariposa Grove, and—at $25,000, the costliest item by far—an upgrading of the road by which visitors reached the valley from Stockton, more than a hundred miles away. Without these amenities, he warned, the park "will remain, practically, the property only of the rich."[27]

To back up that last claim, Olmsted cited figures. Getting from Stockton to Yosemite was a three- or four-day affair costing between $30 and $40, and once there a family would incur expenses "of from $3 to $12 per day for themselves, their guides and horses." (Put all this together, and you have a sum well in excess of the $37.85 complained of by that farmer whose visit to Niagara Falls with his family was recorded in chapter 3.) A good road from Stockton, Olmsted estimated, would cut down the travel time to a single easy day and the cost to $10 or $12.

What had inspired Olmsted to call for a hands-off approach to Yosemite as opposed to the fevered engineering project makeover that he and Vaux had given Central Park? For one thing, the Sierra park's remoteness and great size ruled out a grand construction project of the kind that had molded its big-city eastern cousin; a single-file parade of one-horse cartloads of soil and rock thirty thousand miles long would have gained no traction in 1860s Yosemite. Also on Olmsted's mind was the cautionary tale of Niagara Falls (mentioned by name twice in his report), where multiple exploiters were adding new structures all the time—and making a holy mess of the place. Indeed, with its plethora of attractions and vantage points, Yosemite had the potential to be an even hotter bed of entrepreneurial rivalry than the more self-contained Niagara Gorge, and Olmsted wanted to forestall that.

But Olmsted had another, more profound reason for keeping the park as natural as possible. Playing armchair psychologist, he warned readers that if they neglected their capacity to appreciate nature, it might atrophy in much the same way as an unexercised group of muscles. Olmsted went on to teach a lesson in the mind's workings. The heaviest contribution to mental fatigue, he declared, is made by applying the mind "to the removal

In Praise of Diligent Indolence

of something to be apprehended in the future, or to interests beyond those of the moment."[28]

A century ahead of self-help gurus, Olmsted was urging beleaguered Americans to disarm their calculating and scheming powers by immersing themselves in wild natural scenery—a practice that, like doodling, is benignly pointless in that "the attention is aroused and the mind occupied . . . without a continuation of the common process of relating the present action, thought or perception to some future end." The nonutilitarian enjoyment of wild nature, he summed up, "employs the mind without fatigue and yet exercises it, tranquilizes it and yet enlivens it; and thus, through the influence of the mind over the body, gives the effect of refreshing rest and reinvigoration to the whole system."[29]

Olmsted was crediting the appreciation of nature with an undriven innocence, a freedom from agendas, a disregard for anything other than how we interact with our immediate undeveloped surroundings. It offers escape from goal setting, surcease from getting and spending, relief from the opinion of others, deafness to the call of self-improvement (though, of course, the experience can hardly help but be good for the average goal-oriented Jack or Jill), freedom from the packaging of our fun by others.

Few Americans have better exemplified such indifference to getting ahead, caring about others' opinions of them, and playing by the rules than Thoreau, who paid for his sins shortly after his death. In a eulogy published in the *Atlantic Monthly*, Emerson sang his protégé's praises, only to cancel them out with a startling misreading of what Thoreau stood for: "I so much regret the loss . . . that I cannot help counting it a fault in him that he had no ambition. Wanting this, instead of engineering for all America, he was the captain of a huckleberry party."[30]

Thoreau had been ambitious enough to publish two books and several essays while he lived, and huckleberry partying may have been just the thing for overworked Americans of the 1860s. At any rate, Olmsted wanted to head off the kind of hucksters who were trashing Niagara Falls before they descended on and commodified Yosemite, too, deterring visitors from seeing it unsupervised, at their own pace, by their own lights, with maximal benefit to their psyches and minimal drain on their wallets. And in presuming that his lifelong habit of wandering unsupervised through nature could be of help to almost anyone, Olmsted was honoring his conviction that government should make the best opportunities in life available to all.

Let's circle back to Olmsted's description of Yosemite, which he unrolled in his own idiosyncratic way. He didn't mention the valley's rock stars—El Capitan and Half Dome—by name or describe either one in detail. Rather shockingly, he even suggested that they might be altered without anybody minding all that much: "It is conceivable that any one or all of the cliffs of Yosemite might be changed in form and color, without lessening the enjoyment which is now obtained from the scenery." After all, he pointed out, "There are falls of water elsewhere finer, there are more stupendous rocks, more beetling cliffs, there are deeper and more awful chasms, . . . there are larger trees." The real charm of the place, he asserted, is the way its cliffs and rocks "are banked and fringed and draped and shadowed by the tender foliage of noble and lovely trees and bushes, reflected from the most placid pools, and associated with the most tranquil meadows, the most playful streams, and every variety of soft and peaceful pastoral beauty."[31]

Olmsted's indifference to the colossi that today, more than a century and a half later, serve as backgrounds to selfies galore surely has something to do with—again—the sorry state of Niagara Falls, which he had visited twice as a boy. The more you idolize a park's individual features, the less likely you are to submit to the overall impression it makes or notice the environs to which it belongs. But Olmsted was also indulging his personal taste. He simply didn't care much for what a character in André Gide's novel *The Counterfeiters* was to call "declamatory" scenery.[32]

The report paid relatively little attention—a single paragraph, to be exact—to the park's other sector, the Mariposa Grove. Olmsted noted that it was home to some six hundred giant sequoias, among them the "one known through numerous paintings and photographs as the Grizzly Giant," which he considered "probably the noblest tree in the world. . . . [I]t will not seem strange that intelligent travelers have declared that they would rather have passed by Niagara itself than have missed visiting the grove."[33]

Fine, but Albert Richardson of the *Tribune* evoked the grove's big trees more dramatically by comparing them with the neighboring pines, many of which "are two hundred feet high. Elsewhere *they* would be kings of the forest; but among these hoary giants they become puny, insignificant children." Letting his imagination range further, Richardson declared the sequoias "the oldest and most stupendous vegetable products existing upon the globe."[34] Richardson was right about "most stupendous" but wrong about "oldest"—as we have since learned, *Pinus longaeva*, a species of bristlecone pine found in Nevada and eastern California, is longer-lived than *Sequoiadendron giganteum*. Be that as it may, the reporter's paean to the Mariposa trees seems beyond Olmsted's interests or ability to express. Equally un-Olmstedian is Richardson's impassioned opening to the Yosemite section of his own book on the Colfax junket: "See Yosemite and die!"[35]

Olmsted wasn't myopic. To the contrary, his report shows that, his amateur status notwithstanding, he could be a more perceptive geologist than Josiah Whitney. "At certain points," Olmsted wrote, Yosemite Valley evinces "the terrible force with which in past ages of the earth's history a glacier has moved down the chasm from among the adjoining peaks of the Sierras."[36]

But his heart belonged to Yosemite's "luxuriant and exquisite herbage," "flowering shrubs of sweet fragrance," "banks of heartsease and beds of cowslips and daisies," "the broad parachute-like leaves of the peltate saxifrage"—in all, "a larger number of species of plants within the district than probably can be found within a similar space anywhere else on the continent."[37] Olmsted made the valley sound almost bucolic, the kind of place where you might come upon a woman sitting under a tree, sewing and minding a child.

He also slighted Yosemite's wildlife, although he could hardly have visited the valley three times without sighting at least some of its indigenous species—mule deer, grizzly bears, yellow-bellied marmots, water ouzels. The report's only mention of an animal is almost parenthetical: "The water of the streams is soft and limpid, as clear as crystal, abounds with trout and, except near its sources, is, during the heat of the summer, of an agreeable temperature for bathing." What really impressed him was not any single peak, waterfall, tree, view, or animal, but Yosemite as a whole: "This union of the deepest sublimity with the deepest beauty of nature, not in one feature or another, not in one part or scene or another, not any landscape that can be framed by itself, but all around and wherever the visitor goes, constitutes the Yo Semite the greatest glory of nature."[38]

Olmsted's genius lay in peering into the heart of each landscape he came across and finding ways to bring out its best. Yosemite Valley struck him as an entirely different case from Manhattan Island, in that Yosemite's best had *already* been brought out, by such agents as that glacier grinding away at its granite, and he fashioned his report accordingly. Nor was Yosemite the only landscape for which Olmsted prescribed inaction. When, in 1883, the mayor of Newport, Rhode Island, asked him how a local beach might be improved, Olmsted told the mayor that with its "rocky, wild, sea-beaten" look, the beach was fine as it was. "Nothing better can be done than to let it alone."[39]

In 1903, the year of Olmsted's death, President Theodore Roosevelt gazed out over the Grand Canyon and implored his audience to "leave it as it is. You cannot improve on it. The ages have been at work on it, and man can only mar it."[40] Almost forty years earlier, Olmsted had reached the same conclusion about Yosemite and, by extension, every American national park to follow.

Josiah Whitney was seen, in the introduction to this book, presiding over the Olmsted report's premature burial. Whitney came from a good family—as advertised by his middle name, Dwight, he was related to the early Yale College president Timothy Dwight. Well educated, too; after graduating from Yale himself, Whitney had studied geology in France and Germany. Early in his career, he wrote a well-regarded book, *The Metallic Wealth of the United States: Described and Compared with That of Other Countries* (1854).

As California's state geologist, he called attention to a fun fact about the young state: it contained, within sixty miles of each other, the nation's highest and lowest points, Mount Whitney (named after you-know-who) in the Sierra Nevada and Badwater Basin in Death Valley. When one of Whitney's survey colleagues made so bold as to challenge that claim, Whitney wouldn't back down, and the matter became a cause célèbre because the two sites lay within a borderline area being contested by California and Nevada. Federal surveyors declared Whitney right on both counts: the

In Praise of Diligent Indolence

disputed territory was in California, and it took in both the national high and the national low. Also, Whitney had reacted appropriately on learning of Yosemite's designation as a park, letting out a cheer because it would now be spared the fate of Niagara Falls, which he called "a gigantic institution for fleecing the public."[41] As that line demonstrates, Whitney had a way with words, on fine display in his description of Yosemite's Bridal Veil Fall: "As it is swayed backwards and forwards by the varying force of the wind, it is constantly altering its form, so that it seems, especially as seen from a distance, to flutter like a white veil; hence the name, which is both appropriate and poetical."[42]

We can even sympathize with Whitney for the rough time he was having at the geological survey. He'd gotten off on the wrong foot with his choice of the agency's first big project: a two-volume tome on the state's paleontological resources, published at a time when Californians craved information on precious metals and how to find them, not on old bones. After that miscue, the legislature had cut the survey's budget, a slap that Whitney groused about in a letter to his brother: "It is terribly up-hill work to drag this concern which I have been pulling at for five years, up the hill of difficulty. It is hard enough work to . . . carry on the Survey even if it were appreciated and no obstacles were placed in my way. While I could not help being secretly gratified, or at least relieved, if the Survey were stopped, yet my scientific instincts make me fight for its continuance."[43] Funding kept dropping until 1874, when it dried up completely, and the survey was indeed stopped. After hanging on as state geologist for a few more years, Whitney forsook the West to teach geology at Harvard.

So Whitney can almost be excused for having sneakily urged Governor Low to suppress Olmsted's pathbreaking Yosemite report, and the same goes for Whitney's colleague Ashburner, who concurred in the maneuver—they were bureaucrats guarding their turf. But what about the third member of the cabal, Israel Raymond, the visionary who had done more to save Yosemite than anyone else except John Conness? What made Raymond betray Olmsted, whose very presence on the board of commissioners had come about at Raymond's suggestion? Perhaps Raymond, who had not attended the Yosemite Valley powwow, resented what had gone on there without him: Chairman Olmsted's public presentation of his elaborate blueprint for the park as almost a fait accompli. In the fourth paragraph, moreover, Olmsted had proposed that after submitting the report, the commissioners should all resign "in order to render as easy as possible the pursuance of any policy of management" the state legislature saw fit to adopt.[44] This suggested mass retirement may have stuck in Raymond's craw. Whatever his motive may have been, Raymond came out of the episode looking like a turncoat.

In Praise of Diligent Indolence

1. At or near Yale College, ca. 1847. Frederick Law Olmsted is at bottom right with his arm around his friend Charley Brace. Directly behind Fred stands his brother, John. Courtesy of Frederick Law Olmsted National Historic Site.

2. Olmsted as a cape-wearing young dandy. Courtesy of Frederick Law Olmsted National Historic Site.

3. Carleton Watkins's 1861 photo of Cathedral Rock, which helped make Yosemite Valley a tourist attraction. Courtesy of Wikimedia and the Metropolitan Museum of Art.

4. (*opposite top*) California senator John Conness, who unwittingly spun a fable to get the Yosemite Park bill passed in 1864. Courtesy of the Library of Congress.

5. (*opposite bottom*) Massachusetts newspaper editor Samuel Bowles, whose books and articles kept alive the essence of Olmsted's sidelined Yosemite report. Courtesy of Wikimedia.

6. (*above*) Geologist Ferdinand Hayden, a prime mover in the campaign to make Yellowstone the first national park. Courtesy of Smithsonian Institution Archives.

7. (*above*) Stereoscopic view of Old Faithful by William Henry Jackson. Images such as this one helped persuade Congress to set aside Yellowstone as the world's first national park. Courtesy of Wikimedia.

8. (*opposite top*) Olmsted in his later years. Courtesy of Frederick Law Olmsted National Historic Site.

9. (*opposite bottom*) Yellowstone superintendent Horace Albright (*left*) with explorer Charlie Cook in 1922, at the fiftieth-anniversary celebration of the park's establishment. Courtesy of Wikimedia.

10. Photograph of Mammoth Hot Springs by William Henry Jackson, which would have shown Congress the wonders of what became the first national park. Courtesy of the National Park Service, Yellowstone National Park, YELL #36590-63-447.

11. Nathaniel Langford. After leading an exploring party to Yellowstone in 1870, Langford promulgated what is widely known as the campfire myth of the park's conception. Courtesy of the National Park Service, Yellowstone National Park, YELL #15761.

The Nervous Promoter 8

Olmsted recognized a kindred spirit in one of the scribes embedded with the Colfax party: the House speaker's admirer Samuel Bowles, owner-editor of the *Springfield Republican*. On discovering they were fellow New England Yankees, nature lovers, and sometime nervous wrecks, Bowles and Olmsted began comparing symptoms and swapping remedies.

After starting out as a printer, Sam's father and namesake had founded a weekly newspaper in 1824. A year after leaving school at age seventeen, Sam Jr. urged his father to expand the *Republican* into a morning daily. Sam Sr. agreed on one condition: you take charge of the transformation. This the young man did, but at a cost. He drove himself so hard that he suffered a breakdown and dragged himself off to Louisiana to recuperate.

On his return he worked harder than ever, especially after the emergence of a Springfield competitor, the *Evening Gazette*, which took the same evolutionary path as the *Republican*—from a weekly to a daily—albeit less successfully. Under Sam's leadership, the *Republican* won plaudits for its coverage of state elections, and in July 1848 it absorbed the faltering *Gazette*. By the spring of 1850 the *Republican* could boast the largest circulation of any New England daily outside of Boston. Upon the father's death the following year, the son took over, making it the paper's goal "to give the gist of everything transpiring at this active period of the world's history, and to do it in such a shape and with such directness as to suit in particular the tastes and wants of the people of western Massachusetts."[1]

The series of crises leading up to the Civil War skewed that mission statement away from "the tastes and wants of the people of western Massachusetts" and toward "the gist of everything transpiring at this active period of the world's history," especially during and after the presidential campaign of 1856. Though independent (its name long predated the founding of the Republican Party), the paper backed the Republican candidate, the indefatigable Frémont, who lost to the Democrat, James Buchanan. Nonetheless, the *Republican* had made such a strong impression that the *New York Tribune* called it "the best and ablest country journal ever published on this continent."[2] The paper's circulation continued to grow, and it hired correspondents in Boston and Washington.

In 1857 the U.S. Supreme Court handed down the *Dred Scott* decision, in which the majority quashed Scott's bid for freedom, holding that "a negro, whose ancestors were imported into [the United States], and sold as slaves," could not be a citizen of the United States; the court also struck down a portion of the Compromise of 1850. This excerpt from a *Republican* editorial on the decision shows how perceptive and forthright a "country journal" could be: "The majority of the Court . . . rushed needlessly to their conclusions, and are justly open to the suspicion of being induced to pronounce them by partisan or sectional influences." The decision had increased the likelihood that the current territories would become free states, the editorial pointed out—an outcome that was almost sure to lead to violence.[3]

Bowles was no saint. In one of his books he spoke of American Indians in terms reeking of racist smugness: "We know they are not our equals; we know that our right to the soil, as a race capable of its superior improvement is above theirs. . . . Let us say to [the Indian], you are our ward, our child, the victim of our destiny, ours to displace, ours also to protect." A few lines lower down, he put into words what savvy Indians had already figured out on their own: "You must not leave this home we have assigned you; the white man must not come hither; we will keep you in and him out; when the march of our empire demands this reservation of yours, we will assign you another; but so long as we choose, this is your home, your prison, your playground."[4] That bullyragging tirade's only redeeming feature was its candor. Bowles was surely speaking for the majority of Americans at the time (1869), as well as accurately representing U.S. Indian policy, and he didn't mince words.

Bowles deserves credit for something else, though: the part he played in enriching American literature. One of his best friends was a Massachusetts lawyer whose reclusive sister wrote poems, often on the backs of envelopes. She denounced publication as "the Auction of the Mind of Man," but Bowles talked her into letting him print a few of her poems in the *Republican*, although not before he (or someone on his staff) had tinkered with some of her more cryptic phrases. She was a poet to the core, whose very letters were greenhouses for verse. "Good night, Mr. Bowles!" she wrote in one probably dating from August 1858. "This is what they say who come back in the morning, also the closing paragraph on repealed lips. Confidence in Daybreak modifies Dusk." In late June 1874 she ended another missive to him with this charming paragraph: "Come always, dear friend, but refrain from going. You spoke of not liking to be forgotten. Could you, tho' you would? Treason never knew you."[5]

Bowles's biographer, George Merriam, devoted a full page to the newspaperman's interactions with this small-town family—"he would occasionally come to spend a Sunday, often driving up through the beautiful mountain gap; sometimes arriving unannounced . . . and give himself up to lazy enjoyment"—without mentioning the poet in the house.[6] That's forgivable: Merriam's book came out in 1885, seven years after Bowles's death and a year before the poet's, but not until 1890 did the publication of her collected poems proclaim Emily Dickinson's genius to the world.

In the next chapter, we'll rejoin Olmsted in 1868 as he makes available a portion of his sidetracked blueprint for a wilderness park to a New York newspaper for its campaign to rid Yosemite Valley of squatters. Yet even before that partial resuscitation, the report was less defunct than it seemed. After hearing Olmsted read it in Yosemite Valley on August 9, 1865, Bowles did his job—he gave the gist of the report in a dispatch to the *Republican*'s readers. Later that year Bowles converted his articles about the junket into a book. Bearing one of those prolix titles beloved of nineteenth-century publishers, *Across the Continent: A Summer's Journey to the Rocky Mountains, the Mormons, and the Pacific States with Speaker Colfax* is a lively and authoritative evocation of the early West. In the passage that concerns us most, Bowles recycled what he had written for the *Republican* a few months earlier.

He began by noting that although the journey to the park from San Francisco was arduous and costly, this season's attendance of three thousand souls was already three times the previous year's total. After summarizing how the park came to be, Bowles praised the "laudable and promising effort [now in progress] under the lead of Mr. Frederick Law Olmsted, the manager of the Mariposa estate, to secure an appropriation from the State treasury for improving the means of access, laying out paths among its beauties, and providing cheap yet agreeable accommodations for visitors."[7]

Bowles called for more such set-asides in the future: "This wise cession and dedication by Congress . . . furnishes an admirable example for other objects of natural curiosity and popular interest all over the Union. New York should preserve for popular interest both Niagara Falls and its neighborhood and a generous section of her famous Adirondacks, and Maine one of her lakes and its surrounding woods."[8] Bowles was thus ahead of Olmsted in perceiving that the "wise cession and dedication" that occasioned the latter's report could be replicated elsewhere—Yosemite need not be a one-shot deal.

In the introduction to his book, Bowles mentioned a finding from an informal survey he made before setting out: "There was in our literature no connected and complete account of this great Western Half of our Continent."[9] Written to fill the gap, *Across the Continent* sold fifteen thousand copies, ensuring that despite the shunting aside of Olmsted's Yosemite report, a rough sense of his recipe for taking care of a wilderness park reached a wide audience. Wide enough to include residents of Montana Territory, home to most of the participants in the famous 1870 campfire discussion of what should be done with Yellowstone (see chapter 10). Take, for instance, an editorial that ran in the territory's first newspaper, the *Montana Post*, on July 14, 1866. "The scenery of Yosemite Valley," it read, "as described by Bowles in his new book, 'Across the Continent,' though very grand and peculiar, is not more remarkable than the scenery at the passage of the Yellowstone [River] through the Snowy Range. . . . We should like to have Brierstadt [*sic*] visit this portion of our Territory. He could make a picture from this piece of scenery surpassing . . . his other views of the Rocky Mountains."[10]

The audience for Bowles's condensation of Olmsted's report expanded further when, four years later, the editor toured Colorado and other points

The Nervous Promoter

west, once more under the aegis of that happy wanderer Colfax, who was now vice president under Ulysses S. Grant. The overworked Bowles took this partially redundant trip for the mental relief it promised during a period in his life when "it seemed as if the bottom was falling out."[11] This time around, the group traveled mostly by train, ranging as far as British Columbia and having another look at Yosemite. Again, Bowles chronicled the journey in articles for the *Republican*, which he gathered into a book, *The Switzerland of America: A Summer Vacation in the Parks and Mountains of Colorado* (1869). He then bundled his two travelogues together as *Our New West: Records of Travel between the Mississippi River and the Pacific Ocean* (also 1869), which sold twenty-three thousand copies.

In *Our New West*, Bowles repeated his call for Yosemite to be a trend-setter: "It is a pity that other great natural objects of interest and points of attraction for travelers in our country could not be similarly rescued from subjection to speculating purposes, or destruction by settlement."[12] In the next sentence, he renominated Niagara Falls, the Adirondacks, and a representative chunk of interior Maine as candidates for that rescue.

If we were to create a category labeled Literary Forerunners of the National Park Movement, into it would go Catlin's two-volume North American Indian *Letters and Notes*, Thoreau's *Atlantic* article, Olmsted's report, Bowles's three books, and the newspaper articles written about Yosemite by him and other journalists attached to the two Colfax parties. The chances are excellent, then, that one or more of the well-heeled Montanans whose exploration of Yellowstone in 1870 set in motion its designation as the first true national park had imbibed the park-generating elixir from one or more of those sources.

Bowles's health worsened. At times he was so fatigued that he could hardly stay on his feet long enough to brush his hair. "There were difficulties of the stomach and liver," wrote Merriam, "but all ran back to a common cause—nervous exhaustion."[13] In the autumn of 1877 Bowles went to Philadelphia to consult the eminent physician S. Weir Mitchell, who prescribed one of his patented rest cures. The advice came too late—early in the new year, the patient had a stroke. On January 16, 1878, at age fifty-one, Samuel Bowles died.

Among the many tributes to him afterward, two stand out. Emily Dickinson wrote to his widow, Mary, "As he was himself Eden, he is with Eden, for we cannot become what we were not."[14] (Dickinson had worked a variation on that theme into a letter to Bowles while he was still alive: "You have the most triumphant face out of Paradise, probably because you are there constantly, instead of ultimately.")[15] The *Chicago Times* editorial on the deceased was more earthbound: "To say of a man that he edited the model provincial newspaper in the most newspaper-reading country on the globe, that he gave this provincial paper national influence and importance . . . is to say all that could be claimed for a journalist." This "all," the *Times* concluded, rightfully belonged to the late Samuel Bowles.[16]

The *Times*, however, left out some of the deceased's signal achievements. Bowles had not only kept alive something of his friend Olmsted's suppressed Yosemite report. He had also insisted that a wilderness park need not be a one-off; that the Yosemite precedent could expand into a category, to be added to as other natural wonders were discovered, publicized, coveted by squatters, and threatened with becoming, in Whitney's memorable phrase, "gigantic institution[s] for fleecing the public." Bowles had foreseen that national parks might be what Olmsted later called them: a movement.

Nor, with Dickinson's poetry still languishing in obscurity, did the *Times* allude to Bowles's friendship with her. Today, however, we might sum up the nerve-racked life of Samuel Bowles in this way: one could do worse than be a promoter of Frederick Law Olmsted and Emily Dickinson.

The lot in store for Bowles's idol Schuyler Colfax was disgrace. Having been elected vice president in 1868, he was poised to climb to the highest rung of all. In the runup to the 1872 election, though, he announced his retirement from politics—a move that mystified some of his fellow Republicans. Colfax must be positioning himself so as to wrest the presidential nomination away from Grant, they supposed, or to make a run four years later. The 1872 Republican Convention took Colfax at his word and left him off the ticket. Then the Crédit Mobilier bribery scandal broke, implicating Colfax and ending his political career.

The Nervous Promoter

Despite the suppression of his Yosemite report, Olmsted left marks on California. While continuing to oversee the transfer of the Mariposa Estate to its new owners, he moonlighted as a landscape designer. Two of his commissions were for private estates; a third for the grounds of Mountain View Cemetery in Oakland; a fourth for the campus of a private liberal arts college that was relocating from Oakland to Berkeley; a fifth for a public park in San Francisco. The estates and the cemetery were laid out according to Olmsted's specifications. The San Francisco park fell through. The college campus plan was superseded—except for one small but seminal detail.

In trying to make Yosemite Valley more accessible to the public, Olmsted had run into a problem of topography: certain trees were impeding a desirable right-of-way for carriages. Rather than lay out a single, tree-sacrificing road, he hit upon the idea of splitting it into two strands with a median, thereby reducing the damage. When the college trustees asked him to add a residential subdivision to the plan for their campus, that Yosemite element came to mind. To link the subdivision and campus, Olmsted mapped out what would have been the world's first residential parkway: a divided road leading up to the college grounds from the south.

Later, after Olmsted had moved back to New York, lack of funding caused the trustees to give up on relocating the college; in 1869 it merged with a state agricultural, mining, and mechanical arts college. The Berkeley plot became the campus of this new institution, the future University of California, but the state started over with a new architect. Thus the university's present-day campus bears no resemblance to the one designed by Olmsted. Yet somehow a few blocks of the divided road he envisioned for that adjacent subdivision got built, on a stretch of what is now Piedmont Avenue. By driving or, better, walking the few blocks of Piedmont between Gayley Road and Dwight Way, which the state designated as a historic landmark in 1989, you can travel the remnant of a stylish innovation: the residential parkway with median.

By mail in the spring and summer of 1865 Vaux had sounded out Olmsted on the possibility of extending their partnership. Vaux dangled a couple of temptations: one to design a park for Brooklyn, the other to pick up where they'd left off at Central Park. Olmsted admitted how much he cared for what Vaux called "the big art work of the Republic": "there is no other place in the world that is as much home to me." Brooklyn had its appeal, too, but the financial side of things made Olmsted chary. "I should like very well to go into the Brooklyn park, or anything else—if I really believed I could get a decent living out of it—but in landscape work in general I never had any ground for supposing that I could. You used to argue that I might hope to—that's all. I never could see it."[17]

Vaux kept at him, pointing out that Andrew Green, of all people, wanted them back because he was fighting a lonely battle against his fellow members of the Central Park board, who intended to sanction departures from the Greensward Plan. "[Green] has been a main prop in [this] one sense," Vaux wrote to Olmsted on June 3, "and I cannot reconcile myself to the idea of any man who has stood by the plan being left in the lurch."[18] In July Vaux wrote again to present Olmsted with a definite offer: they could return to Central Park as landscape architects advising the board, with annual salaries of $5,000 apiece. Before setting out for the Yosemite Park Commission's rendezvous with the Colfax party in early August, Olmsted mailed Vaux a letter of acceptance, albeit with the reservation that he still had affairs in California to wind up. That fall Olmsted finally resigned from the commission and moved back to New York with his family.

Samuel Bowles had announced Olmsted's leave-taking in *Across the Continent*, the collection of his western dispatches that came out later that year. "The great Mariposa mining company . . . has come to grief. Its most worthy superintendent and manager, Mr. Frederick Law Olmsted, who was beguiled out here [California] under a gross misapprehension of the situation of affairs, and the duties he was to perform, is going home disgusted, to resume more congenial occupation in the East."[19]

"Most congenial" would have been a better adjective. From among the many occupations Olmsted had tried on for size—store clerk, office clerk, sailor, travel writer, farmer, editor, park superintendent, landscape architect, director of an NGO, mining executive—he was now returning, at age forty-three, to the one that suited him best. Although he wasn't fond of the label, for the rest of his life Frederick Law Olmsted would be a landscape architect.

Superficial observers might have been inclined to write off Olmsted's three years in California as a term in purgatory, about which the best you could say was that having taken a wrong turn, he found his way back to where he belonged and what he should be devoting himself to. Yet by and large the Golden State had agreed with him, and he'd made a good deal of money there. He'd also gotten to know and work with a climate and natural features very different from the East's.

Most important, during his time in California Olmsted had greatly expanded his artistic range, as witness his Yosemite report and his conception of the parkway. He emerged from the shambles that was the Mariposa Estate with his reputation intact, his bank account flush, and his career headed in the right direction.

Contested Ground 9

In *Our New West*, the book covering both of his western swings, Samuel Bowles raised, only to dismiss, a misgiving about California's new park: "The idea is a noble one, and, though somewhat obstructed temporarily by the claim of several squatters in the Valley to nearly all its available lands, we cannot doubt it will in time be fully realized."[1] Bowles was right: the squatters failed to get their claims legitimized, and the noble idea *was* fully realized, but "in time" stretched into a long time. Merely creating the first wilderness park was not enough; it had to be protected from the same kinds of opportunists that were ruining Niagara Falls.

The valley's early settler and booster James Hutchings didn't see why the 1864 Yosemite law should interfere with his occupancy or livelihood; on the contrary, he expected to get rich on the tourists the new park was sure to attract. True, he didn't have a piece of paper giving him title to the hundred-plus acres of valley land he called his own, but in those days the authorities often looked the other way as go-getters helped themselves to slices of the public domain. Why should it be any different this time, especially for a go-getter who thought of himself as Mr. Yosemite? In a similar position was James C. Lamon, a former Virginian who had staked out a plot of land at the valley's eastern end, built a cabin there, and planted an orchard.

Yet both Jameses had the same weakness to contend with. Under U.S. law, public land could not be homesteaded (*preempted* was a synonym for the process) until it had been surveyed, and the Sierra Nevada's remoteness and ruggedness had made it a low surveying priority. Israel Raymond had spelled out the region's desolation in his letter to Senator Conness: "The summits are mostly bare Granite Rocks [and] in some parts the surface is covered only by pine trees and can never be of much value. It will be many years before it is worth while for the government to survey these mountains."[2]

As explained by the historian Alfred Runte, "Until Yosemite Valley had been legally surveyed and further designated for settlement exclusive of any other public use, neither Hutchings nor Lamon had a binding claim to permanent ownership."[3] The survey requirement was no technicality. The United States would have been foolish to let public property go into private hands without having a pretty good idea of its potential. Not until the fall of 1864, *after* it had become a park, was Yosemite surveyed. Clarence King and the engineer-topographer James T. Gardner did the job by arrangement with then-commissioner Olmsted, who paid them out of his own pocket because the state legislature had yet to appropriate funds for this or any other Yosemite-related purpose.

Hutchings and Lamon pled their case jointly before the Yosemite Commission, which rejected it but offered them each the consolation prize of a ten-year lease at a nominal rent. No dice, said Hutchings and Lamon; we deserve title to the land we've been treating as our own and working so hard to make pay.

In his capacity as the commission's secretary, Josiah Whitney defended its policy toward Hutchings and Lamon by framing the issue as "whether the State really is the proprietor of the grant made by Congress, or, in short, whether the United States have authority to dispose of the unsurveyed and unsold public land."[4] The stakes, however, were even higher than that. Recognition of the two men's claims might lead not only to fractionated ownership and piecemeal exploitation of Yosemite Valley but also to the smothering of the national park idea in its crib. Why should Congress give away any more federal tracts as parks if they were just going to be chipped away at by opportunists?

Hutchings and Lamon turned to the state legislature, which took their side. Low's successor as governor, Henry Huntly Haight, vetoed the legislature's recognition of Hutchings's and Lamon's claims, but the veto was overridden. There was a hitch, though: in deference to the land's federal birthright, the legislature made its decision subject to congressional approval.

Contested Ground

The House of Representatives took up the matter in the summer of 1868. Supporters of Hutchings and Lamon parroted their appeal for equity: they were the good guys here, whose efforts to publicize Yosemite and cater to visitors had helped establish the park in the first place. A home-state congressman thundered that neither the Constitution nor the laws of the United States countenanced "the creation of fancy pleasure grounds by Congress out of citizens' farms" and that the dashing of these claimants' hopes would make the United States "not a Government of law, of justice, or of right between man and man; but . . . a plundering despotism, robbing its own citizens."[5] A bill to convey "their" land to Hutchings and Lamon passed the House.

As the Senate considered the bill, Olmsted chimed in—an intervention that was to cause some head-scratching in the 1950s. It was then that Laura Wood Roper went looking for Olmsted's Yosemite report for her biography in progress. She found an incomplete copy, handwritten by his California secretary, in the Olmsted firm's archives in Brookline, Massachusetts; missing from the fifty-two-page manuscript were pages 5 through 14, the ones describing the valley's scenery. The resourceful Roper discovered that Olmsted had removed that section to make quick work of writing a letter to the editors of the *New York Evening Post*, evidently at their request.

On page 2 of the *Post*'s June 18, 1868, issue, those editors weighed in against the claims of Hutchings and Lamon. The headline, "The Yo Semite Bill before the Senate," was anodyne; what followed, however, was anything but: "An extraordinarily impudent proposition is now urged upon Congress, which is asked to repeal or disregard a law passed by itself in 1865 [*sic*] to prevent the Yo Semite valley from falling into the hands of private speculation." The editors then compared Yosemite to the crown jewels that empires have and hold rather than let them "be given over to the chances of private caprice or cupidity. There are those who think it would have been well had Congress fifty years ago been thus wisely conservative of the banks of the Niagara." For readers who had not had the pleasure of seeing Carleton Watkins's "wonderful photographs" of Yosemite, the editors offered in their stead "a description of the scenery which will be found in another column, from the pen of an accomplished and accurate observer, whose signature will be recognized by many of our readers."[6]

The recognizable signature in another column was Olmsted's, abbreviated as his trademark "FLO"; his letter was headlined "The Great American Park of the Yosemite / *To the Editors of the Evening Post.*" Olmsted began by laying out his reason for writing: with the transcontinental railroad nearing completion, it is certain that the new park in California "will be resorted to from all parts of the civilized world. Many intelligent men, nevertheless, have hardly yet heard of it, and hence an effort to give an account of the leading qualities of its scenery may be pardoned, however inadequate it is sure to be." Then came the text of the pages lifted from his three-year-old report: "The main feature of the Yo Semite is best indicated in one word as a chasm," and so on, with fulsome praise of the valley's "luxuriant and exquisite herbage."[7] Thus, although Olmsted may or may not have played an advisory role in drafting the law that made Yosemite a park, he unquestionably joined the effort to repulse the Hutchings-Lamon attack on its integrity. This was another means by which his report withstood the attempt by Commissioners Whitney, Ashburner, and Raymond to make it go away.

The *Post* editors brought their argument to a caustic conclusion: "a more absurd proposition [than the Hutchings-Lamon bill] never came before a legislative body; and yet we find that the bill has slipped through the House without attention, and has been read twice and gravely referred to a Committee of the Senate."[8] The Senate rose to the occasion. Its committee report on the House bill hammered home the point that because Yosemite had yet to be surveyed, the grabby Hutchings and Lamon had relied on no more than "an *expectation* that at some subsequent time they could obtain title from the United States."[9] Yet as pointed out by the committee report's author, Oregon senator George H. Williams, the "remarkable features" that had drawn the two interlopers to Yosemite in the first place should have put them on notice that it would not be treated like a run-of-the-mill federal tract.

Senator Williams went on to accuse the California legislature of violating the letter and spirit of the 1864 act by voting to allow land earmarked for "public use, resort, and recreation [to] go into the hands of those who would levy tribute upon the travelling public, and make this beautiful valley odious for the extortions of its greedy and sordid possessors." Vindicating these two squatters, the senator asserted, would mean "[giving] up the idea of the public enjoyment of the valley, and surrender[ing] it wholly to the purposes of private speculation." Williams also restated the proviso first attached to Yosemite by Raymond in 1864: that the land going to the state should be kept "inalienable for all time."[10]

Williams's rhetoric worked: the House-passed bill died in the Senate. But Hutchings wasn't giving up yet. He sued the state. A California trial court found in his favor, the state supreme court overturned that ruling, and Hutchings appealed to the U.S. Supreme Court.

The court's unanimous opinion in the case, *Hutchings v. Low*, was written by Justice Stephen J. Field, a former member of the California legislature and former chief justice of the state's supreme court.[11] He was also a crony of Whitney's. Whitney, in fact, owed his appointment as state geologist to Field's insertion of his name into the 1860 bill creating the California Geological Survey; another state legislator, John Conness, had steered that bill to passage. (Today a justice in Field's shoes would almost certainly recuse himself from the Hutchings case so as not to appear biased, but standards were laxer then.)

Not far into the opinion, Field tipped his hand. Accepting the sought-after limitation on Congress's power to dispose of federal land, he observed, could lead to dire consequences. The legislative branch might find itself similarly thwarted when it tried to earmark public land for such necessities as "arsenals, fortifications, lighthouses, hospitals, custom-houses, court-houses, or for any other of the numerous public purposes for which property is used by government."

Hutchings's lawyer had made heavy weather of a previous case brought by a man named Cloyes. Cloyes had met all the requirements for perfecting a claim on federal land open to settlement, only to be frustrated by inaction on the part of federal officials; in these circumstances, the Supreme Court had ruled in the claimant's favor.

Field had no trouble distinguishing the two cases. Cloyes's claim covered land that was eligible to be claimed; Hutchings's claim did not. Field continued with a raised judicial eyebrow. "It seems to us little less than absurd to say that a settler or any other person by acquiring a right to be preferred in the purchase of property, provided a sale is made by the owner, thereby acquires a right to compel the owner to sell." The court had one more blow to rain on Hutchings's cause. The 1868 California law attempting to give Hutchings what he wanted was inoperative by its own terms unless ratified by Congress. No such ratification had thus far been made, and "it is not believed that Congress will ever sanction such a perversion of the trust solemnly accepted by the State."

Hutchings and Lamon dropped their quest for title but continued to believe they had been sorely used. They went back to the California legislature, which consoled Hutchings with an award of $24,000—a tidy sum at the time—and Lamon with half that amount.

Well, good for them. And good for parks too. The Supreme Court had done more than just dot every *i* in upholding the federal government's power to dispose of its property as it saw fit. By calling Yosemite and the Mariposa Grove a "trust solemnly accepted by the State," the court had in effect endorsed the Bowlesian view that the idea of a public park in the wilds was a "noble" one.

Hutchings was unrepentant. "Thus ended the unequal contest, of many years, between the Board of the Yo Semite Commissioners and the Yo Semite settlers," he whined in print after pocketing his $24,000. "Comment would be superfluous, as facts not only tell their own story, but suggest their own inferences."[12] After extracting a lease from the park commission, he continued to run his hotel and crank out new editions of *Scenes of Wonder and Curiosity in California*.

It had taken eight years, but the preservationists' vision for Yosemite had won out. Thanks to the 1864 Yosemite Act and the Supreme Court's upholding of federal authority to allocate federal property, a precedent for saving other nationally significant scenic wonders from trespassers and would-be appropriators was now firmly in place.

For all its nobility, the new park could hardly run itself, but without the benefit of Olmsted's report, the state commissioners had little to go on. When in doubt, they did the bidding of visitors and the businesses serving them, with chaotic results. "Under lax state management," writes the

Contested Ground

historian Richard West Sellars, "the Yosemite Valley emerged as a crazy quilt of roads, hotels, and cabins, and pastures and pens for cattle and hogs, mules, and horses. Tilled land supplied food for residents and visitors, and feed for livestock; irrigation dams and ditches supported agriculture; and timber operations supplied wood for construction, fencing, and heating."[13] One concession could lead to another. "I would be very glad if there were no blacksmith's shop in the valley," a park commissioner grumbled in the 1880s. "I would be glad if people could go in on wings."[14]

Olmsted's beloved foliage took repeated hits. Some stands of greenery were being trampled or harvested for fodder; others were growing amok. Where Indians had once set periodic fires to thin out trees and bushes, the authorities now tolerated only campfires. Tree canopies blocked certain views of peaks and waterfalls, to the frustration of visitors; innkeepers took it upon themselves to cut down the offending trees. And the California legislature seldom deigned to give the Yosemite Commission more than a bare minimum of funds to work with.

Concessionaires were quick to take advantage of the dearth of regulation. A modern Galileo named James McCauley began teaching a daily gravity lesson at Glacier Point, where he ran a hotel: he would throw items over the edge and challenge guests to follow their progress all the way down to the valley floor, a distance of thirty-two hundred feet. Over the edge McCauley chucked stones and boxes and—the toss de résistance—a live hen, all of which dwindled to invisibility before reaching bottom. When an onlooker scolded McCauley for his cruelty, he told her not to worry; the bird could take it. "And, sure enough," wrote an eyewitness, "on our road back we met the old hen about half up the trail, calmly picking her way home!"[15]

Another McCauley stunt was to shove glowing embers over the point and let them make their sparky way down, to the beat of dynamite blasts. The blasts later gave way to the soothing strains of a violin, but the so-called firefall became a nightly ritual, maintained well into the twentieth century. (I took in the firefall—sans dynamite or violin—on my first visit to Yosemite, in 1965; three years later the National Park Service closed the show down because the crowds it drew were destroying vegetation and leaving litter behind.) Olmsted's notion to minimize the damage to trees by splitting carriage roads had faded into oblivion; instead, scattered living giants were hollowed out at the base until the opening was big enough to drive a carriage—and later an automobile—through. "Tunnel trees" they were called.

Still managing the park by whim, the commissioners prevailed upon the state engineer, William Hammond Hall, to inspect the valley and tell them what to do with it. In his 1882 report, Hall cited the dictum that improvements should be kept to a minimum, but his idea of "minimum" was flexible enough for the valley to accept a grand hotel built of rustic materials. Calling for the structure to be "massive," Hall ticked off the details he wanted it to have: "a wide portico and a great reception room, fireplaces each as big as an ordinary boudoir, and inside house finish of plain hard wood; outside of stone and tiles; the yard disposed and cultivated to appear as a bit of the natural woodland scenery with its Spring dress on." The rationale for all this pomp was to impress upon the guest how well "his immediate surroundings [complemented] the natural features of the place," making it an inn to match Yosemite's mountains.[16]

And so the valley got the monumental Ahwahnee Hotel. As it was going up, the last trickles of influence from Olmsted's report ("the restriction . . . within the narrowest limits consistent with the necessary accommodation of visitors, of all artificial constructions") were draining out of the valley.

As the rest of California was settled, the Sierra Nevada felt pressure. Farmers in the San Joaquin Valley wanted to irrigate their crops with the region's water, and San Franciscans were shopping for a river that could be dammed to augment the city's water supply. The irrepressible James Hutchings, other Yosemite Valley businessmen, the Southern Pacific Railroad, and nature lovers all found common cause in trying to keep Yosemite green. Nonetheless, the Interior Department opened up public land just outside the park to timbering, pursuant to a law by which logged tracts could end up in private ownership.

At the same time, sheep were safely grazing throughout the region, doing so much damage that one of the shepherds, the Scottish-born immigrant John Muir, turned against his métier and quit. For a while Muir supported himself by running a sawmill for Hutchings. Muir spent his free

Contested Ground

time getting to know Yosemite Valley, and thus Hutchings unwittingly furthered the conservation cause. The more Muir saw of the Sierra, the more it appealed to him in its natural state, "so gloriously colored, and so radiant [that] it seemed not clothed with light, but wholly composed of it, like the wall of some celestial city."[17] Moved to write about the region, he placed his first published article, "Yosemite Glaciers," with the *New York Times* in December 1871.

Compounding the park's problems was infighting among the members of the body tasked with solving them, the Yosemite Park Commission. In 1880 a new state governor, George C. Perkins, reckoned he should be able to work with commissioners of his own choosing. He sought and obtained a state law limiting a commissioner's term to four years. But when Perkins named a replacement for William Ashburner, the lone holdover from the Olmsted era, Ashburner refused to step down. Some of his colleagues sided with him, and Ashburner sued the state. From September 1880 to March 1881, as his case made its way through the courts, Yosemite's plight harked back to the Middle Ages, when there were rival pretenders to the papacy: Yosemite had two park commissions, each claiming sole authority to govern.

The case went all the way to the U.S. Supreme Court, which again found itself refereeing a Yosemite dispute. In *Ashburner v. California*, the court held the state's term-limit law "not repugnant" to the federal statute establishing Yosemite as a park, thereby making Commissioner Ashburner a has-been. The court also issued a reminder: "[The park] must be kept for the use to which it was by the terms of the grant appropriated. . . . So long as the State keeps the property, it must abide by the stipulation, on the faith of which the transfer of title was made."[18] This sounds like a warning: influential outsiders were keeping an eye on Yosemite and none too pleased with what they saw there.

One such observer was Robert Underwood Johnson, an energetic young editor at the *Century* magazine in New York. Johnson kept the Olmsted-Yosemite connection alive by lamenting that the primordial chairman's advice had fallen on deaf ears. What had been set aside as "natural pleasure grounds," Johnson complained, had been "ignorantly hewed and hacked, sordidly plowed and fenced, and otherwise treated on principles of forestry which would disgrace a picnic ground." In reply, one commissioner said he "would rather have the advice of a Yosemite road-maker in the improvement of the valley than that of Mr. Frederick Law Olmsted."[19]

When Johnson went west to see for himself the place he'd been defending in print, he got in touch with Muir, who offered to show him around. During the tour, Johnson wondered what had become of all the wildflowers his guide had raved about in print. Muir's answer—that "hoofed locusts" (his contemptuous term for sheep) were grazing and trampling on flowers throughout the Sierra—gave Johnson an idea. "Obviously," he said, "the thing to do is to make Yosemite National Park around the Valley on the plan of Yellowstone," which Congress had set aside as the first full-fledged national park in 1872. Muir elaborated on Johnson's recommendation in a pair of articles written for the *Century*, offering a stripped-down rationale for the creation of any national park: to satisfy "the lover . . . of wilderness pure and simple."[20]

After doing his bit for the *New York Evening Post*'s campaign against the Hutchings-Lamon claims, Olmsted had kept quiet about Yosemite and its problems. He broke his silence in 1890, at the request of Muir's friend Johnson. The state of California was contemplating a wholesale massacre of Yosemite Valley's young trees, Johnson charged, and Olmsted should write an article of protest for the *Century*. When Olmsted begged off due to the press of other business, Johnson said he would write the piece himself but would like to incorporate Olmsted's views. Olmsted agreed to be quoted as calling the state's proposed cut "a calamity to the civilized world." When the article came out, California's governor, Robert W. Waterman, made the wild assertions that Johnson was Olmsted's nephew and that the piece was designed to help Uncle Fred wangle a landscaping assignment from the Yosemite Commission. Nonsense, retorted Olmsted in a self-published pamphlet titled *Governmental Preservation of Natural Scenery*. "I have never been so unfortunate as to need to solicit public employment, or to have any one solicit it for me." Olmsted didn't dignify with a reply the falsehood that he and Johnson were kin. In the same pamphlet, Olmsted reemphasized a principle common to his 1865 Yosemite report and a Niagara report he had coauthored in 1887—namely, that no artificial addition to a park should be allowed "the presence of which can be avoided consistently with the provision of necessary conditions for making the enjoyment of the natural scenery available."[21] (For more on Olmsted's role in cleaning up Niagara Falls, see chapter 14.)

In 1890 ex-commissioner Josiah Whitney was so incensed by Yosemite's plight that he despaired of the arrangement he'd once been a part of. "If the Yosemite could be taken from the State and made a national reservation," he opined, "I should have some hope that some good might be accomplished."[22] Johnson, reluctant to advocate this solution lest it alienate Californians, proposed a halfway measure: leave the existing state park as is, but protect the land and watersheds around it. He and Muir found themselves on the same side as a player that Muir wasn't very fond of at first but begrudgingly came to appreciate. "Even the soulless Southern Pacific R.R. Co., never counted on for anything good," he recalled, "helped nobly in pushing [the resulting bills] through Congress."[23]

In fact, the Southern Pacific *did* have a soul, and its name was William H. Mills, the railroad's vice president and land agent, who was also a member of the Yosemite Park Commission. The enlightened Mills took what today would be called an ecosystemic approach to Yosemite: he wanted to surround the state park with as many federally owned Sierra Nevada acres as possible.

In the 1880s an eastern firm had proposed building a railroad into Yosemite Valley. Although the Southern Pacific's own line nearby might well gain ridership as a result, Mills inveighed against the project in the *Sacramento Record-Union* (which the Southern Pacific owned), arguing that it would "destroy all the picturesqueness and charm of the magnificent scenery, and . . . rob that marvelous valley of its poetry and majesty."[24] The project was abandoned. Mills also arranged for the *Record-Union* to run environmental essays by Muir, and the paper led a successful campaign to outlaw the dumping of debris from hydraulic mining into streams in California's Central Valley.

In one respect, Mills proved himself a more discerning conservationist than Muir. From talking with local Indians, Mills had learned of the fires they had periodically set to thin out foliage and reduce the likelihood that a wild blaze would burn out of control. Mills talked his fellow commissioners into approving a revival of that practice, but the uncomprehending Muir condemned it as "unnatural," and the commission's reputation suffered as a result. (In 1929 a visitor to the park was to comment on the poor condition of Yosemite Valley. Her opinion mattered because of who she was: Totuya, probably the last surviving member of the Ahwahneechees who had once lived in the valley. The main difference from the old days was that for lack of purposely set fires, vegetation had grown unchecked. Later in the twentieth century, controlled burning regained favor; it is now an acceptable and useful, if sometimes unpopular, tool for park managers.)

When, in 1890, Congress considered whether and how to preserve more of the Sierra, another Southern Pacific land agent, Daniel K. Zumwalt, worked closely with California representative William Vandever. In keeping with the compromise policy of leaving the state park alone, the pair urged creating a larger, adjacent national park to protect High Sierra watersheds. Zumwalt and Vandever got what they wanted and more, thanks to some legislative sleight of hand. The congressman amended the relevant bill to increase the size of the adjunct Yosemite National Park fivefold, and Zumwalt saw to the insertion of language establishing another new national park, Sequoia, to protect some of the namesake giant trees. Amid a rush toward adjournment, Vandever worked more magic. Passed all but sight unseen was a beefed-up law tripling the size of Sequoia and adding a new national park, General Grant, to save a majestic big-tree grove named after the late warrior-president. For help in managing the new entities, the secretary of the interior tapped a source that was already taking care of Yellowstone National Park: the military. The secretary of war obligingly detailed a cavalry troop to each new national park in California. (For more on the military management of both Yosemite and Yellowstone, see chapter 13.)

Yosemite's bifurcated status made it a test case for ascertaining which level of government was the better land manager, the state or the feds. The feds won, again thanks in large part to support from businessmen. A major force at the state level was the California State Board of Trade, which had been founded in 1887 at the suggestion of Mills. He saw to it that pro-Yosemite essays by Muir were included in the Board of Trade's promotional material.

Mills, Muir, and Johnson were now in accord: it was time for Yosemite state park to go fully national. In 1905 the California assembly easily passed a bill to return Yosemite Valley and the Mariposa Grove to the United States, but over in the state senate a battle of civilian titans took place. Favoring retrocession was Edward H. Harriman, latest owner of the Southern Pacific Railroad; opposing it was newspaper magnate William Randolph Hearst, whose *San Francisco Examiner* had made a name for itself by opposing the railroad, a.k.a. the "Octopus," at every turn. Harriman and Muir had become friends after the tycoon invited the conservationist along on his 1899 yachting tour of Alaska. Heeding an appeal from Muir, Harriman ordered his lobbyists to go all out. The retrocession bill passed the senate by a single vote, and the conservation-minded governor, George Pardee, signed it into law.

The one step remaining was for the U.S. government to accept the retrocession. The battle was joined again at the federal level a year later, when Harriman took time out from directing the Southern Pacific's relief efforts for victims of the San Francisco earthquake to promote the conservationist cause. Once again Harriman outlobbied the formidable Hearst. On June 11, 1906, President Theodore Roosevelt signed into law a bill accepting the retrocession and merging the former state park with the adjacent national one. Federal law had at last caught up with popular nomenclature: Yosemite was unequivocally and wholly a national park.

A few years later Muir's lucky streak ended. San Franciscans chose the Tuolumne River in Yosemite Park's Hetch Hetchy Valley as their supplementary water source. By now president of the Sierra Club, which he had founded in response to Johnson's call for a "Yosemite and Yellowstone defense association," Muir described Hetch Hetchy as "a grand landscape garden, one of Nature's rarest and most precious mountain temples." Railing against the water project, Muir resurrected an old theme: that America's natural wonders were its chief works of art. "Dam Hetch Hetchy!" he wrote. "As well dam for water-tanks the people's cathedrals and churches, for no holier temple has ever been consecrated by the heart of man."[25]

Muir's eloquence availed him not. In 1913 Congress passed and President Woodrow Wilson signed a bill authorizing the project. At least Muir was spared the pain of having to witness the valley's flooding. He came down with pneumonia and died in 1914, his death hastened, his friends had no doubt, by his grief over the Hetch Hetchy defeat.

Whiffs of Sulfur 10

In contrast with the long and incremental maturation of Yosemite into a truly national park, Yellowstone seemed to have shot up quickly, with less than two years elapsing between the most thorough exploration of the region to date, by a group of self-appointed Montanans, and its debut as the world's first national park on March 1, 1872. That, however, is a deceptive impression, left in large part by the participants in the 1870 venture, none of whom cited George Catlin, Henry David Thoreau, or Frederick Law Olmsted as an influence. Indeed, some of the Montanans acted as though the national park idea had originated with them, perhaps while they shot the breeze around a campfire on a summer night in 1870. But as we have seen, the concept had been taking shape and circulating for decades until by the late 1860s it was, to paraphrase Olmsted, an offspring of the Genius of Civilization.

Indians knew of Yellowstone country, and one tribe lived there: a band of Shoshones known as the Sheepeaters for the centrality of bighorn sheep to their diet. Yellowstone was reputed to be theirs by default, a place shunned by other tribes for its horrific natural features and rank odors, but put up with by the lowly Sheepeaters because they didn't know any better. Both elements of that theory have since been debunked. Other Indian bands in the region don't seem to have avoided Yellowstone, and the only "lowly" thing about the Tukudika, the Sheepeaters' name for themselves, was that they hadn't gotten around to taming horses. They stayed in Yellowstone until 1871, when they moved to an existing reservation in Wyoming because the removal of so many other Shoshonean bands had left the Tukudika feeling isolated.

William Clark (of Lewis and Clark) had followed the Yellowstone River upstream in 1806, though not far enough to reach even the outskirts of the future park. (From its source in the Absaroka Range south of today's park, the seven-hundred-mile-long Yellowstone flows north and then northeast to join the Missouri just upstream of Lake Sakakawea, a reservoir in what is now North Dakota.) A legend grew up around another member of the party, the trapper and guide John Colter. Haring off to do some exploring on his own, he outran hostile Indians who had stripped him naked and given him a head start—a feat that some believed took place in Yellowstone. We know better now; the thermal area through which Colter ran for his life was actually on the Shoshone River, a good fifty miles east of the park. But a fully clad Colter almost surely visited Yellowstone sometime later, becoming the first white man to see it.

The most frequent early visitor to Yellowstone was the famed trapper and guide Jim Bridger, who first got there circa 1825, when he was barely out of his teens. He returned several times over the course of his long career, bringing back tales of hot springs, inland water spouts, smoking fumaroles, a pervasive smell of sulfur, and the gaudy canyon after which the river and then the region as a whole were named: Roche Jaune, French for "yellow stone." Perhaps the best homage to the canyon's signature color came from the pen of the army engineer-turned-historian Hiram Martin Chittenden in 1895: the Grand Cañon of the Yellowstone, he wrote, is "distinguished . . . by the marvelous coloring of its walls. Conspicuous among its innumerable tints is yellow. Every shade, from the brilliant plumage of the yellow bird to the rich saffron of the orange, greets the eye in bewildering profusion. There is indeed other color, unparalleled in variety and abundance, but the ever-present background of all is the beautiful fifth color of the spectrum."[1]

Bridger had a well-deserved reputation for verbal embroidery—it was said that his epitaph should read "Here LIES Jim Bridger"—so his genuine sightings of hot springs and geysers in Yellowstone country were generally disbelieved. This was the case as late as 1856, when Col. R. T. Van Horn, editor of the *Kansas City Journal*, listened to Bridger describe Yellowstone as "a place where hell bubbled up." According to one of Van Horn's successors, "The Colonel was much interested in the matter at the time and took notes of the account, but did not print it because a man who

Whiffs of Sulfur

claimed to know Bridger told him that he would be laughed out of town if he printed 'any of old Jim Bridger's lies.'"[2]

The first visitor to describe Yellowstone with straight-faced accuracy was Daniel T. Potts, a trapper from Pennsylvania. In a letter to his brother, forwarded to and published by the *Philadelphia Gazette and Daily Advertiser* in 1827, Potts recounted an adventure he'd had after the most recent rendezvous of trappers with their fur-buying factors. Potts had followed the Yellowstone River to "a large fresh water lake . . . on the south borders of [which there] is a number of hot and boiling springs some of water and others of most beautiful fine clay and resembles that of a mush pot and throws its particles to the immense height of from twenty to thirty feet in height. The clay is white and of a pink and [the] water appears fathomless as it appears to be entirely hollow under neath. There is also a number of places where the pure suphor [*sic*] is sent forth in abundance."[3] Merrill J. Mattes, from whose 1949 scholarly article that quotation is taken, identified the site in question as Yellowstone's West Thumb thermal area.

Other visitors, many of them fur-trapping mountain men, brought back similar reports, whose cumulative weight made them hard to ignore. But as beaver hats went out of fashion and the fur trade declined, the profession of mountain man died out. Renewed interest in the region came from a different source in the early 1860s, when the discovery of gold in western Montana Territory set off a rush to the Upper Yellowstone River. Tall tales and reliable rumors alike gained a second wind, which blew in both serious explorers and frivolous vagabonds.

One such vagabond was Sir St. George Gore, baronet, from County Donegal in Ireland. As described by the historian George Black, Gore's retinue sounds like a caravan from the Arabian Nights: "Forty servants; ox wagons and mule wagons; twenty-one horse-drawn French carts painted a fetching shade of red; a linen tent with a striped lining and a brass bedstead; one vehicle for his guns and two for his fishing tackle and his personal fly-tier." During his two seasons in the region, with Bridger as his guide, Gore slaughtered animals in numbing profusion. "His tally ran to 2,000 buffalo, 1,600 elk and deer, 105 grizzly bears, uncounted pronghorn and small game. Most were left on the ground to rot."[4]

In the summer of 1856 Gore and Bridger paused at Fort Union, a trading post on the Missouri River in what is now western North Dakota. There they met Lt. Gouverneur Kemble Warren of the Army Corps of Topological Engineers and Ferdinand Vandeveer Hayden, a civilian geologist and naturalist attached to the expedition Warren commanded. On hearing that Warren, Hayden, and company had been on the Powder and Yellowstone Rivers, Bridger regaled them with tales of the marvels he'd seen farther up the Yellowstone. Bridger's bombast rang true for Hayden, who resolved to see Yellowstone country for himself.

His first chance came in 1860, when another Corps of Topological Engineers outfit, this one led by Capt. William Franklin Raynolds, set out for Yellowstone with orders to scout the best route there from the east. Bridger again served as guide, and Hayden came along as a naturalist. On a tight schedule and impeded by snowdrifts, the party had to turn back short of Yellowstone's thermal features, but Bridger filled them in on what they'd missed. In his official report, Raynolds tried to head off possible objections to one of the guide's most outlandish claims: that water from a spring near the top of a mountain in the region gushed forth "cold as ice, but it runs down over the smooth rocks so far and so fast that it is *hot at the bottom*." "That such stories should have been regarded with skepticism, is not surprising," Raynolds admitted; "yet, as the sequel proved, there was in them a curious matter of fact and fiction."[5] The possibility of cold water heated by friction alone sounds remote even today, but all the same Bridger's credibility was trending upward.

It's probably just as well that Raynolds, Hayden, and company failed to reach Yellowstone's hot spots that year. The published formulations of the national park idea up to that point—those of Catlin and Thoreau—were more like pipe dreams than concrete proposals, and Yosemite's designation as a quasi–national park still lay a few years ahead. In that milieu, a credible report on Yellowstone might have set off a Niagara-esque scramble to claim and market the region's hot springs, geysers, and vantage points—the very threat that, as we shall see, helped spur action to save the place a decade later. At any rate, Raynolds rounded out his report with a prescient forecast: "At no very distant day the mysteries of this region will be fully revealed. . . . I regard the valley of the upper Yellowstone as the most interesting unexplored district in our widely expanded country."[6]

In 1863 a large private party of gold-seekers made an incursion into that most interesting unexplored district. Under the leadership of a civil engineer named Walter Washington De Lacy, the prospectors undoubtedly reached Yellowstone proper, as shown by the fairly accurate map of the region he drew for the Montana Territorial Legislature on his return.

A decade later De Lacy worked up his 1863 notes into a vivid account of the region's thermal assets. We join him and his colleagues as they follow a stream as it zigzags through a network of hot springs:

> [The springs] were so thick and close that we had to dismount and lead our horses, winding in and out between them as we best could. The ground sounded hollow beneath our feet, and we were in great fear of breaking through, and proceeded with great caution. The water of these springs was intensely hot, of a beautiful ultramarine blue, some boiling up in the middle, and many of them of very large size, being at least twenty feet in diameter and as deep. There were hundreds of these springs, and in the distance we could see and hear others, which would eject a column of steam with a loud noise.

De Lacy ended the paragraph by identifying the area as "what was afterward called the 'Lower Geyser Basin' of the Madison, by Prof. Hayden."[7]

In the winter of 1864–65 a Jesuit priest, Francis Xavier Kuppens, was posted to a mission on the Missouri River. On hearing of Yellowstone's marvels, Father Kuppens got some Piegan Indians to take him there. Three decades afterward Kuppens recalled seeing "the Grand Cañon, hot and cold geysers, variegated layers of rock, the Fire Hole, etc." In the spring of 1865, he added, the acting territorial governor, Thomas Meagher, and several other reconnoitering Montanans got caught in a snowstorm. Taking shelter in his mission, they were enthralled by the priest's account of his recent visit to thermal Yellowstone. "None of the visitors had ever heard of the wonderful place," Kuppens noted. "Gen. Meagher said if things were as described the government ought to reserve the [Yellowstone] territory for a national park. All the visitors agreed that efforts should be made to explore the region and that a report of it should be sent to the government."[8]

Although this vignette suggests that the national park idea had been making headway with wide-awake Americans, it's possible that in 1897, when Kuppens penned his account, his recollection was colored by intervening events. Traveling with Meagher had been a lawyer named Cornelius Hedges, later the central figure in the famous campfire tale of Yellowstone park's origin. We'll take a close look at that episode later in this chapter, but for now suffice it to say that Kuppens may have unwittingly read Yellowstone's subsequent history back into the remarks of the men he hosted in 1865.

An 1866 investigation of Yellowstone by a small group led by one George Huston is noteworthy for the favorable comparison it elicited from the editor of the *Montana Post*. Huston's description of Yellowstone, the editor wrote, put the region's scenery in the same league with Yosemite's, as recently touted by Samuel Bowles in his book *Across the Continent*.

Three years later the *Helena Herald* ran an item about a Yellowstone expedition being put together by men who counted in Montana. The news came to the attention of Charles W. Cook, originally from Maine, now running a company that supplied water to placer mines. Cook made up his mind to take part in the venture. On failing to secure a military escort through Indian country, the Montana mandarins canceled the trip, but Cook was undeterred. "Shorn of the prestige attached to the names of a score of the brightest luminaries in the social firmament of Montana," he self-deprecatingly wrote in his diary, "[the expedition] has assumed proportions of utter insignificance, and [is] of no importance to anybody in the world except the three actors themselves."[9] The "three actors" were David E. Folsom, after whom the expedition was named; William Peterson; and Cook himself. They more or less dared themselves into making the trip.

After the fact—indeed, half a century after the fact—Cook held a more exalted opinion of the expedition's importance. On the occasion of Yellowstone's golden anniversary in 1922, the eighty-three-year-old re-created a pregnant conversation held more than fifty years earlier at the trio's camp in Lower Geyser Basin. His mate Peterson had observed that "probably it would not be long before settlers and prospectors began coming into the

Whiffs of Sulfur

district and taking up land around the canyons and the geysers, and that it would soon be all in private hands."

"I said that I thought the place was too big to be all taken up," Cook recalled, "but that, anyway, something should be done to keep the settlers out, so that everyone who wanted to, in future years, could travel through as freely and enjoy the region as we had.

"Then Folsom said: 'The Government ought not to allow anyone to locate here at all.'

"'That's right,' I said. 'It ought to be kept for the public some way.'"

"It was probably from this suggestion," Cook added, "that the recommendation for the creation of the national park later arose in the minds of the members of the [1870] Washburn-Langford Expedition."[10]

Lest all this be written off as the self-serving garrulity of an old man, it was more or less confirmed by the chief disseminator of the campfire origin story, Nathaniel P. Langford, although again not until long after the fact. "On the eve of the departure of our expedition from Helena," according to Langford's diary, kept as events unfolded in 1870 but not published until 1905, Folsom passed along to the expedition's leader, Henry Dana Washburn, the notion of setting aside Yellowstone for some form of public use.[11]

Langford's interest in Yellowstone had been kindled by an article on the three-man 1869 expedition that Folsom had placed with the Chicago-based magazine *Western Monthly* after journals closer to home turned it down as too outlandish to publish. The article had inspired Langford to comb "the social firmament of Montana" for recruits to a bigger and better expedition—a task made easier by his own fairly high place in that firmament.

Langford had been working for a bank in St. Paul, Minnesota, when the prospect of gold lured him to Idaho and then to Virginia City, Montana. Upon Montana's organization as a territory in 1864, Langford exploited a connection with Salmon P. Chase, Lincoln's secretary of the treasury, to get himself appointed as the territory's collector of interval revenue. Langford relinquished that post in 1868 on the understanding that he would be named the next territorial governor, but that honor eluded him. He then entered into an arrangement with the Northern Pacific Railroad to advance its interests. Chase may have been responsible for that hiring too. As Lincoln's secretary of the treasury, Chase had relied heavily on the Philadelphia banker Jay Cooke to finance the Union's Civil War effort, which Cooke had done by selling and standing behind government bonds with an aggregate value of more than $1.6 billion. Despite not knowing beans about trains, Cooke was now performing much the same service for the Northern Pacific. The line's projected route from Minnesota to the Pacific Northwest would bring it within fifty miles of the fabled region, and a sorting out of Yellowstone fact from Yellowstone fiction could help the railroad realize its plan to make the Wonderland (a nickname bestowed on Yellowstone in honor of Alice's adventures) a hot ticket for tourists.

Langford invited Folsom to lecture on his Yellowstone adventures to a gathering of Montana nabobs at the First National Bank of Helena. Reluctant at first because he didn't want to be hooted down as a fibber, Folsom pulled himself together, and in Langford's words, "The accounts which he gave . . . renewed in us our determination to visit that region in the following year."[12] Folsom then took a job with Montana's surveyor-general, the aforementioned Henry Washburn. In his new capacity, Folsom collaborated with Walter De Lacy on the best map of Yellowstone yet, which came to Washburn's attention.

As a former officer in the Union Army, Washburn was the clear choice to take charge of the nascent expedition. Langford signed on, as did Cornelius Hedges, who in 1864 had given up his law practice in Iowa and made the long journey to Montana on foot, arriving in time to get snowbound with the Meagher party and be entertained by Father Kuppens's tales of Yellowstone. Another addition to the 1870 roster was Truman C. Everts, at fifty-four the graybeard of the bunch, currently footloose after losing his patronage job as the territory's assessor of internal revenue. But fear of Indians, Crows in particular, remained a stumbling block, and to be viable the expedition needed a critical mass of participants. As one skittish fellow put it on being told that the party numbered a mere eight, "That is not enough to stand guard, and I won't go into that country without having a guard every night."[13]

Washburn solved that problem by lining up a military escort headed by Lt. Gustavus C. Doane of the U.S. Cavalry, who arrived with a detachment of five men. In addition to its Montana bigwigs (nine of them, as it happened, not eight), the party included two packers and two African-American cooks, for a total of nineteen men.

On the morning of August 17 the expedition got off to a sloppy start. A few hundred yards out of town, three packs fell off the horses, and it took the better part of the day to get everything trussed up again. In the interim, some of the wayfarers had misbehaved. As reported by the *Helena Herald*, "Several of the party, we are informed, were 'under the weather' and tarried in the gay Metropolis until 'night drew her sable curtain down,' when they started off in search of the expedition.'"[14]

The Washburn Expedition's renown rests in no small part on a peripheral incident featuring the antihero Truman Everts. Without adding anything concrete to what was known of Yellowstone, Everts's colorful account of his adventures greatly enhanced public awareness of the region's fantastic weirdness.

One day early on, Everts ate too many wild berries and lagged behind while his tummy settled. By the time he got going again, his companions were nowhere to be seen. After spending the night alone, he caught up with them in the morning. Such separations weren't particularly alarming. Hedges went through several but said, "[I] never had any difficulty in finding my way back."[15] The second time Everts wandered off, though, on September 9, about five weeks into the trip, he fared less well. As he wrote in an article for *Scribner's* magazine, this is what happened:

On the day that I found myself separated from the company, and for several days previous, our course had been impeded by the dense growth of the pine forest, and occasional large tracts of fallen timber, frequently rendering our progress almost impossible. Whenever we came to one of these immense windfalls, each man engaged in the pursuit of a passage through it, and it was while thus employed, and with the idea that I had found one, that I strayed out of sight and hearing of my comrades. We had a toilsome day. It was quite late in the afternoon. As separations like this had frequently occurred, it gave me no alarm, and I rode on, fully confident of soon rejoining the company, or of finding their camp.[16]

When neither of those desired outcomes came to pass, and with darkness coming on, Everts pitched camp and again spent the night alone.

In the morning, he packed up and rode off but couldn't get his bearings. He dismounted to see if he could make out any tracks on the ground.

Leaving my horse unhitched, as had always been my custom, [I] walked a few rods into the forest. While surveying the ground, my horse took fright, and I turned around in time to see him disappearing at full speed among the trees. That was the last I ever saw of him. . . . My blankets, gun, pistols, fishing tackle, matches—everything, except the clothing on my person, a couple of knives, and a small opera-glass were attached to the saddle.[17]

Half a day of futile searching later, Everts fashioned signs indicating where he intended to go next and then moved on. Several miles away, his colleagues were posting similar notices for him, and that night they climbed a peak, lit a fire, and shot off guns to let him know where they were—all to no avail. Next morning the sight of his undisturbed signs had a sobering effect on Everts. "For the first time," he admitted, "I realized that I was lost."[18]

At midday he came to a region of hot springs with a lake that was a magnet to wildlife. "Deer, elk, and mountain sheep stared at me," he recalled, "manifesting more surprise than fear at my presence among them."[19] A little later, Everts's poor eyesight fooled him:

Imagine my delight while gazing upon the animated expanse of water, at seeing sail out from a distant point a large canoe containing a single oarsman. It was rapidly approaching the shore where I was seated. With hurried steps I paced the beach to meet it, all my energies stimulated by the assurance it gave of food, safety, and restoration to friends. As I drew near to it[,] it turned towards the shore, and oh! bitter disappointment, the object which my eager fancy had transformed into an angel of relief stalked from the water, an enormous pelican, flapped its dragon-wings as if in mockery of my sorrow, and flew to a solitary point farther up the lake. This little incident quite unmanned me.[20]

That day had another unmanning incident in store for Everts—the approach of a mountain lion, which treed him.

At this point it's tempting to dismiss Everts as a proto–Mr. Magoo, the nearsighted animated cartoon character who bumbles his slapstick way through life. Yet from time to time, Everts proved to be a clever and resilient wilderness traveler, more of a Crusoe than a Magoo. He discovered what the Tukudika already knew, that the taproot of a locally occurring species of thistle was both "palatable and nutritious," especially when cooked by immersion in a handy thermal pool. Later, when his boots were falling apart, he turned the boot legs into pouches for the storing of thistle roots. As alpine winter came on, he hit upon a way to keep himself constantly supplied with water—in the form of snowballs harvested from ice fields and stuffed in his pockets. One day he caught a bird with his bare hands and ate it raw. Another time inspiration struck as he was resting by a lake. "A gleam of sunshine lit up the bosom of the lake, and with it the thought flashed upon my mind that I could, with a lens from my opera-glasses, get fire from Heaven. Oh, happy, life-renewing thought!"[21] He could now make fire as needed—until, that is, he lost the lens too. From then on, he carried fire with him from camp to camp in the form of a burning stick—until a snowstorm doused it, putting an end to his fires.

When possible, Everts bedded down alongside hot springs for warmth, although one night he rolled over too far in his sleep and scalded his hip. He figured out roughly where he was by climbing a peak and looking around, but he saw no sign of his fellow travelers. They meanwhile were doing all they could on his behalf, blazing trees to mark their route, sending out search parties, and caching food for him. A bird flying over Yellowstone might have witnessed two or three occasions when the hunters and the hunted just missed converging. The rest of the party finally concluded that, in the words of Langford, taken from a surviving copy of a lecture he gave on the subject, "Mr. Everts had been shot from his horse by some straggling Indians, or had followed down a tributary of [the] Snake River on which we camped the day he was lost, and had reached some settlement."[22]

When not looking for Everts, his comrades had close calls of their own. One day Langford and Washburn investigated the Crater Hills on foot.

A violently boiling spring had undermined the adjacent terrain, which, as Langford confessed in his diary,

> I did not at first perceive; and, as I was unconcernedly passing by the spring, my weight made the border slough off beneath my feet. General Washburn noticed the sudden cracking of the incrustation before I did, and I was aroused to a sense of my peril by his shout of alarm, and had sufficient presence of mind to fall suddenly backwards at full length upon the sound crust, whence, with my feet and legs extended over the spring, I rolled to a place of safety.[23]

Hazards aside, each day served up something new and captivating: a spewing geyser or a witchy hot spring or a grotesque formation calcified around the lip of a fumarole. Doane boasted that next to these features, "the geysers of Iceland sink to insignificance."[24] At the same time, food was scarce and the men's stamina was flagging. When the expedition ended, Langford's weight had dropped from 190 pounds to 155, and Washburn was suffering from a cold that worsened the case of tuberculosis he'd contracted in the Union Army trenches at Vicksburg. (A few weeks later, at his father-in-law's home in Indiana, Washburn died.)

Throughout his ordeal, Everts somehow managed to keep his spirits up. He dwelled on the examples set by two plucky American forerunners in similar straits, Isaac Strain in South America and Elisha Kent Kane in the Arctic. As food became scarcer, the starving Everts began to hallucinate. "An old clerical friend, for whose character and counsel I had always cherished peculiar regard, in some unaccountable manner seemed to be standing before me, charged with advice which would relieve my perplexity"—advice that Everts thought he heard the old friend proffer out loud.[25]

On October 16, 1870, his thirty-eighth day of solitude, with the weather bitterly cold and Everts at his lowest ebb, he was found—a deliverance that, thanks to the historian Lee H. Whittlesey, we can follow from dual perspectives, the sufferer's and that of one of his finders. A sleet storm hit, raising in Everts's mind "[a] solemn conviction that death was near, that at each pause I made my limbs would refuse further service, and that I should sink helpless and dying in my path. . . . Amid all this tumult of

Whiffs of Sulfur

the mind, I felt that I had done all that man could do. . . . Groping along the side of a hill, I became suddenly sensible of a sharp reflection, as of burnished steel. Looking up, through half-closed eyes, two rough but kindly faces met my gaze.

"'Are you Mr. Everts?'

"'Yes. All that is left of him.'"

After a bit more back-and-forth, as Everts recalled, "I fell forward into the arms of my preservers, in a state of unconsciousness. I was saved."[26]

His rescuers were two volunteers motivated by the offer of a $600 reward. The historian Aubrey Haines sums up one of them, Collins J. (Jack) Baronett, as "a fabulous character" whose multifaceted past made him the quintessential soldier of fortune. "Yet, he was always a gentleman: soft-spoken, competent, and utterly reliable."[27] In Baronett's telling, the man whose life he saved was a mere shadow of the glib wisecracker in Everts's *Scribner's* article, "[his] clothing nearly stripped and worn from his person, which was reduced to skin and bones; hair long, and matted with dirt; eyesight nearly gone; unable to speak; and crawling on hands and feet among the rocks, looking for grasshoppers and bugs for food." On another occasion, Baronett described the abject creature he'd found as practically comatose and near skeletal: "The bones protruded through the skin on the balls of his feet and thighs. His fingers looked like bird's claws."[28]

Carried to a nearby cabin, Everts managed to swallow and keep down a pint of oil squeezed from the fat of a freshly killed bear—a nostrum that weaned him from his thistle-heavy diet. So complete was his recovery that he lived for thirty more years. His finders never saw a penny of their reward, though, and Baronett said he wished he'd "let the son-of-a-gun roam."[29] Still, Baronett did all right for himself. He was soon collecting tolls—a dollar per man or beast—from users of a bridge he'd built over the Yellowstone River. As noted in the diary of Albert C. Peale, a former student of Hayden's who accompanied him to Yellowstone as a geologist the following summer, Baronett lived in "a log cabin on the shore above [his bridge]. . . . It is substantial and quite pretty, spanning the river just before it is joined by the East Fork, and immediately after its emergence from the Grand Canyon."[30] In 1883 Baronett had the honor of guiding through Yellowstone a party headed by U.S. president Chester A. Arthur, and Hayden named a peak after him, although misspelling his name as Baronnette.

The most extraordinary aspect of Everts's ordeal was the public reaction to his article about it in *Scribner's*, which at the time was edited by Dr. Josiah Holland, Samuel Bowles's former assistant editor at the *Springfield Republican*. Slanted to make its author look like a capable outdoorsman rudely plunged into an unprecedentedly hostile environment, "Thirty-Seven Days of Peril" not only generated publicity for the nascent campaign to preserve Yellowstone but also made its author famous. Everts had a mixed record as an outdoorsman—yes, he'd shown intelligence and grit, but time and again he'd lost a belonging that might have made the difference between life and death. Even so, when it came time to pick a first superintendent for Yellowstone National Park, Everts was the people's choice. On learning, however, that "there was no appropriation to pay for such an officer," he took himself out of the running, stating, "I could not afford to take it solely for the honor tho I wanted to very much."[31] Yet measured against the men who served as Yellowstone's first few superintendents (discussed in chapter 13), he might not have been such a bad choice after all.

Because of the timing of its publication—November 1871—Everts's account may have acted as a softening agent for Yellowstone. Readers would already have consumed Langford's two-part article on the expedition in *Scribner's* May and June issues, learning how religiously its members posted guards at night and that one day they had sighted half a dozen Indians on horseback. Langford's article had also contained such thrilling passages as this:

> Entering the basin cautiously, we found the entire surface of the earth covered with incrusted sinter thrown from the springs. Jets of hot vapor were expelled through a hundred natural orifices with which it was pierced, and through every fracture made by passing over it. . . . [The springs] were all in a state of violent ebullition. Throwing their liquid contents to the height of three or four feet. . . . The central spring seethed and bubbled like a boiling caldron.[32]

Against that background, the appearance of "Thirty-Seven Days of Peril" a few months later may have been paradoxically reassuring. Rugged and violent as Yellowstone might be, old Truman Everts had survived it—and without his glasses. The combined effect of the three *Scribner's* articles was to give readers the shudders while also holding out the possibility that someday they, too, might be able to travel through some of this one-of-a-kind wilderness. Yes, Yellowstone had a hellish side. But if they were careful, it could also be the adventure of a lifetime.

Another contribution from the Washburn Expedition was nomenclature—several of Yellowstone's major attractions, Old Faithful included, bear names given them by Washburn, Langford, and company. And shortly before breaking up, the group, minus Everts, held an after-hours exchange of views that became both cherished and controversial.

The setting was a campfire, the date September 19, 1870. As Langford recorded in his next day's diary entry (which he may or may not have revised for publication thirty-five years later), one member of the group proposed that they exploit their inside knowledge by claiming land across from "the falls of the Yellowstone" and charging the public for admission thereto. Others suggested additional features as worthy of the same treatment. To avoid conflict, a diplomatic member recommended holding a lottery, with each member writing down his own preferred tract, "and in order that no one should have an advantage over the others, the whole should be thrown into a common pool for the benefit of the entire party."

"Mr. Hedges then said that he did not approve of any of these plans—that there ought to be no private ownership of any portion of that region, but that the whole of it ought to be set apart as a great National Park, and that each one of us ought to make an effort to have this accomplished." Every camper but one endorsed this civic-minded suggestion, and Langford's enthusiasm for it was such that he confessed to having lain awake half of that night "thinking about it," adding, "and if my wakefulness deprived my bed-fellow (Hedges) of any sleep, he has only himself and his disturbing National Park proposition to answer for it."

"Our purpose to create a park," Langford wrote in conclusion, "can only be accomplished by untiring work and concerted action in a warfare against the incredulity and unbelief of our National legislators when our proposal shall be presented for their approval. Nevertheless, I believe we can win the battle."[33]

It's a heartening story: heeding their better nature, the Montana trail-blazers replaced their greedy first impulses with enlightened principles. Most historians, though, now regard it as more of a pious afterthought than an accurate rendition of what was said. They refer to it as the camp-fire myth, whose most formidable purveyor was Horace Albright, deputy and eventually successor to Stephen Mather, the first head of the National Park Service.

In 1922, to mark the fiftieth anniversary of Yellowstone's establishment, Albright emceed an on-site celebration. Before an audience that included Charley Cook of the three-man 1869 expedition and two sons of Cornelius Hedges, Albright conjured up that long-ago discussion around a camp-fire and its altruistic climax. "And right there," Albright concluded, "the National Park Idea was born. These men were big enough, broad enough, and public spirited enough to lay aside all their personal ambitions and the wealth that was before them, and it was unanimously agreed then that a national park should be created."[34]

Oddly, though, Langford had made no mention of the campfire colloquy in the article he had published in two successive issues of *Scribner's* in the spring of 1871. (The illustrations for that article were by Thomas Moran, soon to visit Yellowstone in person as an artist attached to Hayden's 1871 expedition; for Langford's piece, Moran had only the author's written descriptions to go by, and some of his drawings distort the phenomena they purport to depict.) The omission is surprising in that by dangling before *Scribner's* readers the prospect of Yellowstone becoming a national park, Langford could have enhanced the appeal to investors of the railroad Jay Cooke was financing, and for which Langford was working as a PR man.

The Northern Pacific, Langford *did* write in his *Scribner's* piece, should be complete within three years. At that point "the traveler will be able to make the trip to Montana from the Atlantic seaboard in three days, and thousands of tourists will be attracted to both Montana and Wyoming in order to behold with their own eyes the wonders here described."[35] How easy—and effective—it would have been to tack on to the end of that sentence a phrase such as "and being promoted as a national park by myself and other far-seeing Montanans" if the campfire discussion had indeed gone as Langford and, after him, Albright, portrayed it. There is no record of anyone having seen the Hedges brainstorm passage in Langford's original diary, which is no longer extant, nor does the campfire discussion figure in any of the surviving diaries kept by other members of the Washburn party or in the leader's official report.

Langford finally went public with the campfire tale in the 1890s, while being interviewed by someone who was writing a Yellowstone guidebook, and to repeat, not until 1905 did Langford get around to publishing his diary from the expedition, from which the above replay of the campfire debate is taken. On the other hand, by the 1890s Langford would have known that "incredulity and unbelief" had *not* been a sticking point for "our National legislators" in 1872; rather, they had questioned the advisability of taking such a large and possibly valuable chunk of federal land out of circulation. (For a detailed treatment of the Yellowstone Park bill's enactment, see the next chapter.) One can argue that if Langford were going to doctor his diary to make Hedges, himself, and the others look nobler than they actually were, he would also have corrected his forecast of the kind of resistance a national park proposal would meet with.

In his 1895 history of Yellowstone, Hiram Chittenden asserted that on January 23, 1871, Langford had been quoted in the *New York Tribune* as favoring national park status for Yellowstone, but nobody has ever been able to track that citation down or find such a remark attributed to Langford in the *Tribune* or any other New York paper of the time. Hedges's role is equally iffy. Albert Matthews addressed the problem in a 1904 paper he read before the Colonial Society of Massachusetts. After confirming that Hedges's journal from the period fails to mention the park project, Matthews cited a note dated August 1904 in which Hedges wrote, "It was at the camp after leaving the lower Geyser Basin when all were speculating which point in the region we had been through would become most notable, that I first suggested uniting all our efforts to get it made a National Park, little dreaming that such a thing were possible."[36]

Hedges's best claim to have had a hand in saving Yellowstone from private exploitation can be found in one of a series of articles he wrote for the *Helena Herald* between October 6 and November 9, 1870. He pointed out that Yellowstone Lake was located in the far northwest corner of Wyoming without access to the rest of that territory, "Hence the propriety that the Territorial lines be so readjusted that Montana should embrace all that lake region west of the Wind River Range, a matter in which we hope our citizens will soon move to accomplish, as well as to secure, its future appropriation to the public use."[37] As that passage shows, Hedges's primary concern was to enlarge Montana Territory at Wyoming's expense, and in any case, "future appropriation to the public use" is a wobbly synonym for "national park." Yet he was on more or less the right track.

It's easy to see why Albright made the campfire tale his preferred origin story—it teaches a lesson on the value of civic virtue and is easy to grasp. And even if in 1922 Albright had been well versed in the evolution of the national park idea from Burke to Catlin to Thoreau to Conness to Whitney to Olmsted to Bowles to Meagher to Folsom and beyond, the deputy director couldn't have done justice to the material without speaking at such a length as to lose his audience. The campfire story had legs because it was crisp, catchy, and emblematic of human nature at its best.

To Aubrey Haines goes the credit for carefully examining and ultimately rejecting the campfire-origin tale, and he paid for his heresy by being roundly criticized in National Park Service circles, especially by Horace Albright, who was still very much alive when Haines's histories of the park came out in the 1970s. Haines even had an answer for the question of why, if Langford were going to manufacture a creation myth for Yellowstone National Park, he would have cast Hedges, rather than himself, as the park's main begetter. In an exchange with Robert Utley, the National Park Service's chief historian in the 1970s, Haines looked to Langford's character for the answer; he was, Haines summed up, "never more than a coattail-rider, dependent on family and friends for the influence which got him jobs and favors."[38]

Fascinating as the dispute about the campfire tale may be, for purposes of this book its resolution may not matter all that much. By 1870 the idea of a national park could hardly have come as a bolt from the blue to members of the Washburn Expedition. Hedges's campfire proposal, assuming it was made, evoked what Langford called "an instantaneous and favorable

Whiffs of Sulfur

response" from his fellow campers because something like it had been floating around and gathering support for decades, even in remote Montana.[39] Indeed, Hedges had been on hand six years earlier when territorial governor Meagher made a similar suggestion at that snowbound Catholic mission in Montana.

There is no need, then, for us to take a definitive position on how much mythologizing license Horace Albright allowed himself on July 14, 1922. The important point is that fifty years previously, the national park idea had been one whose time had come.

On their return to civilized Montana, the members of the Washburn Expedition found their exploits overshadowed for a time by the still-missing Truman Everts. Washburn wrote a fairly detailed account of the expedition, which came out in the *Helena Daily Herald* on September 27 and 28, 1870. The expedition also received coverage in such papers as the *Rocky Mountain News* (Denver), the *St. Paul Pioneer Press*, and the *New York Times*, which said that although Washburn's "record" read "like the realization of a child's fairy tale," its accuracy was not in doubt.[40] Even this much attention alarmed Samuel Wilkeson, secretary of the Northern Pacific Railroad, who complained in a letter to Jay Cooke, "The villains in Helena are wholly uncovering the nakedness of our sleeping Yellowstone Beauty. It breaks my heart."[41] Wilkeson's heartbreak had to do with the possibility that opportunists would rush to claim valuable tracts in the area before the railroad could make its own choices of the land it had been promised by the federal law chartering it.

At the time, Cooke didn't put much stock in Wilkeson's lament. It was at Cooke's suggestion, in fact, that Langford wrote his Yellowstone articles for *Scribner's*. Cooke also commissioned Langford to give a series of lectures on the Washburn Expedition in which he was expected to harp on the Northern Pacific's likely role as the Geyser Express. But a case of bronchitis forced Langford to call the series off after only three performances: one at Ogontz, Cooke's suburban Philadelphia mansion; another in Manhattan, at which an unnamed *New York Tribune* reporter may or may not have heard Langford propose national park status for Yellowstone; and one in Washington DC.

Introducing Langford in Washington was House Speaker James G. Blaine, a Cooke ally, and sitting in the audience was a man with the geological savvy and political clout to trump the amateur Washburn Expedition with a professional one: Dr. Ferdinand Hayden, director of the U.S. Geological and Geographical Survey of the Territories. A few weeks later Hayden was again present when Spencer Baird, assistant secretary of the Smithsonian Institution, read aloud a portion of Lieutenant Doane's report on the Washburn Expedition before the American Philosophical Society in Washington. By then, however, Hayden's itch to make a thorough investigation of Yellowstone had been tingling for fifteen years, and his biographer Mike Foster argues persuasively that Hayden had picked Yellowstone as his project for next summer *before* listening to Langford's lecture or Doane's report. Still, Foster adds, "the rivalry created by [the] recent expeditions only added urgency to [Hayden's] planning."[42]

The Man Who Picked
Up Stones Running

Ferdinand Vandeveer Hayden and Thomas Starr King (the clergyman who first brought the Sierra Nevada's wonders to easterners' attention) would probably have liked, or at least understood, each other. In making names for themselves as interpreters of the American West, they both had to overcome the disadvantages of humble birth and near poverty. King died just as he was coming into his own. Hayden lived long enough to become a trusted authority on the West and the acknowledged leader in the effort to set aside Yellowstone as the world's first national park.

Hayden was born in western Massachusetts in 1828. When he was twelve, his mother, Melinda, divorced his father, Asa (occupation unknown), and sent the boy off to live with his father's sister in Rochester, Ohio. Although Aunt Lucretia was a kind and loving substitute mother, the uprooting left an emotional scar. A college classmate recalled Hayden wearing "a kind of downcast, furtive expression as if ashamed of his circumstances in life. He had a kind of stooping, awkward gait when he walked."[1] (In photographs of him as an adult, Hayden looks not so much downcast or furtive as buffeted by the vicissitudes of life.)

That college was Oberlin, where Hayden's awkward gait had brought him, on foot, at the age of sixteen. Owing to his spotty previous education, he was relegated to a preparatory track, but two years later he made it into the college proper. He graduated in 1850 with what he remembered as "a decided taste for the natural sciences."[2]

After teaching school for a short while, Hayden attended lectures at the Cleveland Medical School. On field trips with one of his instructors, he showed promise as a collector and classifier of botanical specimens. He returned to the East and enrolled in the Albany Medical School in Albany, New York, studying natural history as part of the medical curriculum, as was customary then. In 1854 he graduated with an MD degree.

To compensate for his quasi-orphaned status, at every stage of his education Hayden had charmed one or more of his teachers into making a pet of him. Early in 1853 one of these mentors had written a letter introducing Hayden to Spencer Baird of the Smithsonian. Hayden followed up with an appeal of his own: "I am extremely anxious to spend a few years in the study of natural history. I feel as though I could endure cheerfully any amount of toil, hardship and self-denial provided I could gratify my strong desire to labor in the field of a naturalist. "[3] That summer he was given a place in an expedition to the Badlands of Dakota Territory, where he performed well enough to earn his first morsel of immortality: a newly discovered mollusk was named *Avicula haydeni*. Another benefit of the trip was meeting and working with the leader's assistant, the invertebrate paleontologist Fielding B. Meek. Meek shared his knowledge of fossils, Hayden soaked it up, and they formed an enduring partnership in which Hayden typically found the specimens and Meek took the lead in analyzing and classifying them. Hayden's performance that summer also vindicated the judgment of Baird, who had strings to pull and funds to disburse for his protégés.

It was a bully time to be doing science in the West. Americans craved reliable information about a region reputedly awash in precious metals to be mined, punishingly hot deserts to be skirted, geysers to be marveled at, indigenous people to be feared for their belligerence and envied for their glamorous nomadism, and endless expanses to be crossed and mapped. Almost everything about the West held easterners in thrall, including its very speech and the ambient air. Mark Twain gave "You bet!" and "Oh no, I reckon not!" as just two examples of the Nevada slang he rated "the richest and the most infinitely varied and copious that had ever existed anywhere in the world, perhaps," and Samuel Bowles lauded the air for tempering the sometimes oppressive sunlight with a "constant vitality."[4] Hayden developed into a switch hitter, equally adept at analyzing western wonders as a scientist and popularizing them as a writer.

It was also a period when teams of geologists and naturalists were at large, gathering information on the animal, vegetable, and mineral contents

The Man Who Picked Up Stones

of American land with a view toward exploiting them. Though called surveys, these endeavors relied on exploring, note-taking, and specimen collecting more than on triangulating with telescope and theodolite. Some surveyors went off on their own, as when the future ethnologist Henry Rowe Schoolcraft and a colleague investigated a mineral-rich belt of Missouri and Arkansas in 1817–18. After publishing the results as *A View of the Lead Mines of Missouri* (and setting off a mineral rush to the region), Schoolcraft was hired to do the same thing in Michigan.

Hayden preferred to undertake his surveys with sponsorship. In the spring of 1854 he ingratiated himself with Maj. Alfred Vaughan, an Indian agent who agreed to underwrite the young man's expenses on a yearlong collecting trip to the Upper Missouri River Basin. Whenever the boat taking them upriver stopped, Hayden would rush off to explore, as he described it, "[with] my pick in one hand, my bag in the other, my note book in my side pocket, my bottle of alcohol in my vest pocket, my plant case around my neck, and with all these carry a gun to defend myself from bears and Indians."[5] By agreement, Vaughan and Hayden were each entitled to half of the specimens found, with first pick going to Hayden.

This was probably the journey on which Hayden's hard-charging geologizing led Sioux onlookers to dub him the Man Who Picks Up Stones Running. Hayden's biographer Mike Foster discounts some historians' supposition that the nickname was the Indians' way of dismissing Hayden as a harmless fool, his bustling presence tolerated because he didn't seem quite right in the head. In any event, the Man Who Picks Up Stones Running ably captures Hayden's drive and hectic pace. As the Indians kept tabs on Hayden, he returned the favor, jotting down notes on their customs and languages for an anthropological treatise he never got around to writing.

Even in the informal West, however, Hayden felt the stigma of his straitened circumstances. "I am treated here with respect, yet I am well aware that here a man without money is a bore," he confessed in a letter to Baird. "And my industry only makes me a greater bore . . . because traders can make no money out of me. It seems as if I was excluded from the world, an exile as it were. And I sometimes feel lonely."[6] Yet the lonely outsider racked up some impressive firsts on that 1854–55 trip. He sent back the first known American soft-shelled turtle and several teeth identified as saurian by his latest mentor, Joseph Leidy, an anatomy professor at the University of Pennsylvania; Leidy's verdict made Hayden the first recognized finder of dinosaur fossils in North America. Another milestone was his election as a corresponding member of the prestigious Academy of Natural Sciences in Philadelphia. And in collaboration with Meek, Hayden spun off five scholarly articles from his recent fieldwork.

With Baird's assistance, in the summer of 1856 Hayden caught on with a survey commanded by Lt. Gouverneur Kemble Warren of the Army Corps of Topographical Engineers. Their guide was the garrulous Jim Bridger, whose tales of Yellowstone persuaded Hayden that he had to see it for himself. Their haul of specimens was so impressive that after examining it in Philadelphia, Leidy congratulated Hayden for having discovered "more than half the species brought from the Upper Missouri country, including all explorers back to the time of Major [Stephen H.] Long."[7] The trip was also lucrative: Hayden more than doubled his $1,000 salary by selling choice fossils to the academy.

Though Hayden chafed under the restraints of military supervision, he failed to cobble together a civilian expedition of his own in 1857. Working for Warren again, Hayden correctly pegged the Black Hills as an eastern branch of the Rocky Mountains. Among the fossils he boxed up and shipped back were the bones of sixteen extinct species, including a mastodon, an elephant, a rhinoceros, and a camel—all previously thought to be strictly Old World fauna. Again Leidy parsed the bones, and Baird assured Hayden that his "collections and results [were] prodigious, but not more than past experience would lead us to expect."[8]

To put himself in the field each year with his salary and expenses taken care of, Hayden threaded his way through a maze of surveys and explorations sponsored by the military, the Department of the Interior, the states, the territories, and even private parties. The best he could arrange in 1858, however, was a brief foray with Meek to study rocks and gather fossils in Kansas. Before they set out, a friend warned Hayden of an extracurricular hazard: "Be virtuous among the Shyennes and see that Meek don't get—," with the blank space standing for a venereal disease.[9]

The following summer Hayden was hired as a naturalist, at $120 per month, by Warren's successor at the Corps of Topographical Engineers,

Capt. William Franklin Raynolds. They didn't get along. Hayden disdained Raynolds as a sanctimonious meddler whose opposition to working on the Sabbath weakened the expedition, while Raynolds confided to a friend that Hayden "seems to live only for the world and worldly fame. . . . I fear his whole aim is this world's rewards. God grant he may see his error."[10] (This was the expedition that was turned back by snowdrifts before it could reach any of Yellowstone's hot spots.)

Back in Washington, Hayden roomed with Meek in what may have been the city's second most prestigious digs (after the White House): the Smithsonian Castle. Other institutions of learning opened their doors to Hayden, too, though not as a live-in tenant. He became a member of the Lyceum of Natural History in the city of New York, the American Philosophical Society, the Boston Society of Natural History, the Essex Institute in Massachusetts, the American Association for the Advancement of Science, and the Academy of Science in St. Louis. To put it in West-speak, the ex-outsider was doing "mighty well" for himself.

Pooling their knowledge, Hayden and Meek laid out a stratigraphic column—a diagram showing the layered succession of geological periods in a region. When the partners came to the Cretaceous Period, which climaxed with the extinction of dinosaurs 65.5 million years ago, they broke it down into "five separate layers," setting what the historian William H. Goetzmann called "the standard for all future geologists."[11] And Hayden and Meek declared independence for American science by eschewing European nomenclature for geological units, naming them instead after local landmarks, such as the Fort Benton Group and the Fort Pierre Group.

Two solo publications burnished Hayden's reputation as a scientific hunter-gatherer. First came a "Catalogue of the Collections in Geology and Natural History" amassed by him and Warren during their travels together. As annotated by Foster, here is a rundown of the loot:

77 fossil vertebrates, 50 thought to be new
251 fossil mollusks [186 new]
70 fossil plants [all new but none named in text]
423 mineral and geological specimens
47 recent mammals

186 birds

65 recent mollusks

24 fishes

28 reptiles

1,500 recent plants [49 new, but only 593 listed][12]

Hayden followed this up with *On the Geology and Natural History of the Upper Missouri*, a tome consolidating what he'd learned of the West so far. In it he blended science with travelogue, instructing his professional peers while also entertaining lay readers—a hybrid treatment that would characterize his surveys from then on. By the start of the Civil War, Hayden was known as one of America's most versatile and productive naturalists. Like Olmsted, he had an uncanny gift for sizing up landscapes, albeit with a view toward deciphering their geological and paleontological patterns and assessing their commercial prospects, rather than evaluating their potential to refresh the harried visitor. Unlike Olmsted, though, Hayden tended to drop his mentors when their usefulness to him came to an end and to take a jealous lover's interest in the places he investigated—indeed, in the trans-Mississippi West as a whole.

Hayden dusted off his medical diploma for the Civil War. Enlisting in the Union Army, he served as a surgeon, the director of a hospital, and finally chief medical officer of the Army of the Shenandoah. He resigned shortly after Lee's surrender to Grant in April 1865. Later that year, with Leidy's support, Hayden was appointed auxiliary professor of geology and mineralogy in the University of Pennsylvania's Department of Medicine. The regular salary brought stability and put an end to his poverty. In 1871, at age forty-three, he married Emma Woodruff, the daughter of a prominent Philadelphia merchant.

Hayden seems to have liked lecturing and been good at it, but he resented the academic year's encroachment on his time in the field, especially when the annual spring thaw freed up the Missouri River for boat travel while he was still stranded in Philadelphia. He sometimes skipped out early, and his colleagues took it amiss. After he cut a faculty meeting in mid-March 1870, the dean was "instructed to . . . convey [to Hayden] the desire of the faculty that his course of lectures be completed this year at the same time as the others."[13] In 1872, the year when he played the starring role in establishing Yellowstone National Park, Hayden left Penn for good.

Five years earlier Baird had let Hayden know of an opportunity that was to reshape his professional life. Parked in the treasury of the new state of Nebraska was federal money left over from its territorial days and earmarked for a geological survey. Hayden lined up enough support to take charge of the Nebraska survey under the auspices of the General Land Office, a division of the Department of the Interior. At last he was running his own show, and the government was glad of it. "Your labors cannot fail to promote the public interest," Land Office commissioner Joseph Wilson assured Hayden as he left for Nebraska in 1868, "and will be appreciated by the Department."[14]

From then on Hayden operated as something of an institution—the yearly question was no longer *if* he would lead another expedition, but where it would go. With him at the helm, the Geological Survey of Nebraska morphed into the Geological Survey of the Territories of the United States, then into the U.S. Geological and Geographical Survey of the Territories, and finally the U.S. Geological Survey pure and simple. But to most Americans it was just the Hayden Survey, an eagerly awaited annual event with its namesake as commander in chief. At a time when the national interest ran heavily toward western settlement and development, Hayden was acting as an advance man, bringing order to the vast and astonishing domain beyond the hundredth meridian, sparing would-be settlers and entrepreneurs the burden of westering in the dark, as it were.

In the field, Hayden left no stone unpicked up. One summer, while riding a Union Pacific train from Wyoming to San Francisco, he got permission to borrow a handcar so that he could lag behind, geologize, and catch up with the train later. Congress steadily increased his budget, and he added personnel. For his 1869 survey of Colorado and New Mexico, he brought with him an artist, an entomologist, a mining engineer, a zoologist, and a crew consisting of a cook, a laborer, and three teamsters. His reports expanded to take in supplementary papers written by experts, some of whom traveled with him, others of whom analyzed the items he brought back.

Hayden's flag-waving ebullience pours forth like a geyser in his fourth annual report, covering portions of Wyoming and Utah and published in 1871: "Never has my faith in the grand future that awaits the entire West been so strong as it is at the present time, and it is my earnest desire to devote the remainder of the working days of my life to the development of its scientific and material interests, until I shall see every Territory, which is now organized, a State of the Union."[15] He was in effect marketing the West, a service that prompted Goetzmann to call him "par excellence the businessman's geologist."[16]

Made available to the public free of charge, Hayden's reports were hot items. The one for 1869 had a printing of eight thousand copies, but demand was so heavy that three weeks later they were all gone. Hayden was not the first explorer of Yellowstone or Chaco Canyon, to name just two of the many sites associated with him. Other travelers—Indians, trappers, missionaries, pioneers—had preceded him. But unlike them, Hayden could brief legislators and opinion makers on the West's prodigious natural resources while also enchanting lesser mortals with prose and images that evoked its eye-popping scenery.

To get those images, Hayden relied on artists and photographers. His favorites were Thomas Moran, one of the few painters who could capture not only the outsize physical reality of western peaks and waterfalls but also the impressions they made on the viewer, and William H. Jackson, a photographer with a keen eye for western scenery. Moran, of whom more later, was to join Hayden for the first time on the Yellowstone expedition of 1871. By then Hayden and Jackson had already developed an excellent working relationship.

They had met in a Cheyenne, Wyoming, brothel in 1869. Originally from upstate New York, Jackson started out as a retoucher of photographs—a job, he explained, that consisted of "sharpening and improving certain details of his [employer's] prints with India ink and 'warming them up' with water colors; the paper then used almost always produced photographs of rough appearance, and retouching was indispensable."[17] Jackson headed west after a fight with his fiancée ended their engagement. He settled in Omaha, where he was joined by his brother Ed. The Jackson brothers transformed themselves into photographers, whose early work consisted of what William described as "straight portrait jobs; group pictures of lodges, church societies and political clubs; and outdoor shots that gratified civic pride."[18] The brothers' MO was to present the shop owner or lodge president with a fait accompli—a developed shot of the establishment, which he would naturally want to buy. The outdoor work taught the ex-retoucher that he had a flair for capturing nature.

Jackson was at that Cheyenne house of ill repute on business (though maybe not *exclusively* so). He wanted permission to take pictures of the house and its "girls," who would then, he hoped, buy the finished prints. To close the deal, he plied the madam with wine until she was "hot and heavy for some large pictures to frame."[19] Jackson, who knew Hayden by sight, remembered being "much surprised to see [him] come in with some military friends. He acted like a cat in a strange joint."[20] In that or some other "strange joint," the "cat" contracted syphilis. As the two men got acquainted, a partnership took root.

In his autobiography, *Time Exposure* (1940), Jackson remembered Hayden as "a dynamic, intense man," full of enthusiasm.[21] The photographer rated his inclusion in Hayden's first Yellowstone expedition as "priceless," saying, "It gave me a career."[22] He added, "If any work that I have done should have value beyond my own lifetime, I believe it will be the happy labors of the decade 1869–1878"—the years with Hayden.[23]

The stir caused by interviews with, and articles and lectures by, Washburn Expedition alumni made a scientific investigation of Yellowstone inevitable, and Hayden was the man to lead it. Along with chasing down the rumors of thermal extravaganzas on an unprecedented scale, the undertaking promised to answer a question then perplexing geographers: Did the region encompass the sources of all the rivers—the Snake, the Green, the Yellowstone, and the Missouri—that seemed to emanate from its fastness? You bet it did. As Hayden was soon in a position to explain, "The snows that fall on the summits [of Yellowstone country] give origin to three of the largest rivers in North America"—namely, the Missouri; the Columbia, by way of its tributary the Snake; and the Colorado, by way of its tributary the Green. "From any point of view which we may select to survey this remarkable region, it surpasses, in many respects, any other portion of our continent."[24]

To finance the venture, Hayden lobbied the House of Representatives, where he made allies of James G. Blaine of Maine, the speaker, and Henry L. Dawes of Massachusetts, chairman of the Appropriations Committee. Congress obliged with an appropriation of $40,000, up substantially from Hayden's $25,000 budget for the year before. Hayden was on the receiving end of lobbying too—on behalf of Thomas Moran, who had a patron in the mighty banker Jay Cooke. The go-between was Alvred Bayard (A. B.) Nettleton, a former brigadier general who had fought with Custer but since settled into the more sedentary role of office manager for the Cooke-financed Northern Pacific Railroad.

Nettleton wrote to Hayden proposing an arrangement of mutual benefit: the addition of Moran to Hayden's Yellowstone roster. "Mr. Moran is an artist (landscape painter) of much genius," Nettleton declared, "who goes out under the patronage of Messrs. Scribner and Co., Publishers, NY," for which Moran was working as an engraver at the time, "and our own Mr. Cooke . . . on whom you will confer a great favor by receiving Mr. Moran."[25] Best of all, Nettleton promised, the artist "simply wishes to take advantage of your cavalry escort" and, thanks to a sort of fellowship provided by Cooke, would cost Hayden nothing.[26] Naturally, Hayden said yes. The pieces were falling into place for one of the most influential western expeditions after Lewis and Clark's.

The fortified 1871 edition of the Hayden Survey got off to a smooth start in late May. "Horses, mules, wagons, and all other equipments were in place on freight-cars and taken by rail to Ogden, Utah," Hayden recalled in the letter transmitting his report to Interior Secretary Columbus Delano nine months later. "Here our journey began."[27] At Ogden, Hayden noted in a letter to Baird, they all switched to "5 wagons and 2 ambulances . . . about 50 mules and horses, with 7 wall tents and several flies." "We make a formidable camp," he summed up, "and almost an army on the march."[28]

Besides Hayden, the party consisted of eighteen principals: botanists, a mineralogist, a zoologist, a physician, an entomologist, topographers, artists, Jackson as photographer, and a few general assistants. Support

The Man Who Picked Up Stones

was provided by a staff of fifteen, who took care of such tasks as packing, hunting, and cooking.

Hayden's mineralogist was Albert C. Peale, MD, a former student of his and a great-grandson of Charles Willson Peale, in whose Philadelphia Museum George Catlin had studied the artifacts that inspired his first Indian paintings. The industrious Albert kept a diary throughout the summer; sent regular dispatches to the *Philadelphia Press*, which published them much as the *New York Commercial Advertiser* had done with Catlin's letters four decades earlier; and contributed a thirty-page paper on minerals, rocks, and thermal springs to the expeditionary report. Two of the general assistants were the sons of congressmen: John A. Logan of Illinois and Dawes of Massachusetts.

In addition to Jackson and Moran, Hayden brought along another image maker. This was the adventure-loving Henry Wood Elliott, who had first worked for Hayden two years earlier, at the age of thirty-two. By then Elliott had already compiled a varied and eventful curriculum vitae: studying art at the Smithsonian, helping lay out a route across the Bering Strait for a Russian-American telegraph line, and canoeing 725 miles from the Yukon to Victoria, British Columbia. The highlight of his post-Hayden career was a campaign to save seals, which culminated in the Hay-Elliott Fur Seal Treaty of 1911, the first of its kind to benefit wildlife. Elliott's artistic specialty was the panorama.

Also in the field was an eleven-man party led by Capt. John Barlow, chief engineer of the U.S. Army's Division of Missouri, tasked with surveying and mapping some of the territory being explored by the Hayden party. The two groups often converged, working together tolerably well as they shared a military escort headed by Lt. Gustavus Doane, who had performed the same service for the Washburn Expedition. If we throw in the Barlow and Doane contingents, Hayden's "army on the march" was at times more than eighty strong.

From Ogden the main party traveled by horse, mule, and wagon through western Utah to southern Montana, where they made the Bottler brothers' ranch their staging area. "The three brothers for whom the place was named were Dutchmen," remembered Jackson, "laughing, hearty fellows who kept bachelor hall in a big log house. They set a good table and, to augment their income from a cattle and fur business, they obligingly took in occasional guests like ourselves."[29] Leaving the wagons there, the Hayden army spent the next month—from July 21 to August 25—making a clockwise loop through the Yellowstone region: south from the hot springs near White Mountain (just across the border in Wyoming), to Tower Creek, through the Yellowstone River's Grand Canyon, to its Lower and Upper Falls, to the Mud Springs and Sulphur Cauldron, around Yellowstone Lake, to the Geyser Basins, and back north to the Bottler spread.

Even with so many men at his disposal, the boss was not one to sit by while they carried out his orders. Hayden took part in almost every phase of the exploration, sometimes perilously so, as when he and his men came upon "a mud volcano" with numerous outlets. "I attempted to walk about among these simmering vents," he recalled, "and broke through to my knees, covering myself with the hot mud, to my great pain and subsequent inconvenience."[30]

In a letter inviting his Oberlin teacher George Allen to join the expedition, Hayden had cited the "wild joyous freedom from restraint" that had characterized his earlier trips.[31] The aging Allen did come, but on discovering that he couldn't pull his own weight, he dropped out early. Despite occasional hunger, frequent swarms of mosquitos, and a scary but harmless earthquake, everyone else seems to have had the standard "wild joyous" time.

True to form, rather than cram his part of that season's report with scientific minutiae, Hayden made it a chronological narrative of the expedition's linear progress and major geographic discoveries, leaving technical topics—minerals, agricultural prospects, paleontology, zoology and botany, meteorology—for his experts to elucidate in their supplementary papers. When Hayden slipped into learned jargon, as when he called a rock formation "quaquaversal," he would usually pause and either define it or provide a more readily comprehensible alternative, in this case "an isolated puff or bulge in the crust."[32] In that way, his contribution stands apart from, say, Peale's mineralogical report, which is sprinkled with words like "garnetiferous," "pedicles," and "vesicular," all left undefined; it's the difference between prose written for a general audience and the argot of the specialist.

Occasionally Hayden mined his own past for recondite comparisons, as when the reddish sandstone near the Great Salt Lake took him back to "the Medina sandstone of New York." But the popular touch was never absent for long. Hayden evoked the rocks flanking Tower Falls by calling them "pinnacle-like columns . . . standing like gloomy sentinels or like the gigantic pillars at the entrance of some grand temple" and by wondering if perhaps "the idea of the Gothic style of architecture had been caught from such carvings of nature." And to evoke Yellowstone's thermal features as a whole, he employed a household image: they "are nothing more than the closing stages of that wonderful period of volcanic action that began in Tertiary times. In other words, they are the escape-pipes or vents for those internal forces which once were so active, but are now continually dying out."[33]

When a spectacle amazed Hayden—a not-infrequent occurrence—he let himself go. Yellowstone Lake is "a vast sheet of quiet water, of a most delicate ultramarine hue, one of the most beautiful scenes I have ever beheld." Above the Firehole River, a steaming spring bubbles over its edges and "descends by numerous small channels, with a large number of smaller ones spreading over a broad surface, and the marvelous beauty of the strikingly vivid coloring far surpasses anything of the kind we have seen in this land of wondrous beauty." Like Fanny Trollope at Niagara Falls four decades earlier, Hayden sometimes admitted to being dumbstruck—at White Mountain Hot Springs, for instance, he exclaimed over "a hill 200 feet high, composed of the calcareous deposit of the hot springs, with a system of step-like terraces which would defy any description by words"—only to recover his voice and go on about the hill at some length.[34] (He neglected to define "calcareous," which means "made of calcium.")

It's a tough call, but Hayden's greatest rave may have been occasioned by the Giantess in the Upper Geyser Basin. "[Its] grand eruption continued for twenty minutes, and was the most magnificent sight we ever witnessed," he exclaimed. He was particularly struck by how sunlight "filled the sparkling column of water and spray with myriads of rainbows, whose arches were constantly changing . . . while the minute globules into which the spent jets were diffused when falling sparkled liked a shower of diamonds." In places where clouds of vapor cast shadows on the water column, he marveled at the luminous circles, "radiant with all the colors of the prism," surrounding those shadows. "All that we had previously witnessed seemed tame in comparison with the perfect grandeur and beauty of this display."[35] Breathless as that passage may be, it's also a tour de force of fine-tuned observation (the ever-changing rainbow arches, the light-encircled shadows cast by vapor) and a foretaste of the brio that Hayden soon brought to his lobbying for a Yellowstone park. Moran's accompanying sketch of the erupting Giantess makes her look like a multilevel aqueous tree.

On his own specialty, geology, Hayden went light. Now and then he alluded to vulcanism, as with his "escape-pipes" metaphor. But the contemporary state of knowledge was such that neither he nor anyone else could have suspected how much more dynamism lurked beneath Yellowstone's flimsy crust, including a molten-rock magma chamber eight kilometers down and a hot spot in the earth's mantle some four hundred kilometers below that. Nor could he have been aware that in the last 2.1 million years the region had been rocked and riven by three cataclysmic eruptions, which raised a plateau with an average elevation of eight thousand feet and left behind calderas, the most recent of which had formed 640,000 years ago. Not until geologists studied the region with better instruments than Hayden's, more time at their disposal, and the theoretical framework of plate tectonics on which to hang their findings could Yellowstone's thermal features be satisfactorily explained.

There was plenty to see on the surface, though, including spouting geysers, smoking fumaroles, bubbling mud pots, and boiling-hot springs. Oh, and the same nuisance that had plagued Yosemite Valley in 1864: squatters. Early in the going, the main party came upon a cluster of invalids lolling in a hot spring. This impromptu spa went by the name Chestnutville, after a Col. J. D. Chestnut from Bozeman. Not long after the expedition passed by, one of the Chestnutville bathers got dressed and started building a road projected to run, he said, "from Bozeman to the Yellowstone Lake, by the Mammoth Hot Springs . . . for the benefit of the travel to & from the Wonderland, & to be a toll road."[36] At the terraced hot springs known collectively as Soda Mountain, two men were erecting a cabin. Alongside the Firehole, others had cut poles for fencing off some of the local geysers.

These inroads so alarmed Hayden that he brought them to the attention of Congress that fall.

The flaw in Hayden's fifth annual report is logorrhea. As Goetzmann observed, "Everything was appealing [to Hayden]. Everything had possibilities and must be included, the shoddy and the brilliant alike."[37] Some judicious trimming would have made for a punchier document than the 161-page word flood, illustrated by the drawings of Elliott and Moran, embellished by two glued-in foldout maps, and followed by 275 pages of auxiliary papers, that Hayden formally submitted to Secretary Delano on February 20, 1872; in his defense, though, Hayden had been under pressure to get something out ASAP. The previous fall, for example, Elliott had briefed editors at the *New York Times* on the expedition. Afterward the editors explained in print why they remained on tenterhooks: "The accounts of the Yellowstone country hitherto received . . . have been so extraordinary that confirmatory testimony has been anxiously looked for. Even now, and with every respect for the new witness [i.e., Elliott], part of whose evidence we shall quote, the official narrative of the Hayden Expedition must be deemed needful before we can altogether accept stories of wonder hardly short of fairy tales in the astounding phenomena they describe."[38]

Seen in that light, Hayden's cluttered-cabinet approach looks better. The expedition had been asked to bring back the truth, and here it was, heaps of it, Yellowstone Verified, nearly as outlandish as previous, unofficial accounts had made it out to be.

Even before finishing the report, Hayden was giving his expedition high marks, bragging in an August 28 letter to Delano that thanks to himself and his men, "no portion of the West has been more carefully surveyed than the Yellow Stone basin."[39] In a September 2 letter to his old teacher, the dropout George Allen, Hayden crowed about "having completed our work to our entire satisfaction. We have had an uninterrupted series of successes, without a single pullback."[40]

Two pullbacks were imminent, though. On October 14 Anton Schönborn, the expedition's chief topographer, committed suicide in his rented room in Omaha, a calamity blamed on his heavy drinking and proneness to depression. Schönborn left his topographical notes in good order, but

Hayden had been counting on him for the next step, the drawing of maps, which would now be delayed. And in Chicago, where Captain Barlow and his men made their headquarters, most of their specimens, photographs, and negatives were consumed by the great fire of October 1871. Luckily, Hayden had the images captured by his own people—Moran's watercolors, Jackson's photographs, Elliott's panoramas—to fall back on.

Hayden didn't know it yet, but those artworks would be good for more than simply justifying the confidence Congress had placed in him and his survey. They would also combine with his energetic advocacy to help transform Yellowstone into the world's first national park.

Saving Gravel   12

The participation of Thomas Moran was not Jay Cooke's only stake in the 1871 Yellowstone survey. Before setting out, Hayden gave an interview to the *Helena Daily Herald*. After ticking off his main goals, he added that if possible, he and his men would undertake an extra assignment for Cooke: finding a route to connect Yellowstone with the western half of the transcontinental railroad. As it happened, this task was not carried out, but Hayden's mention of it shows how cavalier nineteenth-century Americans could be about using public money to advance private interests.

Cooke's bond-managing prowess had helped save the Union. Also during the Civil War, President Lincoln had signed into law a bill chartering the Northern Pacific Railroad. Missing from that law were the generous financial subsidies enjoyed by the transcontinental railroad's two components, the Union Pacific and the Central Pacific, but five years later, when Cooke was deciding whether to back the Northern Pacific, he counted on persuading Congress to sweeten the pot. In this he was to be disappointed. As explained by the historian M. John Lubetkin, "The mood of Congress had changed; a northern route served no vital interest [and] most of the land [in the region] was devoid of settlement."[1] Cooke had to rely on his reputation, his salesmanship, and flim-flam.

The first politician to raise the possibility of a Yellowstone park was Rep. William Darrah "Judge" Kelley—a "broad-visioned man," as Aubrey Haines described him, and a longtime ally of Cooke's.[2] Having represented his Pennsylvania district since 1861, Kelley had been a member of Congress when the Yosemite Park bill was debated and passed in 1864. In proposing similar treatment for Yellowstone, he was building on that earlier legislation. He passed his idea on to Cooke's man A. B. Nettleton.

Hayden was in Washington, plugging away at his Yellowstone report, when he received a letter dated October 27, 1871, written on the stationery of Jay Cooke & Co., Bankers, Financial Agents, Northern Pacific Railroad Company, and signed by Nettleton. "Dear Doctor," it read, "Judge Kelley has made a suggestion which strikes me as being an excellent one, viz.: Let Congress pass a bill reserving the Great Geyser Basin as a public park forever—just as it has reserved that far inferior wonder the Yosemite Valley and big trees. If you approve this would such a recommendation be appropriate in your official report?"[3] Nettleton was thus performing the same function for Yellowstone that Israel Ward Raymond had for Yosemite: bringing a proposal to the attention of a man with the know-how and connections to get it enacted into law. Hayden was happy to do Nettleton's bidding.

Cooke, you may recall, had been alerted by the railroad's Samuel Wilkeson to the possibility that a campaign to make Yellowstone a tourist destination would impinge on the Northern Pacific's selection of lands owed it by the federal government. Hayden may have given Cooke a peek at his work in progress, for on October 30 the banker sent a query to the engineer charged with locating the railroad's route through Montana: "It is proposed by Mr. Hayden in his report to Congress that the Geyser region around Yellowstone Lake shall be set apart by government as a reservation as [a] park, similar to that of the Great Trees & other reservations in California. Would this conflict with our land grant, or interfere with us in any way?" Cooke did not hide his ulterior motive in writing: "It is important to do something speedily, or squatters & claimants will go in there, and we can probably deal much better with the government in any improvement we may desire to make for the benefit of our pleasure travel than with individuals." By telegram from Helena on November 21, the engineer flashed the all-clear sign: "Geysers outside our grant advise Congressional reservation."[4]

The Kelley-to-Nettleton-to-Hayden initiative now enjoyed Cooke's full support. The honor of introducing a bill fell to William H. Clagett, Montana Territory's delegate to the House of Representatives. Nathaniel Langford came to Washington, and Hayden put his report aside to join him in lobbying for the bill.

Writing to the secretary of the Montana Historical Society more than thirty years after the fact, Clagett took credit for more than just drafting and introducing the park bill: "Hedges, Langford, and myself formed the same idea about the same time [as one another], and we all three acted together in Montana, and afterwards Langford and I acted with Professor Hayden in Washington, in the winter of 1871–2." He continued: "The fact is that the matter was well under way before Professor Hayden was ever heard of in connection with that measure." The delegate admitted that Hayden had performed "valuable services" in bringing back specimens from Yellowstone that were put on display in the Capitol building and in explaining geological and other features of the proposed park to members of Congress. Nonetheless, Clagett insisted, "the movement which created the Park [originated] with Hedges, Langford and myself; and after Congress met, Langford and I probably did two-thirds, if not three-fourths of all the work connected with its passage."[5]

Few historians have accepted Clagett's fractions. Take, for example, Hiram Chittenden, whose views gain credence from his personal history with the park as a road-building engineer for the Army Corps of Engineers. "Dr. Hayden occupied a commanding position in [the efforts to get the Yellowstone Park bill passed], as representative of the government in the explorations of 1871," Chittenden wrote in his book *The Yellowstone National Park* (1895). "Dr. Hayden gave to the cause the energy of a genuine enthusiasm, and his work that winter will always hold a prominent place in the history of the Park."[6]

There has been some confusion over Moran's part in the campaign. His *Grand Canyon of the Yellowstone*, done in oil, is an unquestionably spectacular painting. But because Moran did not finish it until after the Yellowstone Park bill became law, *Grand Canyon* could have had no direct effect on the legislation. The painting was much anticipated, though, and on delivery it made everyone forget about the long wait. "It rivaled Church and outdid Bierstadt in offering the panoramic thrill that no watercolor can give and the density of substance that no photograph could rival," wrote the twentieth-century art critic Robert Hughes. "It became a prime symbol of wilderness tourism."[7]

Hughes was right: though impressive, Bierstadt's version of Yellowstone's Grand Canyon lacks the scope and vibrancy of Moran's. The work also brought Moran a small fortune; he sold *Grand Canyon* to Congress for $10,000—80 cents per square inch, by Hughes's estimate—and it now dominates a grand staircase in the Smithsonian American Art Museum. (As William Henry Jackson noted, however, the painting we have today is not the original, which was "so badly neglected—and later, so badly restored—as to lose its original character . . . but [is] a fine copy, which Moran made some years afterward.")[8]

Moran's watercolors, done on-site, *were* on hand when the park bill was being debated in the winter of 1871–72, as were Jackson's photos. Because no photographs of Yellowstone had yet been published, Jackson recalled, "Dr. Hayden was determined that the first ones should be good. A series of fine pictures would not only supplement his final report but tell the story to thousands who never read it. Photo-engraving and ten-cent picture magazines were still unknown; but an astonishing number of people bought finished photographs to hang on their walls, or to view through stereoscopes."[9]

Bringing scenery on the scale of Yellowstone into focus had been a challenge for Jackson, who learned much from his fellow artist Moran, especially how to finesse details in favor of the big picture. Jackson would take better photos later in his travels with Hayden, but the 1871 Yellowstone series did what it was supposed to—it gave lawmakers a good look at what they were being asked to preserve—and Jackson satisfied the demand in person. While visiting his parents in Nyack, New York, he learned that he was urgently needed in Washington to develop more prints of his negatives for the Yellowstone campaign. He answered the call.

Hayden also had Elliott's panoramic drawings to show. Though skilled and charming, they have been overshadowed by the more vivid work of Moran and Jackson. A select few of Elliott's panoramas made fine chapter headings for *Yellowstone and the Great West*, Marlene Deahl Merrill's 1999 compendium of documents and images from the 1871 expedition.

A fuller picture of who did what for Yellowstone on Capitol Hill emerges from the legislative history. After introducing the park bill, Clagett apparently forgot about it. It stagnated until January 27, 1872, when Rep. Mark H. Dunnell of Minnesota gave Interior Secretary Delano a nudge, saying that he, Dunnell, would be pleased to receive Hayden's Yellowstone report. Delano passed the word on to Hayden, who obliged by condensing his working draft into a two-page synopsis, which he sent to Dunnell post-haste. Included in that synopsis was the squatter alert mentioned in the preceding chapter:

> Persons are now waiting for the spring to open to enter in and take possession of these remarkable curiosities, to make merchandise of these beautiful specimens, to fence in these rare wonders, so as to charge visitors a fee, as is now done at Niagara Falls, for the sight of that which ought to be as free as the air or water. . . . If this bill fails to become a law this session, the vandals who are now waiting to enter into this wonder-land will, in a single season, despoil, beyond recovery, these remarkable curiosities, which have required all the cunning skill of nature thousands of years to prepare.[10]

Over in the Senate, a Yellowstone bill had been introduced by Sen. Samuel C. Pomeroy of Kansas on December 18 and reported favorably out of committee on January 23. A week later the bill came up for debate on the Senate floor. The only opposition on record came from Sen. Cornelius Cole of California, who professed not to "see the reason or propriety of setting apart a large tract of land of that kind in the Territories of the United States for a public park." In reply, Sen. George F. Edmunds of Vermont cited the difficulty of settling or farming land located "north of latitude forty, and . . . over seven thousand feet above the level of the sea," concluding, "You cannot cultivate that kind of gravel." In rebuttal, Cole plunked down a gotcha: "But if it cannot be occupied and cultivated, why should we make a public park of it? If it cannot be occupied by man, why protect it from occupation?"[11] (The Californian's resistance makes more sense when one considers that he chaired the Senate Appropriations Committee, which took a jaundiced view of any legislation likely to cost money.)

In surrebuttal, Illinois senator Lyman Trumbull taught Cole a lesson he shouldn't have needed:

I think our experience with the wonderful natural curiosity, if I may call it that, in the Senator's own State, should admonish us of the propriety of passing a bill such as this. There is the wonderful Yosemite valley, which one or two persons are now claiming by virtue of preemption. . . .

. . . [And] there is a dispute about it. Now, before there is any dispute as to this wonderful country [i.e., Yellowstone], I hope we shall except it from the general disposition of the public lands, and reserve it to the Government. At some future time, if we desire to do so, we can repeal this law if it is in anybody's way; but now I think it a very appropriate bill to pass.[12]

Minutes later the bill did pass the Senate, without a roll call. History is silent as to whether James Hutchings and James Lamon—whose Yosemite claims were the ones Trumbull meant—ever found out that they were dragged into the Senate's Yellowstone debate as unnamed bogeymen.

Over in the House, Clagett's bill continued to languish, in part because some Yellowstone squatters were seeking grandfathered status for their claim to a tract at Mammoth Hot Springs. Their attempt failed, and Hayden turned up the heat in an article appearing in the February 1872 issue of *Scribner's*: "Why will not Congress at once pass a law setting [the Yellowstone region] apart as a great public park for all time to come, as has been done with that far inferior wonder, the Yosemite Valley?"[13]

The Senate-passed bill reached the House floor on February 27. Speaking in favor, Dunnell said it would be appropriate for the House to pass the Senate bill verbatim. At this point, Haines notes, Dunnell submitted Hayden's synopsis, complete with its no-more-Niagaras plea, as the committee's own report on the park bill.

As the House debated the Senate bill, Yellowstone found the heavyweight spokesman it needed in Dawes of Massachusetts, whose son had been one of Hayden's interns the previous summer. "This bill treads upon no rights of the settler," Dawes assured his colleagues, "infringes upon no permanent prospect of settlement of that Territory, and it receives the urgent and ardent support of the Legislature of the Territory, and of the Delegate himself . . . and of those who surveyed it and brought the

Saving Gravel

attention of the country to its remarkable and wonderful features."[14] The House passed the Senate bill without amendments by a vote of 115 to 65, with 60 members not voting. The enrolled bill then went to President Grant, who signed it into law on March 1, 1872.

Modeled on the operative language of the 1864 Yosemite Act, Section 1 of the new law provided that a specified tract in the Territories of Montana and Wyoming was "hereby reserved and withdrawn from settlement, occupancy, or sale under the laws of the United States, and dedicated and set apart as a public park or pleasuring-ground for the benefit and enjoyment of the people; and all persons who shall locate or settle upon or occupy the same, or any part thereof . . . shall be considered trespassers and removed therefrom." The acreage getting this treatment was tremendous—bigger than the states of Delaware and Rhode Island combined. Section 2 gave "exclusive control" of the park to the secretary of the interior,

> whose duty it shall be, as soon as practicable, to make and publish such rules and regulations as he may deem necessary or proper for the care and management of the same. Such regulations shall provide for the preservation, from injury or spoliation, of all timber, mineral deposits, natural curiosities, or wonders within said park, and their retention in their natural condition. . . . He shall provide against the wanton destruction of the fish and game found within said park, and against their capture or destruction for the purposes of merchandise or profit. He shall also cause all persons trespassing upon the same after the passage of this act to be removed therefrom, and generally shall be authorized to take all such measures as shall be necessary or proper to fully carry out the objects and purposes of this act.[15]

The act set no penalties for violating the secretary's regs, an omission that was to hobble the new park for decades to come.

At the time, though, the law met with near-unanimous approbation. The *Helena Daily Herald* anticipated a regional spillover effect: "[The Yellowstone Act] will redound to the untold good of this Territory, inasmuch as a measure of this character is well calculated to direct the world's attention to . . . such resources of mines and agriculture as we can boast, spread everywhere about us." The *Territorial Enterprise*, the Nevada paper in which the journalist Sam Clemens had restyled himself Mark Twain a decade earlier, filed a less parochial comment: "It is pleasant to see Congressmen turn aside from their sterner duties and vote . . . for a measure looking to the adornment of the Republic. This will be the grandest park in the world—the grand, instructive museum of the grandest Government on Earth."[16] With its "instructive museum" metaphor, the *Territorial Enterprise* was seconding Hayden, who in his completed Yellowstone report had hailed the new law as "mark[ing] an era in the popular advancement of scientific thought, not only in this country, but throughout the civilized world."[17] Back east, the *Nation* magazine rooted for more of the same, although in doing so it mischaracterized the ownership of Yosemite at the time: "It is the general principle which is chiefly commendable in the act of Congress setting aside the Yellowstone region as a national park. It will help confirm the national possession of the Yo Semite, and may in time lead us to rescue Niagara from its present degrading surroundings."[18]

All but overlooked by the press and everyone else was the detail of who would be running the new entity. The Yosemite solution of state ownership and control was inapplicable to this case because Montana and Wyoming were still territories. The park was left in federal ownership, under the care of the secretary of the interior. Yellowstone thus became the first national park in the full sense of the term and the template for others to come.

As for who most deserves the title Begetter of Yellowstone National Park, a good case can be made for a man who did not claim it—Jay Cooke. Had he raised his hand and said something like "I'm the one. The idea originated with my people, and we did more than anybody else to effectuate it," his bid would have been hard to deny. An impersonal way of putting the same idea is Chris J. Magoc's assertion that "Yellowstone [was] created by market capitalism."[19]

To be sure, Cooke had something weightier on his mind than the paternity of a park. He had been uncharacteristically neglectful of the railroad he was now financing, making it possible for the Northern Pacific's president, former Vermont governor J. Gregory Smith, to divert funds to the benefit of another railroad, the Vermont Central, of which Smith was also the CEO.

The Franco-Prussian War had meanwhile slowed sales of bonds in Europe, and Americans began to lose confidence in the railroad after Sioux and Cheyenne warriors led by Sitting Bull tangled with the U.S. cavalry in the summer of 1872. Dispatched to protect surveyors laying out the Northern Pacific's route west from Bismarck, Dakota Territory, the horse soldiers did not disgrace themselves. Yet gloom was sown by a letter from an unnamed Northern Pacific surveyor that ran in the *New York Times* on September 30: "You will hear before this reaches you that the Yellowstone [River] expedition and Northern Pacific Railroad survey is a failure . . . [The Indians] demonstrated the fact that our force was totally inadequate to pass down the Yellowstone Valley."[20] (For an account of how the park's existence affected one group of Indians in the Yellowstone region, see the following chapter.)

After more such trouble a year later, a *Times* editorial posed a grim question: "If several thousand of our best soldiers, with all of the arms of the service, under some of our most dashing officers, can only hold the ground on their narrow line of march for 150 or 200 miles west of the Upper Missouri, [what] will peaceful bodies of railroad workers be able to do, or what can emigrants accomplish in such a dangerous region?"[21] High on anyone's list of the "most dashing officers" would have been George Armstrong Custer, who had commanded some of those ground-holding cavalrymen.

That summer Olmsted's old friend Charley Brace, now a roving correspondent for the *Times*, had some good things to say about the Northern Pacific but also observed that American businesses were "drawing in sail everywhere, discharging men, and making ready for the storm. *Woe to the company now in the West which has to borrow money or place bonds!*"—the very situation in which the Northern Pacific found itself.[22]

Woe, indeed. Having borrowed heavily against an anticipated bull market for Northern Pacific bonds, Cooke was now in a bad way. He had promised his partners that he would advance the railroad no more than $500,000 but in fact had handed over $7 million. He kept up appearances until September 18, 1873, when he learned what his partner Harris C. Fahnestock had unilaterally done that morning: shut the doors of the banking firm's New York branch, walked over to the Stock Exchange, and fessed up. A day later the *Times* described the reaction to Fahnestock's actions in a story headlined "The Panic": "To say that the street became excited would only give a feeble view of the expressions of feeling. The brokers stood perfectly thunderstruck for a moment . . . [then] surged out of the Exchange, stumbling pell-mell over each other in the general confusion, and reached their respective offices in race-horse time."[23]

The turmoil delayed the next rollout of the Hayden Survey. "The Panic of 1873 threw a staggering burden upon the Congress which convened shortly before Christmas," Jackson remembered. "One of the inevitable results was that the Geological Survey should be pushed into the background. The appropriation finally came through so late that we never got out of Washington until July."[24]

The Panic grew into a debacle, an economic contraction that lasted almost six years—arguably the worst of its kind until the Great Depression of the 1930s. Half of the nation's railroads went bankrupt during the earlier period, but the Northern Pacific was not among them. It managed to stay solvent by selling some of the land it had received from the federal government. Indeed, the railroad was flush enough in the fall of 1873 to hire Frederick Law Olmsted to design its terminal city, Tacoma, Washington. Olmsted submitted a plan calling for streets to follow the land's contours, only to have it rejected by traditionalists wedded to the standard grid pattern.

The once-mighty banker was shunted aside. "Ogontz was closed in 1874," wrote Lubetkin, "and Cooke moved into the home of a married daughter who lived nearby. For the next 31 years, he stayed in a child's bedroom, from which he could see the grounds of Ogontz."[25] Still, the Northern Pacific forged ahead, and although the spur line to Yellowstone wasn't built until 1883, the railroad did more than simply maintain its policy of promoting the park. As we shall see in the next chapter, it also schemed to monopolize the park's concessions.

For a number of years, Hayden fared much better than Cooke. Hayden returned to the Yellowstone region in the summer of 1872, bringing along more topographers to finish mapping the new park. A year later, during the summer session cut short by the Panic, he saw enough of

Saving Gravel

Colorado to argue convincingly that the approach of railroads made a thorough exploration of that territory imperative. In 1874 Congress sent him there with a budget of $75,000, allowing him to add personnel until he was juggling six different parties as they braved such hazards as a lack of water, getting lost, forest fires, hostile Indians, and sublimely bad weather. "The [surveyors'] tripod began to 'click like a telegraph machine,'" Goetzmann wrote of a high-altitude electrical storm that hit one group, "pencils in their hands chattered, and their hair emitted a sound 'like frying bacon.'" Stones on the ground were humming, and lightning flashed all around the surveyors, two of whom "slid down the mountain to safety just as a tremendous lightning bolt struck the bald summit where they had been."[26]

For help with managing his growing empire, Hayden turned to James T. Gardner, who had surveyed the brand-new Yosemite Park for Olmsted a decade earlier. Gardner proved to be efficient, but he wanted the world to know it, and Hayden complained of his new hire's tendency to "crowd out the central power." The "central power" took particular exception to Gardner's off-the-books survey of Colorado coalfields for the Denver and Rio Grande Railroad at a time when Hayden was fending off accusations of being too chummy with private interests. Fed up with what he called Hayden's "abusive tirades," Gardner resigned at the end of the 1875 season.[27]

The Colorado survey produced more than just chattering pencils, fried-bacon hair, and Gardner's departure in a huff. Hayden saw into print a handsome book, *Sun Pictures of Rocky Mountain Scenery*, which introduced the world to such marvels as Mesa Verde and the Mount of the Holy Cross, named for a pattern made by snow-filled fissures on its upper slope. With Hayden otherwise occupied, Jackson had led the group exploring Mesa Verde. They didn't discover a thing: the locals had been well aware of the old cliff dwellings' existence. But Jackson's daredevil picture taking—some of the ledges he crawled out on to get shots were no more than twenty inches wide—called attention to this little-known phase of pre-Columbian history. In later seasons, Hayden explored more archaeological sites in the Southwest, among them Canyon de Chelly, Chaco Canyon, and Pueblo Pintado. Jackson not only photographed these but also made models of them for a three-dimensional panorama displayed at the 1876 Centennial Exhibition in Philadelphia.

After a return trip to Idaho, Montana, and Wyoming in 1878, Hayden got busy on what stacked up as his most elaborate publication of all, the five-volume *Report of Progress of the Exploration in Wyoming and Idaho for the Year 1878*—the twelfth and last of the series—which came out in 1883 with what Merrill calls "an accompanying packet containing an array of large, folded geological maps of the area, several in color. Also included were three striking panoramas of the Teton and Wind River ranges by the survey's last topographer-artist, William Henry Holmes."[28]

In the late 1870s Hayden's fame was at its zenith. When the continued existence of rival and sometimes duplicative surveys finally prompted Congress to amalgamate them into a single federal agency, who was better qualified to be its first director than the Man Who Picks Up Stones Running?

Yet a choice that had seemed foregone got bogged down in rivalry and politics. Some of Hayden's fellow scientists denigrated him as a facile crowd pleaser. His most outspoken critic was John Wesley Powell, the geologist famous for having explored the Lower Colorado River, who had lobbied for the new agency's establishment. As Powell's biographer Donald Worster sees it, Powell's animosity was justified: "Having been treated with condescension and contempt by him for years, Powell despised Hayden in every way and was worried that the wily, mean-spirited conniver might once again fool Congress and gain command over a creation that Powell had worked hard—much harder than anyone else—to achieve."[29]

In what Mike Foster calls "a widely circulated memorandum," Powell belittled Hayden as "a charlatan who has bought his way to fame with government money and unlimited access to the Government Printing Office." Also weighing in was the president of Harvard, Charles William Eliot, who dropped this sneering estimate into a letter to President Rutherford B. Hayes: "I have often heard Dr. Hayden discussed among scientific men, but I have never heard either his attainments or his character spoken of with respect. On the contrary, I have often heard his ignorance, his scientific incapacity, and his low habits when in camp, commented on

Saving Gravel

with aversion and mortification."[30] One man's "wild joyous freedom from restraint," it seems, is another's "low habits when in camp."

For all his accomplishments, then, Hayden remained an outsider, an upstart, a ruffian. Where would he have been, though, if he hadn't broken the rule that a gentleman doesn't toot his own horn, if he hadn't asked favors of the elders he so assiduously cultivated, if he hadn't lectured on his surveys in venues as profane as Delmonico's restaurant in Manhattan, if he hadn't written books that were catnip to the average reader? It was a case of damned if you did, never heard of if you didn't. Even Worster acknowledges that Powell "might have been more restrained [in his opposition to Hayden], considering that his own work often had something of the fragmentary and disjoined about it," and that he, too, "had curried favor by furnishing photographs to the wonder-loving committees that controlled his funding."[31]

Hayden also got entangled in the bone war, the infantile feud waged by two brilliant paleontologists, Edward Drinker Cope, a regular contributor to Hayden's reports, and Othniel Charles Marsh, a solid member of the eastern upper class. Preposterous as it may sound, the West was too small to contain the Cope ego and the Marsh ego at the same time, and a series of disputes over scientific findings fueled a mutual hatred that stopped just short of fisticuffs. At one point, Marsh resorted to a heinous method of keeping Cope from combing through a fossil field that Marsh had just finished working: at his order, one of his men blew up the field with dynamite. After the death of the incumbent president of the Academy of Natural Sciences in 1878, Marsh took over; his new position lent authority to his criticisms of Cope and Hayden.

Hayden might still have been named director of the new Geological Survey—he enjoyed a good deal of support, especially from western members of Congress—if he hadn't run short of his famous enthusiasm. He may have been distracted and disheartened by a condition he was suffering from: locomotor ataxia, in all likelihood a symptom of syphilis. For whatever reason, he failed to promote himself with his customary vigor, and President Hayes gave the nod to the well-connected Clarence King. (Josiah Whitney also coveted the job, but he lost out too.) After less than two years in the job, King resigned to concentrate on making a killing as a mining entrepreneur (but failed). His successor, Powell, set the young agency on a firm, if sometimes prickly, course, telling western politicians things they didn't want to hear, such as the likelihood that the region's aridity was a permanent condition. Powell at least had the courtesy to keep Hayden on the payroll so that he could finish his work in progress.

Hayden then retired to Philadelphia, where he wrote portions of two more books for a popular audience. His health stabilized enough for him to make a few more western field trips, and on one of these he took along his wife, Emma, on whom he'd increasingly come to rely. In June 1886, the University of Pennsylvania awarded Hayden an honorary doctorate of laws. Shortly afterward his condition worsened, leaving him bedridden. He died on December 22, 1887, at the age of fifty-nine. By then a new wave of academic specialists was making Hayden's wide-angle kind of science look superficial and antiquated. The physician who had taken a few courses in the natural sciences was giving way to the degreed specialist in a discrete field, such as geology, zoology, or paleontology. Yet any scientist of today who scores a federal grant might well drink a toast to Hayden, whose exploring and popularizing helped make federal funding of science a habit.

Neither Cooke's fall nor Hayden's decline should be allowed to vitiate their contributions to the making of Yellowstone National Park. The aesthetician Burke, the visionaries Catlin and Thoreau, the pragmatists Raymond and Conness, the landscape reader Olmsted and his proselytizer Bowles, the fireball Hayden, the super salesman Jay Cooke, the countless visitors to Niagara Falls who came away saying, "We can't let this sort of thing happen again"—all these players and more had helped forge an American consensus: that preserving wildland for public benefit can be sound governmental policy.

A Shaky Start 13

Yellowstone was now the world's first national park, but its success was not assured. Over the next decade and a half, the park wrestled with problems of such severity—inadequate financing, rampant poaching, feeble and sometimes corrupt management, a protracted effort to make it a railroad subsidiary—that the U.S. Army rode to the rescue.

Before the Yellowstone bill passed, a promise had been extracted from Hayden: he would not seek appropriations for the park. The consensus was that Yellowstone would be self-sustaining; the Northern Pacific would reach Montana and build a spur line to the park, droves of tourists would ride in and patronize the concessions, and the government's cut of the fees would pay for the park's operation. As the visiting earl of Dunraven put it, "'When the railway is made' is, in Montana, a sort of equivalent for our phrase, 'When my ship comes home.'"[1] But as the tracks stayed unlaid while the Northern Pacific shook off the Panic it had ignited, tourists continued to travel the last leg of their trip to the park by stagecoach—a long and costly ordeal over steep and rocky roads—and not until 1877 did annual visitation exceed five hundred souls.

That was also the year when Yellowstone became a way station in what historian Elliott West has called "the last Indian war." The conflict stemmed in part from the federal government's insistence on dealing with each tribe as if it were a kind of nation-state, led by a prime minister who dictated policy and stifled dissent. But the Nez Perce consisted of interrelated clans and bands that no single leader could unilaterally commit to a course of action, not even one mandated by treaty. Indeed, an 1855 treaty confining the Nez Perce to a reservation in Idaho had split them into two factions, treaty and nontreaty Indians.

Eight years later the superintendent of Indian affairs for Washington Territory faced the unenviable task of persuading the Nez Perce to give up a big chunk of their reservation. The government was bending to pressure from white intruders who flouted the 1855 treaty by prospecting and settling on reservation land; in the words of a local newspaperman, "The logic of events is stronger than parchment." The superintendent tried to tell the Nez Perce he had their interests at heart. It is not for our benefit, he said, presumably with a straight face, "so much as it is for yours, that we have proposed to make your reservation smaller."[2]

The nontreaty Indians were hardly likely to inhabit a shrunken version of the reservation they had already spurned. In 1874 Gen. Oliver Otis Howard was named commander of the army's Department of the Columbia and ordered to bring in the holdouts. Three years of fruitless negotiating later, Howard issued an ultimatum: come willingly, or we'll make you. Rather than submit or fight, several hundred nontreaty Indians packed up their belongings and fled east, trusting the Crows, a traditional ally, to take them in.

At peak strength, the fugitives could muster about 250 warriors, Howard four times that many. The Nez Perce were crack horsemen, marksmen, and exploiters of their surroundings. As an American officer complained, "They ride up behind little elevations, throw themselves from their ponies, fire, and are off like rockets. Lines of them creep and crawl and twist themselves through the grass until within range. . . . They tie grass upon their heads, so that it is hard to tell which bunch of grass does not conceal an Indian with a . . . globe-sighted rifle."[3] Also, they answered to a first-rate tactician, a man called Poker Joe. As for the plodding Howard, he got his nickname, General Day after Tomorrow, from another renegade leader, known as Joseph. In skirmish after skirmish, from western Idaho to Yellowstone National Park and beyond, the fugitives outwitted and outfought their pursuers.

Adhering to the myth that superstitious Indians would shy away from spooky Yellowstone, the army's western commander, Lt. Gen. Philip Sheridan, assured worried tourists they would be safe in the park. The Nez Perce exploded both the myth and Sheridan's warranty by entering the park, staying there two weeks, and crossing paths with tourists. Although harmless in themselves, the tourists couldn't be trusted not to reveal the Indians' whereabouts to the army. Still, the vacationers would probably have gone unharmed if young Nez Perce hotheads hadn't acted on their own, killing two men and wounding three others.

After exiting the park, the Nez Perce pulled off their most brilliant maneuver. Seemingly trapped in high country with Howard's force behind them and a patrol led by Col. Samuel Sturgis up ahead, the Nez Perce feinted toward a relatively easy way down (at the bottom of which Sturgis was waiting for them) and took a fiendishly difficult one instead. Then they rode their mounts back and forth, leaving a maze of hoofprints impossible for Howard to sort out. The fugitives got away only to be brought up short in Crow country. Manifest Destiny had become manifest even to the Crows, who saw no sense in unnecessarily angering their white overlords. Hence, no sanctuary for the Nez Perce, who were now down to their last option: pivoting north and making for Canada, where they could join Sitting Bull and a contingent of Sioux who had preceded them some weeks earlier.

Forty miles short of the border, the fugitives pulled up to debate the issue of timing. Poker Joe was for riding on, but another leader, Looking Glass, thought they needed a rest. Too risky, Poker Joe replied; let's push on to safety in Canada, where we can rest all we like. When Looking Glass held firm, Poker Joe gave in. But the latter's instincts were right; unbeknownst to the Nez Perce, another group of soldiers—infantry and cavalry under Col. Nelson Miles—was rushing toward them on a diagonal from the southeast.

Miles's men took the Indians by surprise on a plain below the Bear Paw Mountains of Montana. As always, the Nez Perce fought well, but the soldiers drove off enough of their horses to foreclose escape. (About two hundred fugitives split off, however, and made it safely to Canada.) Looking Glass and Poker Joe were killed, leaving Joseph to broker the surrender on October 5. While surrendering, Joseph probably said something like "From where the sun now stands, I will fight no more," but an aide to Howard touched up the declaration until it ran to 150 valedictory words, ending with "Hear me, my chiefs. I am tired; my heart is sick and sad. From where the sun now stands I will fight no more forever." Howard found this rendition so moving that he inserted it in his report on the campaign to the secretary of war.

The speech helped inspire a reassessment. The *Milwaukee Sentinel* praised the nontreaty Nez Perce for having "turned a new leaf in Indian warfare by scalping no dead, killing no wounded, treating captives with kindness, generally sparing women and children, [and] invariably respecting the flag of truce." The *Sentinel* must have missed one warrior's boast that he would gladly have scalped an African American cook in Yellowstone because "colored man's hair is good medicine for sore ears," except that the intended victim got away. The *New York Times* summed up the war as "in its origin and motive nothing short of a gigantic blunder and a crime"—on the government's part, that is.[4] All too true, though easy to say after the fact. Sympathy for the Nez Perce and esteem for Joseph were outbreaks of the early-onset nostalgia that allowed Sitting Bull to perform in Buffalo Bill Cody's shows and Geronimo of the Apaches to make money by signing autographs. Today the 1877 campaign is commemorated in the Nez Perce National Historical Park, a unit of the national park system established by Congress in 1965 and encompassing dozens of sites associated with the tribe in four northwestern states.

Yellowstone needed strong, honest managers in its early years; rarely did it get them. After Truman Everts begged off, Nathaniel Langford stepped in as the park's first superintendent. During his five-year tenure, he deigned to visit the place only three times. Granted, he was serving without pay (he made his living as a federal bank examiner), but he shouldn't have accepted a post to which he could not do justice. He assigned a lofty motive to his policy of turning down applications to run concessions in Yellowstone: preventing greedy businessman from "[securing] possession of the most important localities in the Park" and then charging exorbitant fees to visit them.[5] But there is another, less altruistic explanation: he may have been saving those concessions for his longtime supporter, the Northern Pacific, to take over once its spur line was up and running. Regardless, while Langford was busy inspecting banks, miscreants were poaching Yellowstone's wildlife at will and chipping off pieces of what the visiting Rudyard Kipling called "the fretted treasury of the formations."[6]

Capt. William Ludlow, commander of a military party sent in to investigate the vandalism, went into more detail on the damage suffered by one geyser: "The ornamental work about the crater and the pools had been broken and defaced in the most prominent places by visitors, and the pebbles were inscribed in pencil with the names of great numbers of the most unimportant persons. . . . The visitors prowled about with shovel and ax, chopping and hacking and prying up great pieces of the most ornamental work they could find; women and men alike joining in the barbarous pastime."[7] To put an end to these depredations, Ludlow recommended creating a mounted police force. Congress did not listen.

Among the fixes suggested by Langford in his single report to Congress was for Wyoming to hand over its sector of the park to Montana, which would have been a case of the tail wagging the dog: the sliver of Montana within the park amounted to a small fraction of its then 3,348 square miles. Congress ignored this suggestion too.

Langford was gone by the time it dawned on Congress that a self-supporting park was unlikely to come about any time soon. In 1878 Yellowstone got its first annual appropriation, in the amount of $10,000. That was a start, but Langford's replacement as superintendent, Philetus W. Norris, was hamstrung by a near-perfect inability to deter poachers and vandals. Norris turned to Wyoming for help. Extend your laws into the park, the superintendent urged, and my ability to protect it will be much enhanced. In 1884 the territorial legislature cooperated.

A not bad idea in theory became a scandal in practice. Local constables and magistrates saw how money could be made from the new arrangement. When a later park superintendent declared war on visitors who accidentally started forest fires by failing to extinguish their campfires all the way, Wyomingites became the world's strictest fire marshals. Campers who left behind so much as a single live coal could find themselves arrested and fined. This sort of thing might have gone on indefinitely if an officer of the law hadn't messed with a group that included Joseph Medill, editor of the *Chicago Tribune*. Arrests were made, and the ensuing trial reached a farcical climax when Medill called the judge "a damned old Dogberry" and His Honor sent for a dictionary. Medill wired his paper that "in a national park the national laws and regulations should be enforced by a national tribunal."[8] In 1886 Wyoming took back its laws.

Norris now made a strategic error, complaining to his superiors in Washington of the Northern Pacific's attempts to monopolize park concessions. Several of those same superiors were beholden to the railroad; they saw to it that Norris was canned and replaced by a weakling. Meanwhile, the Yellowstone Park Improvement Company, an avaricious group closely tied to the Northern Pacific, was gathering support for its position that entrusting park concessions to a single provider—namely, itself—would further the long-sought goal of a self-financing park. The Improvement Company's hold over Yellowstone was based on ten-year leases of 640-acre tracts containing some of the park's signature features. General Sheridan concluded an inspection tour of the park by reporting that he "regretted exceedingly to learn that the national park had been rented out to private parties."[9]

The railroad owed its ultimate defeat in part to the callously utilitarian policy it adopted toward wildlife. Both the general and his acquaintance George Bird Grinnell, the wealthy easterner who edited *Forest and Stream* magazine, had reviled poachers who slaughtered elk for their hides, which could bring as much as $6 apiece. Now the Improvement Company was proposing a hecatomb of elk, deer, bighorn sheep, and buffalo to feed its workers. Grinnell, an avid conservationist who flourished at a time when hunting for sport was touted as an antidote to what Teddy Roosevelt called the "effeminization" of American life, chose Yellowstone as the place to make a last stand. "There is one spot left," he editorialized, "a single rock about which the tide will break, and past which it will sweep, leaving it undefiled by the unsightly traces of civilization. Here in this Yellowstone Park the large game of the West may be preserved from extermination." Broadening his attack to include what he called "the Park Grab," Grinnell joined the long line of those who cited Niagara Falls as a disgrace: "How would our readers like to see [Yellowstone] become a second Niagara—a place where one goes only to be fleeced, where patent medicine advertisements stare one in the face, and the beauties of nature have all been defiled by the greed of man?"[10]

The Improvement Company's kingpin was Rufus Hatch, a Wall Street financier who in the summer of 1883 set out to woo potential investors by taking them on a deluxe western excursion. In Montana, the *Livingston Enterprise* poked fun at the spectacle put on by Hatch's guests: "One earl came with thirteen trunks; another had a retinue of servants; and there were enough monocles, tight pants, and effete manners to thoroughly amuse the natives." Not that the *Enterprise* objected to Hatch's underlying purpose. Calling Yellowstone his "leasehold property," the paper observed that "doubtless the members of the party, as well as outsiders, understand the fact that their presence here is the grandest advertising scheme ever inaugurated and carried to a successful conclusion."[11]

The Hatch crowd crossed paths with another group of easterners touring Yellowstone that summer. Its leaders were Sheridan and Missouri senator George Vest, who, as their honored guest, had snagged no less than the president of the United States, Chester A. Arthur. Vest, an ex-Confederate congressman, had so thoroughly reconciled himself to the South's defeat as to glory in the first national park, which he'd seen for himself on a fact-finding tour the previous fall. While dining in a saloon, he'd overheard men at a nearby table boast of outfoxing Uncle Sam in negotiating a deal for concessions at Yellowstone. Now Vest and Sheridan were double-teaming the president.

The tour had its intended effects. POTUS rested up, he fished, he cut an appealing figure as a man happy to dispense with luxuries and rough it for days on end. (When the two Yellowstone parties crossed paths, Hatch and his fellow dudes snickered behind the president's back at his slovenly appearance.) Best of all, Arthur sympathized with the antimonopolists' complaints.

On returning to Washington, however, Vest found that some of his colleagues were ready to end the national park experiment and throw Yellowstone back into the pool of claimable federal land. A senator from Kansas professed not to "understand what the necessity is for the Government entering into the show business in the Yellowstone National Park." In reply, Vest took aim at Gilded Age America. Our citizens are world famous, he complained, for wanting to acquire money "at the expense of all esthetic taste and of all love of nature and its great mysteries and wonders. . . . [Yellowstone] answers a great purpose in our national life. There should be [available] to a nation that will have a hundred million or a hundred and fifty million people a park like this as a great breathing place for the national lungs."[12]

A provision added by Vest to the Sundry Civil Appropriation Act for fiscal year 1884 voided all existing contracts pertaining to Yellowstone, whittled the Improvement Company's leaseholds down to ten acres apiece, and supplied authority long sought by Sheridan: the secretary of the interior could call on the secretary of war for help in running the park. Grinnell headlined his editorial on the subject "Mr. Vest's Victory."

Hatch had wildly overspent on his Yellowstone boondoggle, and his guests must have seen clearly through their monocles: few of them invested in the Yellowstone Park Improvement Company. Hatch filed for bankruptcy, and in 1885 the company was sold outright to—surprise, surprise— officials of the Northern Pacific Railroad.

Speaking of which, a third group of junketeers had paid Yellowstone a visit that summer of 1883. Their host was Henry Villard, the Northern Pacific's president, who hoped to entice his guests into investing in the railroad or writing about it in such glowing terms that others would do so. In the party was German journalist Nicolaus Mohr, who did not cooperate. "The name 'National Park' could lead one to believe that the landscape surrounding the volcanic wonders has been artificially constructed to give it the look of a park," Mohr wrote in his travelogue, *Excursion through America*. "Nothing could be further from the truth. Except for a very few primitive paths, a few dikes through the gulleys, and some timber trestle bridges, not a thing has been touched. . . . [Y]ou won't believe how much dust and dirt we have swallowed, or how many bumps and bangs we have endured in the buggies, or what dubious and dangerous paths we have crossed in order to reach the Upper Geyser Basin and return."[13]

To us, Mohr's disdain seems based on a gross misconception, but at the time, who was to say? In the absence of Olmsted's Yosemite report or any other agreed-on principles for managing a national park, the prediction made about Yosemite by an irate California congressman during the Hutchings-and-Lamont controversy was in danger of coming true: if the Northern Pacific had its way, Yellowstone would become "a fancy pleasure ground."

Happy to lend a hand was Robert Emmett Carpenter, a venal superintendent who took part in a scheme to have Congress excise land from the northeast portion of the park for the benefit of a railroad (though not the Northern Pacific). As soon as a bill to that effect became law in Washington, Carpenter was supposed to wire the news to a confederate in Montana who would share it with selected cronies over a newfangled apparatus called the telephone. The clued-in few would then file claims to desirable parcels of ex-parkland. The overeager Carpenter sent his telegram before the fact, which turned out to be no fact at all. The Senate did not pass the bill, the would-be claimants were stymied, and Carpenter was fired.

The secretary of the interior, the splendiferously named Lucius Quintus Cincinnatus Lamar II, used this fiasco as an excuse to invoke the military intervention clause of the 1884 Sundry Civil Appropriation Act. Starting in 1886 and lasting until 1918, Yellowstone National Park was a responsibility of the U.S. Army. How sorely no-nonsense governance of the park was needed can be gauged from the welcome awaiting its first soldier superintendent, Capt. Moses Harris, when he rode in at the head of a fifty-man detail in the summer of 1886: multiple fires set by spiteful poachers. The arson stopped almost immediately, but it took more time to curtail the poaching.

In 1890 Yosemite, too, came under military control. Though little poaching was going on there, the park had a different animal-related problem: the "hoofed locusts" railed against by Muir. Yosemite's and Yellowstone's acting superintendents, as the military commanders were called, shared a handicap: a lack of authority to punish offenders. The only available sanction, expulsion, was a joke—nothing stopped an ejected miscreant from reentering the park—until officials at both parks hit upon the same makeshift solution. Instead of ushering a poacher or shepherd over the nearest boundary line, they would frog-march him across the park and out the other side, leaving him footsore and apt to think twice before misbehaving again. This penalty worked a special hardship on the Yosemite herders, whose flocks were apt to disperse in their absence, but its legality was questionable.

The 1887 holdup of a stagecoach carrying passengers to Yellowstone led to a reformation. Among the victims was John F. Lacey, soon to be elected a congressman from Iowa. Seven years later, after another precipitating incident—the killing of five buffalo inside the park—Lacey introduced a bill "to protect the birds and animals in Yellowstone National Park, and to punish crimes in said park, and for other purposes." With a push from Vest in the Senate, the bill became law on May 7, 1894. Six years later, Lacey was instrumental in the enactment of another landmark law: the eponymous Lacey Act, which prohibits trafficking in illegally taken birds and animals.

Still hobbling Yellowstone was a condition that army administration could not solve: even after the Northern Pacific's spur line was in place, merely getting there took so much time and cost so much money that the park continued to be, if not a fancy pleasure ground, at least what Aubrey Haines describes as "a semi-exclusive haunt of middle-and upper-class vacationers. It was . . . operated in a manner to discourage 'sage-brushers' (visitors who came in their own rigs and camped by the wayside) and 'independents' (outsiders who conducted visitors through the Park in a similar manner), and the success of the methods used to exclude such unremunerative use (from the concessioner's viewpoint) is evident from available records."[14]

The equation changed with the advent of the automobile—or, rather, with Henry Ford's determination to make the contraption cheaper and more affordable. Fittingly, the first car allowed into Yellowstone, on July 31, 1915, was a Model T Ford, the assembly-line vehicle priced low enough for middle-class Americans to buy. Cars had been denied entry until then, and the policy change ended the park's bias toward the carriage trade. In justifying the decision, the soon-to-be first overseer of the National Park Service, Stephen Mather, might have been channeling Olmsted: "We've got to do what we can to make sure that nobody stays away because he can't afford it."[15]

For all its helpfulness, military rule was less than ideal. A soldier might relish his stint in Yellowstone, Yosemite, or one of the other parks established in the late nineteenth and early twentieth centuries but still regard it as a pothole in his career path. Moreover, a 1907 study suggested that civilian guardians would cost about a third as much as the military kind. Five years later President William Howard Taft recommended that Congress establish a Bureau of National Parks. With the creation of the National Park Service in 1916, the army pulled out of every park except Yellowstone. (The soldiers at Yosemite and Sequoia National Parks had already handed the parks over to civilian rule in 1914.) Under pressure from the Montana legislature, which looked upon a military installation as a cash cow for neighboring towns, Congress agreed to keep the soldiers on duty in Yellowstone a while longer. The park was finally transferred to the National Park Service on October 31, 1918.

The new agency carried forward a number of policies introduced by its military predecessors, including dedicated campgrounds (bringing to an end park visitors' habit of tenting wherever they pleased), educational talks and walks for visitors, and uniformed rangers. Many soldiers who had fallen in love with the ranger's life took discharges from the army and joined the Park Service, keeping their expertise in the parks.

In both Yellowstone and Yosemite, the soldiers had extended the protection of resources to resident wildlife. In Yellowstone, that policy begat a campaign to save the American bison from extinction—a fate predicted for it as early as 1846 by a perceptive Cheyenne named Yellow Wolf. Once numbering an estimated 60 million head, the buffalo were down to a wild population of 541 by 1886, many of them hanging on in Yellowstone itself. In 1893 the acting superintendent, Capt. George S. Anderson, called for introducing domesticated buffalo into the park to keep the wild herd from inbreeding itself out of existence. By the time this suggestion was acted on, Yellowstone was down to its last 22 head, but eventually the project succeeded. "By 1916," writes historian H. Duane Hampton, "the [Yellowstone] herd had increased to 273 animals and it had become possible to transfer some buffalo to other game refuges and municipal parks throughout the country. The American bison had been saved from total extinction and the military commanders of Yellowstone National Park had played an important role in its preservation."[16]

Let the military presence in national parks be summed up by a pair of comments from Muir. The first paints a before-and-after picture: "In pleasing contrast to the noisy, ever-changing management or mismanagement, of blustering, blundering, plundering, money-making vote-sellers who receive their places from boss politicians as purchased goods, the soldiers do their duty so quietly that the traveler is scarcely aware of their presence." The second quotation represents the high priest of the Sierra at his sloganeering best: "Blessing on Uncle Sam's soldiers. They have done the job well, and every pine tree is waving its arms for joy."[17]

We've already looked at some of the legal complexities arising from the American federal-state-territorial system of government as applied to parks. There was—and still is—one more. The 1872 act had described Yellowstone as located in the territories of Montana and Wyoming, but later, more careful surveys showed that the park took in a strip of Idaho too. This tristate existence has given rise to an anomaly, as explained in "The Perfect Crime," a 2005 scholarly article by the law professor Brian C. Kalt.

In 1894, when Congress created a federal court for the District of Wyoming, it put the entire park in that district, the Montana portion and the Idaho strip included. "This makes the District of Wyoming the only district court that includes land in multiple states," Kalt writes. Other national parks sit astride more than one state, among them Great Smoky Mountains in Tennessee and North Carolina and Death Valley in California and Nevada, but none of these parks "are shoehorned into a single federal district, and no undue travesties have resulted." Congress's 1894 action was "constitutionally fateful," as Kalt puts it, because Article III, Section 2, of the U.S. Constitution provides that "the Trial of all Crimes, except in Cases of Impeachment; shall be by Jury; and such Trial shall be held in the State where the said Crimes shall have been committed."[18]

Kalt then poses a gnarly hypothetical:

Say that you are in the Idaho portion of Yellowstone, and you decide to spice up your vacation by going on a crime spree. You make some moonshine, you poach some wildlife, you strangle some people and steal their picnic baskets. You are arrested, arraigned in the park, and bound over for trial in Cheyenne, Wyoming, before a jury drawn from the Cheyenne area. But Article III, Section 2, plainly requires that the trial be held in Idaho, the state in which the crime was committed.[19]

Suppose further that you—the notorious Picnic Basket Strangler—get your case transferred to Idaho. Good move, for the Sixth Amendment to the Constitution guarantees "the right to a speedy and public trial, by an impartial jury of the State and district wherein the crime shall have

A Shaky Start

been committed," and unless something has changed in recent years, the Idaho portion of Yellowstone National Park is unpopulated. That makes it impossible to empanel a jury from the state and district in which the crime was committed. Having gone on your spree in no-man's-land—"the zone of death," in Kalt's words—you are between a rock and a soft place, and your case must be dismissed.[20]

Kalt suggests a simple cure: amend the 1894 law establishing the Wyoming district court so that every crime committed in Yellowstone is allotted to whichever of the three states (and federal judicial districts) it occurred in. Congress has yet to act, but so far this chance to commit the perfect crime has remained only theoretical. Before going on a Yellowstone rampage, no malefactor has thought to square a park map with his or her location while also juggling copies of the U.S. Constitution and the U.S. Code.

Cleaning Men 14

On returning to the East from California in 1865, Olmsted had thrown himself into what might be called nostalgic work. With Vaux, he went back to advising the commissioners of Central Park and supervised the making of Prospect Park in Brooklyn, where he introduced a modification of his parkway idea. On his own, Olmsted renewed his interest in the American South by joining the executive committee of the Southern Famine Relief Commission. Again with Vaux, he incorporated parkways into the design of a network of parks for Buffalo, New York.

While visiting that city in August 1869, Olmsted returned to an old haunt: Niagara Falls. Accompanying him were William Dorsheimer, a Buffalo lawyer then serving as U.S. district attorney for northern New York, and thirty-year-old Henry Hobson Richardson, the architect of Dorsheimer's new house. Richardson's revival of elements from twelfth-century architecture was coalescing into an influential style called Richardson Romanesque. He and Olmsted hit it off and eventually collaborated on several projects, notably the new state capital at Albany. Looking back on the 1869 visit, Olmsted noted that his involvement with Yosemite had left him wondering whether something similar couldn't be done for Niagara Falls. While taking a walk on Goat Island that August, he, Dorsheimer, and Richardson set in motion a save-Niagara campaign that would drag on for two decades.

Goat Island was a fitting birthplace for the effort. The thirty-acre island's location between the American mainland and Canada's Horseshoe Falls underscored a basic truth: neither nation could restore Niagara satisfactorily on its own. Although the island—long owned by a family named Porter—was in a near-pristine state, there was no telling how long it would stay that way. Writing in the *Nation*, Henry James passed along a rumor that the Porters were being courted by a developer eager to buy them out. James hoped that some level of government would step in and acquire the property first. "It is the opinion of a sentimental tourist," he added, "that no price would be too great to pay."[1]

The island's ample greenery harmonized with Olmsted's theme that visitors should not allow their enthusiasm for a great natural spectacle to blind them to its less flashy environs. A few years later he and Richardson came back for a more leisurely tour. "We were out several hours without coming in sight of the Falls," Olmsted recalled, "—did not see them fairly, indeed, till the next day. When we did, [Richardson] had caught the idea of throwing curiosity aside and avoiding amazement, and was willing to sit for hours in one place contemplatively enjoying the beauty."[2] Vaux seconded Olmsted's opinion of Goat Island, declaring it "a beautiful example of natural landscape design."[3] Scientists who studied the island concluded it was home to a greater number of botanical species than anywhere else of its size in the eastern United States or, for that matter, in all of Europe.

The Canadians took the plunge first, appointing a Royal Commission to study the falls. In 1873 the commission reported back that the hounding of visitors by "cabmen, fancy and variety store keepers, guides, sight showers, picture takers, oil clothes furnishers, conductors under what is alleged to be the sheet of water, hotel keepers and runners, all working to plunder . . . has been so great as to elicit comments of travelers and the criticisms of the public press throughout the civilized world."[4] The commission urged the Canadian government to intervene but met with resistance from the premier of Ontario, Oliver Mowat.

A renowned American painter now took up the cause: Frederic Church, who a generation earlier had captured the falls in all their dizzying grandeur. In the summer of 1878 Church broached the idea of a joint Canadian-American cleanup with Frederick Hamilton-Temple-Blackwood, Lord Dufferin, who was on his way out as governor general of Canada to become Britain's ambassador to Russia. Dufferin was receptive—and such a publicity hound that before releasing copies of his speeches to the press, he would pencil in how the audience had reacted ("Laughter," "Applause"). After sharing the international park idea with New York governor Lucius Robinson, his lordship gave it its first public tryout in a speech to the Toronto Society of Artists.

The laugh-and-clap tally for that occasion has not survived, but the speech bowled over a reporter for the *New York Herald*: "Lord Dufferin's untiring efforts to cultivate pleasant relations between Canada and the United States were beautifully illustrated in his speech yesterday. . . . He mentioned his meeting . . . with the governor of New York when he had proposed to establish an international park around the Falls of Niagara [which would] create a pleasant bond of sympathy between American and Canadian visitors." Governor Robinson did his part, urging the state legislature to recognize the falls as "the property of the whole world," a status that made it "incumbent on both governments to protect . . . travelers from improper annoyance on either side."[5]

But Robinson was a lame duck, too, as was his lieutenant governor, former district attorney Dorsheimer. Doubtful that New Yorkers were ready to commit to an international park, Dorsheimer pushed through a compromise bill: the State Survey (a geographic one, responsible for mapping) should look into the matter. Olmsted had drafted that bill, and he took part in the investigation, which was headed by the survey's director, James T. Gardner—the same chap Olmsted had hired to survey Yosemite with Clarence King a quarter century earlier and who had more recently clashed with the "central power" better known as Ferdinand Hayden.

Working together amicably, in March 1880 Gardner and Olmsted delivered a tripartite package. The *Special Report of the New York State Survey on the Preservation of the Scenery of Niagara Falls* consisted of a main body written by Gardner, "Notes" added by Olmsted, and a petition addressed jointly to the governor of New York and the governor general of Canada.

In his section, Gardner warned that the outcome feared by Henry James might be imminent: the Porters were entertaining offers for Goat Island. "I made careful inquiry concerning the nature of the proposals for purchase," Gardner wrote. "By some it has been proposed to cut the woods off the Island and make a race-course of it; others think it a favorable site for a great summer hotel; others wish to make a rifle range upon it, while another and more practical party suggests cutting a canal down the center of the Island and building a row of factories along its front between the American and Canadian Falls."[6] Gardner was willing to concede that "the Falls themselves man cannot touch; but he is fast destroying their beautiful frame of foliage, and throwing around them an artificial setting of manufactories and bazaars that arouses in the intelligent visitor deep feelings of regret and even of resentment."[7] Gardner spoke too soon: man soon proved that he *could* touch "the Falls themselves" to produce hydropower, and in 1969 the U.S. Army Corps of Engineers shut the water off for five months to see about removing rubble that was marring views of the American falls; in the end, the engineers abandoned the effort.

In his supplementary "Notes," Olmsted credited Church with having first alerted him to "the rapidly approaching ruin of [the area's] characteristic scenery." Olmsted drew a contrast between visitors like himself, who were inclined to hang around for several days, returning to the falls again and again, taking it in at their own pace, and more docile tourists who were "so much more constrained to be guided and instructed, to be led and stopped, to be 'put through,' and so little left to natural and healthy individual intuitions."[8] He was polishing a plank from his Yosemite report: the value of letting people see and experience nature on their own terms if they were so disposed, rather than have it sliced and packaged for them. A century before the term "bucket list" was coined, Olmsted was advising against the reduction of tourism to a string of hits, to be seen, photographed, and collected like charms on a bracelet. He would have scorned some of the Yellowstone guidebooks published in later years. One laid out the best route for visiting "the wonders of the Park . . . in sequence . . . until the crowning glory of the entire region is reached in the Grand Canon."[9] And a timetable for geyser eruptions became a standard feature of any Yellowstone guidebook. A phrase Olmsted coined when the United States and Canada got down to planning their respective Niagara parks captured the end result he hoped to avert: a "Coney Island Big Elephant affair."[10]

Last came the petition. Titled "Memorial Addressed to the Governor of New York, and the Governor-General of Canada," it acknowledged how hard it was to spoil the sublimity of mountains (this was before the invention of strip mining). Waterfalls, however, were another matter, as current conditions at Niagara made clear. "The river's banks are denuded

Cleaning Men

[of] the noble forest by which they were originally covered, are degraded by incongruous and unworthy structures, made, for advertising purposes, willfully conspicuous and obtrusive, and the visitor's attention is diverted from the [natural] scenes . . . by demands for tolls and fees, and the offer of services most of which he would prefer to avoid." Unless remedial steps are taken, the petition warned, "the loss to the world will be great and irreparable."[11]

The petition ended on a global note, placing objects of great natural beauty "among the most valuable gifts which Providence has bestowed upon our race. The contemplation of them elevates and informs the human understanding. They are instruments of education. They conduce to the order of society. They address sentiments which are universal. They draw together men of all races, and thus contribute to the union and peace of nations." The recommended solution was to bring the falls under the "joint guardianship" of the governments of New York State and Canada.[12]

Like Olmsted's application to be superintendent of Central Park, the petition came with a roster of prestigious endorsers. Washington Irving was long gone, but Olmsted and his friend the art critic Charles Eliot Norton rounded up Francis Parkman, Ralph Waldo Emerson, Henry Wadsworth Longfellow, John Greenleaf Whittier, Oliver Wendell Holmes, Thomas Carlyle, Charles Darwin, John Ruskin, and more. Olmsted fretted over the correct order and style for the signers like a hostess filling out the seating chart for a state dinner. "Can I resolve [the problem] by the Alphabet?" he wondered. "If so shall I jump as the alphabet requires from Oxford to Buffalo, Buffalo to Caribou & Caribou to Washington? Finally, shall I give each man his proper tail? Shall I write 'Lord Houghton'?" In a footnote to the volume of Olmsted's papers in which that passage appears, the editors helpfully supplied Houghton with his rightful head and tail: "Richard Monckton Milnes, First Baron Houghton."[13]

The petition won over Premier Mowat, although he wanted the Canadian federal government to pay all the Canadian costs. When the maritime provinces balked at being taxed for a project that to their way of thinking would benefit Ontario almost exclusively, Prime Minister Sir John A. Macdonald proposed a cost share by the federal government and Ontario. Mowat wouldn't have it. On the other side of the border, the governorship of New York was in the hands of a philistine, Alonzo Cornell (eldest son of Ezra, the founder of Cornell University). In rejecting the petition, Governor Cornell prated, "I don't see that it will make any difference—the water will run over the falls all the same."[14]

Olmsted and Dorsheimer now marshaled their publishing experience—the former with *Putnam's Monthly* and the *Nation*, the latter with the *Atlantic Monthly*, for which he had written articles—to wage a precursor to the modern public-relations campaign. They got good help from Henry Norman, a recent Harvard graduate who was clever with a pen, and the journalist Jonathan Baxter Harrison. To make the case for saving the falls, Norman employed sarcasm. Who could blame New Yorkers for objecting to even a minuscule tax increase "for the sake of a few persons whose nerves are so delicate that the sight of a tremendous body of water rushing over a precipice is spoilt for them by a pulp-mill standing on the bank"?[15]

In 1882 Olmsted and Norton were among the founders of the Niagara Falls Association, which called attention to the Niagara problem, drumming away until, in Olmsted's words, there was "a reverberation filling the air."[16] Harrison, who served as the association's secretary, wrote save-Niagara magazine articles, some of which were republished as pamphlets, and lectured widely on the topic. The association shelved the idea of a binational reservation and concentrated on getting the American bank cleaned up, but even with its narrower focus, the cause was slow to make headway. Norton prepared for defeat with New England rectitude, vowing to keep fighting, "not so much to save the Falls, as to save our own souls. Were we to see the Falls destroyed without making an effort to save them—the sin would be ours."[17]

Norton's gloom lifted after the 1882 New York State election. The new governor, former Buffalo mayor Grover Cleveland, was a friend of Dorsheimer's. After dining with those two portly politicians, Richardson—no scarecrow himself ("Mein Gott, how he looks like his own buildings," a German admirer once exclaimed)—had good news to report: Cleveland was "strongly in favor of Niagara."[18] In 1883 the association drafted, the legislature passed, and Governor Cleveland signed into law a bill authorizing "the selection, location and appropriation of certain lands in the village of Niagara Falls for a State reservation and to preserve the scenery

Cleaning Men

of Niagara Falls."[19] One of the five commissioners appointed to carry out the law was Dorsheimer. Another was Andrew Green, the czar of Central Park, whose reentry into his life rattled Olmsted so hard that he almost jumped ship. When the commissioners asked him and Vaux to advise them informally, however, Olmsted gritted his teeth and agreed to serve.

Sure enough, Green made trouble, though in an un-Greenish way. As the state legislature considered a bill to authorize a bond issue for purchasing the land described in the 1883 law, Vaux and Green proposed throwing in the gorge downstream of the falls, too, thereby greatly increasing the total cost. You might be morally right, Dorsheimer told them, but you are politically wrong. Harrison agreed and said so in a letter published in the *New York Sun*: "This enormous enlargement of the proposed reservation, and of its cost, . . . would, I think, insure the defeat of the original enterprise."[20] In a spat that Olmsted called "ugly to the last," he and Dorsheimer prevailed: only land in the falls' immediate vicinity was targeted for acquisition. The Niagara Falls Association rallied its members and others friendly to the cause with a mass mailing; Harrison kept lecturing; Cleveland, now president of the United States, sent a message urging action. The legislature passed the bill, and on April 30, 1885, Gov. David B. Hill signed it into law. On July 15 the state held an opening ceremony. Thirty thousand people from both sides of the border showed up to enjoy the Niagara Reservation free of charge and unvexed by hawkers and touts. Its first superintendent, Thomas Vincent Welch, saw to it that nearly all the structures were gone from the reservation by 1887.

Olmsted's two closest allies in the campaign agreed on the magnitude of his contribution. "I congratulate you, prime mover," Norton wrote after the funding bill became law. "I hail you as the Saviour of Niagara!"[21] A decade later Harrison elaborated on that rave: "Success was obtained by the cooperation of multitudes; but the indispensable factor was Mr. Frederick Law Olmsted's thought. He was the real source, as he was the true director, of the movement, and but for him, there would be no State Reservation at Niagara today."[22]

Over in Canada, however, the authorities were inclined to do no more than consolidate ownership of the riverbanks. Premier Mowat had been approached by syndicates whose sweeping claims about their desire to clean up "the prevailing disfigurements and extortions which have brought the beautiful neighborhood into worldwide disrepute" didn't quite obscure their ulterior motive: to hog the tourist trade. These were boom times in Canada, which, like the United States, was crawling with would-be robber barons, especially among the ranks of railroad men. According to an insider paraphrased by the Canadian journalist Pierre Berton, one day "when the Speaker's bill rang for a division in the Ontario legislature, the majority of members were to be found in the apartments of an influential railroad contractor, where the champagne flowed like sarsaparilla."[23]

Confronted with rival proposals and public opposition to awarding another monopoly to an outfit that already had one (a railroad route), Mowat prevailed on the legislature to establish—what else?—a commission to study the issues. To chair it, Mowat chose Casimir Stanislaus Gzowski, a Polish émigré and wealthy former railroad man with glittering credentials (among other things, he was an honorary aide-de-camp to Queen Victoria). Mowat seems to have misjudged his man—Gzowski was no patsy for vested interests. The best outcome for the Canadian side of the falls, he and his fellow commissioners agreed, would be public ownership as a park "laid out and planted, not as a showy garden or fancy grounds, but as nearly as possible as they would be in their natural condition."[24] It was a recommendation after Olmsted's own heart—indeed, he had personally lobbied Canadian officials to create a sister park to New York's and later advised Gzowski on the Canadian-side landscaping.

When Mowat dithered, the commissioners urged action, insisting that with visitation increasing all the time, government ownership was "the only policy worthy of being adopted."[25] Mowat finally gave in, supporting the bill that became the Queen Victoria Niagara Falls Park Act of 1887. The preferred solution of joint guardianship has never materialized, but the two nations have long consulted each other on the managing of the Niagara Reservation and Queen Victoria Park.

Olmsted and Vaux had dissolved their partnership in 1872, but the Niagara Reservation coaxed them into a reprise. The new state possession had been called a "reservation" rather than a "park" because to most people the latter term still implied extensive landscaping and improving. Unadorned as it

Cleaning Men

might be, however, the Niagara Reservation needed careful planning, if only for the laying out of roads and trails. To carry out the assignment, Commissioner Green recommended Vaux. Commissioner Dorsheimer suggested Vaux *and* Olmsted, and over Green's dissent, Dorsheimer prevailed.

The dual appointment drew plaudits from the *New York Times*: "The commissioners seem to think that the restoration of the river banks and the islands will never be complete till these have felt the magic touch of those famous landscape architects, Messrs. Olmsted and Vaux."[26] Olmsted welcomed the task, which for him was the fulfillment of a long-standing desire to do right by an attraction he'd admired since boyhood. His ardor surfaced in a letter to a friend: "I can no more write what is on my mind about [Niagara Falls] than a crow can sing."[27]

Somehow, though, the *General Plan for the Improvement of the Niagara Reservation* (1887) got written. In it Olmsted and Vaux took care to "make a suitable provision of roads and walks, of platforms and seats, at the more important points of view, and of other accommodations, such as experience has shown to be necessary to decency and good order when large numbers of people come together."[28] That being said, the coauthors reaffirmed the Olmstedian principle that "nothing of an artificial character should be allowed a place on the property, no matter how valuable it might be under other circumstances and no matter of how little cost it may be had, the presence of which can be avoided consistently with the provision of necessary conditions for making the enjoyment of natural scenery available."[29] To show they meant business, Olmsted and Vaux cited the Statue of Liberty, which had been dedicated with great fanfare in New York Harbor while they were drafting their plan. If France had conditioned the gift of that grand landmark on its being "set up on Goat Island," Olmsted and Vaux declared, "the precept to which our argument has tended would [require] a declension of the gift as surely as it would the refusal of an offer to stock the Island with poison ivy or wolves or bears."[30]

In another throwback to Olmsted's Yosemite report, he and Vaux urged visitors to look beyond the reservation's tumultuous centerpieces and take in an "incomparable greater beauty of a kind in which nearness to the eye of illumined spray and mist and fleeting waters, and of the intricate disposition of leaves, with infinitely varied play of light and shadow, refractions and reflections, and much else that is undefinable in conditions of water, air, and foliage, are important parts."[31] As always, Olmsted was carrying the torch for nature's subtler, gentler effects.

Perhaps owing to Green's presence on the reservation's commission (he eventually served as its president), Olmsted had nothing more to do with the falls after he and Vaux submitted their report. Yet by all accounts, Green was a worthy Niagara czar who, in a speech delivered in 1903, sounded almost Olmstedian: "The lesson of which Niagara Falls may be said to have been a pioneer teacher, is the State's right of eminent domain over objects of great scientific interest and natural beauty—the inherent right of the people to free enjoyment of the wonders of nature."[32] Later that year the eighty-three-year-old Green was returning to his house in Manhattan for lunch when a man stepped out of hiding and shot him dead. It was said to be a case of mistaken identity.

Three years previously William Dean Howells had exulted in the falls' rescue: "I will not even try to recall the stupid and squalid contrivances which defaced [the scenery] at every point, and extorted a coin from the insulted traveller at every turn. They are all gone now, and in the keeping of the State the whole redeemed and disenthralled vicinity of Niagara is an object lesson in what public ownership, whenever it comes, does for beauty."[33] If Howells made that outcome seem almost predestined, one of the reservation's early commissioners, Charles Mason Dow, set the record straight: "Indeed, when we consider the business and manufacturing possibilities which Niagara offered, . . . we marvel, not that the achievement of a free Niagara took so long, but that it did not take longer."[34]

Cleaning Men

Going Out with Two Bangs   15

Among the projects Olmsted took on late in his professional life, two stand out from his previous work as sharply as Yosemite had from Central Park: the landscaping of the 1893 World's Columbian Exposition in Chicago and the founding of American commercial forestry at the Biltmore Estate in Asheville. Also during those years, second-guessers interfered with his designs; the meddlers were typically either civic boosters who regarded urban parks as prime sites for outdoor sports and decorative structures or average Americans ill at ease with open space, which seemed to get on their nerves until it was well seasoned with man-made objects. Olmsted continued to generate new designs and fight rearguard actions on behalf of old ones until he succumbed to a slow, inexorable descent into senility.

Departures from the Greensward Plan for Central Park had been proposed as early as the 1860s, which ended with New York City reduced to a fiefdom of the Tweed Ring. The park commissioners were asked to rule on a zoo (yes), an opera house (no), the Metropolitan Museum of Art (yes), statues (yes, yes, yes, yes, yes . . .). Most disturbing to Olmsted, his carefully calibrated plantings came under siege—bushes were thinned out and trees stripped of their lower branches—to improve the circulation of air. "How will it be," he wondered aloud, "when a 'free circulation of air and light' beneath every bush and brooding conifer has been secured; when the way of the lawn-mower has at all points been made plain, and the face of nature shall everywhere have become as natty as a new silk hat?"[1] Although Andrew Green was no longer the park's comptroller, he had stayed on the board of commissioners, trying to stave off harm but being regularly outvoted by his colleagues. Olmsted didn't change his opinion of the man, however.

After the Tweed Ring was dethroned (temporarily) in 1871, Frederic Church joined the park commission, and Olmsted and Vaux returned as landscape architects. "The appointment of Church," a relieved Olmsted wrote to Charley Brace, "signifies . . . that offices (for the present) are not for sale . . . but are to [be filled by] the best men." "For the present" was the operative term. As administrations came and went at the city and state levels, park policies vacillated accordingly. Things got so bad that, complaining to a journalist, Olmsted called into question the very idea of a park like Central. Not only was the park "going to the devil" but Olmsted wondered if it hadn't been "a mistake . . . doomed to failure because of the general ignorance of the conditions of success and the impossibility of getting proper care taken of it."[2]

In 1876, with the Ring back in power, the commissioners ended Olmsted's ties with the park and held firm against a campaign to have the action overturned. Six years later Olmsted aired his grievances in a long, self-published pamphlet called *The Spoils of the Park: With a Few Leaves from the Deep-Laden Note-Books of "A Wholly Unpractical Man."* In the twenty-second of his indictment's twenty-three counts, Olmsted recounted one of the many attempts to burden the park with a speedway for carriages. While meeting with a speedway proponent and the president of the Central Park board in the latter's office, Olmsted raised "the landscape considerations. At the first mention of the word the gentleman exclaimed, . . . 'Oh, damn the landscape!' then, rising, he addressed the president to this effect: 'We came here, sir, as practical men, to discuss with your Board a simple, practical, common-sense question. We don't know anything about your landscape, and we don't know what landscape has to do with the matter before us.'" In the same pamphlet, Olmsted deplored the many hours wasted on dealing with job seekers and the politicians sponsoring them: "I do not remember ever to have seen the office of the Board without a poster, reading, 'No laborers wanted;' and I do not believe that there has in twenty years been a time when nine-tenths of the intellectual force and nervous energy of the Board has not been given to recruiting duty."[3]

In 1892 a recurring fear of Olmsted's nearly came to pass. The state legislature passed, and the governor signed into law, a bill authorizing construction of a road for fast carriage driving on the park's west side. The press cried foul, and a protest meeting was held at the Cooper Union, where a surrogate read an antiracetrack statement by Olmsted to a packed house. Taken aback by the uproar, the park commissioners convened a public hearing, at which, Laura Wood Roper relates, "the only advocates of the speedway were a scant dozen trotting-horse owners, with their lawyer."[4] Bowing to the people's will, the board asked the legislature to rescind the law, which it did.

Constant vigilance and frequent frustration are the lot of anyone working to save something beautiful or wild or historically significant, whether it be a vintage railroad station, a free-flowing river, an endangered species of wildlife, or an expanse of open land. No triumph is ever final, no positive outcome ever safe from being undone. What made Olmsted's plight so poignant was that the vulnerable items were his own works of art.

The late Sam Bowles had given Olmsted a piece of good advice: instead of hanging around in New York to watch your masterpiece be unraveled before your eyes, why don't you go live somewhere else? Olmsted complied in stages, first summering with his family in Cambridge, Massachusetts, then in 1881 moving the household and the firm to another Boston suburb, Brookline. "I enjoy this suburban country beyond expression," he told Brace, "and the older I grow [the more] I find my capacity for enjoyment increasing."[5]

One source of that increase was his children. His stepson, John Charles Olmsted (the son of Fred's late brother), graduated from Yale's Sheffield Scientific School and joined the firm in 1875. Five years earlier Fred and Mary had had a son of their own, Henry Perkins Olmsted. When Henry was seven, his name was changed to Frederick Law Olmsted Jr. The grown-up Rick, as he was called, graduated magna cum laude from Harvard, but not before working on some of the firm's biggest projects, including the Biltmore Estate and the Chicago World's Fair. Rick, more than John, became his father's standard-bearer; among other accomplishments, Rick helped draft the bill that created the National Park Service in 1916.

In the 1880s and early 1890s F. L. Olmsted and Co. was awash in projects on a grand scale. In addition to Biltmore and Chicago, there were the Stanford University campus, Boston's Emerald Necklace of parks (Olmsted preferred to call it simply "the parkway"), the grounds of the U.S. Capitol, and dozens more.

Olmsted also brought his expertise to bear on the Adirondacks. In 1864 the *New York Times* had called for building a railroad into the region so that it might become "a Central Park for the world."[6] With Charles Eliot Norton, Olmsted worked to establish something new and different there: a state scenic reservation. In 1885 New York placed 681,000 Adirondack acres in the slightly different category of "state forest preserve," in which private landowners could keep title to and continue to live on their property. Seven years later the state folded the preserve into a 2.8-million-acre park, and in 1894 a constitutional amendment prohibited timber cutting on state lands inside the park. The Adirondack innovation of mixed public and private ownership set a pattern that now obtains in many national parks throughout the world.

In the last two decades of the century Olmsted lost some of his closest friends and colleagues. Henry Bellows died in 1882, at the age of sixty-seven, followed in 1887 by Henry Hobson Richardson. Only forty-seven, Richardson had been suffering from Bright's, a disease of the kidneys; Olmsted had paid him a last visit two weeks before the end.

In January 1890 Olmsted received a copy of Brace's new book with a puzzling note attached. "I do not see why you should say it is probably your last [book]," Olmsted wrote back. Later that year, at age sixty-four, Brace died of an illness he'd kept to himself. "His death was a shock to me," Olmsted wrote to a mutual friend, "and the shock has been growing since."[7] In 1895 Calvert Vaux accidentally drowned while visiting his son Downing in Brooklyn.

Olmsted himself was working as hard as ever, thereby deepening the central irony of his career. By incessantly taking on more jobs than he could comfortably manage, he denied himself what his talents were making possible for so many others: restfully aimless exercise and not-for-profit enjoyment of the natural world. It was as if by accepting such a plethora of assignments, Olmsted hoped to better the odds that at least some of them would escape being "arrested, wrecked, mangled and misused," as he had once complained in letter to Brace.[8]

Going Out with Two Bangs

The Chicago fairground must have come as a sweet assignment. The excuse for the fair was the four hundredth anniversary of Columbus's discovery of America, and Central Park had been in the running for the site—a candidacy Olmsted strenuously opposed. Already familiar with Chicago from past projects, he envisaged Lake Michigan as the fair's focal point. The local bigwigs agreed, settling on Jackson Park, within sight of the lake on the city's South Side. In a letter to his landscaping superintendent, Rudolph Ulrich, Olmsted outlined the approach he wanted to take: "Chicago has grown out of a swamp, and as far as I know a swamp without beauty. Let us try to show the possible beauty of a swamp, even without trees."[9] Olmsted accordingly built an on-site lagoon, dressed it with aquatic foliage, and populated it with hundreds of ducks and geese and a sprinkling of such exotics as snowy egrets and flamingos.

Knitting the fair together was the color white, which most of its plaster buildings had to be painted. The White City, it was called, but on one of his prefair site visits, Olmsted saw what he thought was too much of a good thing. "I fear," he wrote to Ulrich, "that against the clear blue sky and the blue lake, great towering masses of white, glistening in the clear, hot, summer sunlight of Chicago, with the glare of water that we are to have both within and without the Exposition grounds, will be overpowering."[10] Olmsted had more plants rushed in, but light-sensitive fairgoers beat the glare by wearing blue-tinted eyeglasses.

Olmsted's presence in Chicago was sporadic, but even from afar he exerted a steadying influence. At the kickoff dinner in the spring of 1893, Daniel H. Burnham, the exposition's director of works, stood up to praise

the name and genius of him who stands first in the heart and confidence of American artists, the creator of your own parks and many other city parks. He it is who has been our best adviser and common mentor. In the highest sense he is the planner of the Exposition—Frederick Law Olmsted. . . . As artist, he paints with lakes and wooded slopes; with lawns and banks and forest-covered hills; with mountainsides and ocean views. He should stand where I do tonight, not for his deeds of later years alone, but for what his brain has wrought and his pen has taught for half a century.[11]

The "best adviser and common mentor" wasn't on hand to blush at that tribute. He'd gone south to check up on some of his firm's other works in progress.

One of these was Biltmore, which coaxed out of Olmsted something his brain had not previously wrought nor his pen taught: an approach to forestry. He'd been handling a couple of routine landscaping projects for George Washington Vanderbilt—one at Vanderbilt's summer house at Bar Harbor, Maine, the other at the family mausoleums on Staten Island—when the plutocrat sounded out Olmsted on a colossus in the making. What should be done with the 125,000 acres of land Vanderbilt had quietly bought in and around Asheville, North Carolina, to ensure privacy for the palatial house he intended to build there?

Writing to the project's bricks-and-mortar architect, Richard Morris Hunt, on March 2, 1889, Olmsted can almost be heard thinking out loud about how to answer that question. "The value of the site is in its outlook; the local scenery is not attractive," he pointed out. "The soil is extremely poor and intractable. There is not a single circumstance that can be turned to account in gaining any desirable local character, picturesqueness, for instance, or geniality. Whatever we aim at must be made 'out of the whole cloth.'"[12] Hunt and Olmsted, by the way, had once been at odds. In the 1860s Hunt, the first American ever admitted to the prestigious École des Beaux-Arts in Paris, had designed gateways for one of the entrances to Central Park. Olmsted and Vaux had objected, and the gates had not been commissioned. A quarter century later at Biltmore, however, Olmsted and Hunt collaborated harmoniously to enhance what had attracted Vanderbilt to the site in the first place: its grand views.

All sorts of figures can be marshaled to give a sense of the Vanderbilt mansion's size and grandeur—the thousand workmen who built it, its 250 rooms, the twenty-three thousand volumes in its library, the banquet hall that can seat sixty-four people—but one of the most telling is the $77,500 spent on putting in a private railroad to ferry construction material from the main line to the house site. "When he considers that the building of this road was a measure of economy," exclaimed a reporter for the *New York Sun*, "it is then that the Tar Heel begins to comprehend something of what it is to be a millionaire."[13]

Going Out with Two Bangs

In July 1889 Vanderbilt received Olmsted's Biltmore report. Early on, the author called for drastic action: "The scope of the scenery to be enjoyed from the house will be much enlarged by cutting down the crest of the hill-top on the East and by breaking into the woods on the North." Toward the end of the document, Olmsted circled back to the house in a section on "The Approach," the road that the visitor would follow through turns and past foliage, not even glimpsing "the Residence, with its orderly dependencies, [until it] breaks suddenly and fully upon him."[14] (To this day, seeing the mansion burst into view at the end of Olmsted's approach road is a highlight of anyone's first visit to Biltmore.)

In between those recommendations, Olmsted unveiled his extraordinary plan for the unpromising land outside the mansion's immediate grounds: make it a profitable forest. The young man chosen to oversee the project, Gifford Pinchot, had studied forestry in France and picked the brains of experts elsewhere in Europe. One of them, Dietrich Brandis, had cautioned Pinchot that his ambition to transplant commercial forestry across the Atlantic couldn't be realized "until some State or large individual owner makes the experiment and proves for America what is so well established in Europe, that forest management will pay."[15] In his report, Olmsted in effect nominated Vanderbilt, a stupendously large individual owner, to be that experimenter. Vanderbilt accepted the challenge.

"Here was my chance," Pinchot wrote in his autobiography, *Breaking New Ground*. "Biltmore could be made to prove what America did not yet understand, that trees could be cut and the forest preserved at one and the same time."[16] The twenty-six-year-old familiarized himself with the estate by tramping through "the wild, wild woods, sleeping on the ground, conversing with moonshiners, and feeding on warmed-up dough."[17]

Yet the Olmsted-Pinchot regime at Biltmore was not a success, at least not on their terms. The inexperienced forester made mistakes, Vanderbilt's interest in the project waned, and the forest did not become a self-sustaining investment. Still, Pinchot prized the experience as a valuable warmup for what he later accomplished: helping found the Society of American Foresters, the Yale School of Forestry, and the U.S. Forest Service, which he served as its first chief. In the 1930s Pinchot worked with Vanderbilt's heirs to keep the forest largely intact, selling the land to the United States, which converted it into the Pisgah National Forest.

In 1893 Olmsted made a confession to his partners: "My health is extremely frail and I may be tipped out any day."[18] He meant his physical health, but his memory was beginning to fail too. In March 1895 Rick Olmsted advised another partner in the firm, "Father is showing his age terribly. He can no longer keep his ideas clearly before his mind from minute to minute. . . . In giving directions he contradicts himself from minute to minute, and forgets completely what he has said on the subject the day before." After several months of resisting his partners' attempts to ease him into retirement, Olmsted wrote to one of them, his stepson, John, "[I have] come to understand the situation and to accept it. I suppose that I am nearly as heart-broken as a man can be and live."[19]

Despite having designed the grounds of several asylums, Olmsted did not want to live in one. In the end, though, he had little choice. He was committed to the McLean Hospital in Belmont, Massachusetts, in 1898. Five years later he died there at the age of eighty-one.

In 1890, before the onset of his mental decline, Olmsted had recapped his legacy in a letter to an old flame:

> There are, scattered through the country, seventeen large public parks, many more smaller ones, many more public or semi-public works, upon which, with sympathetic partners or pupils, I have been engaged. After we have left them they have in the majority of cases been more or less barbarously treated, yet as they stand . . . they are a hundred years ahead of any spontaneous public demand, or of the demand of any notable cultivated part of the people. And they are having an educative effect perfectly manifest to me—a manifest civilizing effect. I see much indirect and unconscious following of them. . . . I know that I shall have helped to educate . . . a capital body of young men for my profession, all men of liberal education and cultivated minds. I know that in the minds of a large body of men of influence I have raised my calling from the rank of a trade, even of a handicraft, to that of a liberal profession—an Art, an Art of Design.[20]

Going Out with Two Bangs

Writing almost a half century after his death, Carl Schenck, the German forester who succeeded Pinchot at Biltmore, remembered Olmsted as "not merely *the* great authority on all landscapism and indeed the creator of landscape architecture in the U.S.A.; he was also *the* inspirer of American forestry. And he was more: he was the loveliest and most loveable old man whom I have ever met."[21]

Missing from these summings-up was any reference to Olmsted's Yosemite report. Yet despite its derailment, the document had seeped into contemporary articles and books, and from there into the minds of men who worked to establish Yellowstone National Park. Moreover, Olmsted had reaffirmed the report's central recommendation—that managers of a wilderness park should keep "improvements" to the bare minimum—periodically throughout his career, including in the report for Niagara Falls he coauthored with Vaux. How the National Park Service has reckoned with that tenet over the years is the subject of the next and final chapter.

The Olmsteds   16

As a park with moving parts—those erupting geysers and pulsating fumaroles—Yellowstone should have been a hard act to follow. Not that moving parts were required for membership in the club. In fact, there *were* no requirements, and establishing new parks was an ad hoc affair. Which is how the honor of being the second one fell to a small, unassuming federally owned tract on Mackinac Island, in Lake Huron. Mackinac National Park took its place beside Yellowstone in 1875 and stayed there for twenty years before being transferred to Michigan as a state park, a status better suited to Mackinac's modest charms.

By the time of that demotion, the national park movement had gone international. Park number three cropped up in 1885 at Banff in Canada's Alberta province, first as a reserve protecting thermal springs and hot pools. Two years later the Dominion of Canada (as the country was then known) enlarged the reserve and rechristened it Rocky Mountain National Park. Today, as Banff National Park, it anchors the Canadian Rocky Mountain Parks World Heritage Site, which also takes in Jasper National Park (in Alberta), Yoho and Kootenay National Parks (British Columbia), and Mount Assiniboine, Mount Robson, and Hamber Provincial Parks (British Columbia). In each case the scenery spoke—no, shouted—for itself: the Canadian Rockies are one of the world's most dramatically scenic ranges. After the national park movement crossed the Pacific in 1887 and made landfall in New Zealand, there was no stopping it.

Three sites in the Sierra Nevada—Sequoia, General Grant, and the highlands above Yosemite Valley—became national parks in 1890. One more American attraction received the honor before the turn of the century: Mount Rainier in Washington State, which elicited what may be the ultimate in New World one-upmanship. "I could have summoned back the whole antique world of mythology and domiciled it upon this greater and grander Olympus," gushed an admirer in the American *Review of Reviews* magazine. Compared with Rainier, the rave of raves continued, "the mild glories of the Alps and Apennines grow anemic and dull," and from its summit, "the tower of Babel would have been hardly more visible than one of the church spires of a Puget Sound city." As a national park, the commentator wound up, the mountain will allow "our great army of tourists [to] gain a new pleasure, a larger artistic sense, and a higher inspiration from the contemplation of the grandeur and glory of this St. Peter's of the skies."[1]

At roughly the same time, a new breed of opportunist was at large on the public domain, prowling Indian ruins in the Southwest and filching artifacts, especially pottery, often with the intention of selling them on the black market. These treasures could be better protected if the sites on which they clustered were designated national parks, but the only way to accomplish that was by act of Congress, a sometimes laborious and time-consuming process. For speedy relief, Congressman Lacey pushed through the Antiquities Act of 1906, which authorized the president to set aside federally owned tracts as national monuments.

Although the law was occasioned by a specific kind of threat, its language was broad: the president could use the new tool to protect "historic landmarks, historic and prehistoric structures, and other objects of historic and scientific interest" on federal land.[2] Occupying the White House then was Theodore Roosevelt, never one to settle for a timid interpretation of executive power. Reasoning that a site can be of scientific interest not just for its artifacts (if any) but also for its geology, biology, and scenery, on September 24, 1906, Roosevelt proclaimed Devil's Tower, a monolith in Wyoming, the first national monument. Since then Republican and Democratic presidents alike have used the Antiquities Act to protect so many pottery-free sites that the law's stop-thief origin has been all but forgotten. Congress has promoted a number of national monuments to national parks, notably the Grand Canyon—a national monument starting in 1908, a national park since 1917. As of this writing, the most recent monument to be ennobled as a park is White Sands in New Mexico.

A national monument need not be managed by the Park Service; two of its sibling agencies in the Interior Department, the U.S. Fish and Wildlife Service and the Bureau of Land Management, take care of several monuments apiece. Other agencies in charge of one or more monuments are the Departments of Energy and Defense, the U.S. Forest Service in the Department of Agriculture, and the National Oceanic and Atmospheric Administration in the Department of Commerce.

The most sweeping use of the Antiquities Act came in 1978, when President Jimmy Carter applied it preemptively in Alaska, establishing 56 million acres' worth of national monuments because Congress could not reach a consensus on the land use decisions called for by Section 17(d)(2) of the Alaska Native Claims Settlement Act of 1971. Congress responded to Carter's action by getting a move on: the Alaska National Interest Lands Conservation Act of 1980 converted most of those monuments—along with more federal land in Alaska, for a grand total of 103 million protected acres—into national parks, wildlife refuges, forests, wild and scenic rivers, and recreation areas.

The question of whether a later president can undo what a predecessor has wrought under the Antiquities Act came up early in 2017, when Donald Trump signed executive orders excising large chunks of land from two national monuments in Utah, Bears Ears (designated by Barack Obama in 2016) and Grand Staircase-Escalante (designated by Bill Clinton in 1996), to allow for their commercial development. Those orders were challenged in court; as of this writing, their legality has yet to be ruled on, but the question may become moot. Soon after taking office as president in 2021, Joe Biden commissioned a study of the two monuments; the end result is expected to be the restoration of much—perhaps all—of the land removed from the two monuments in 2017.

The 1916 law creating the National Park Service, called the National Parks Organic Act, explained what the parks were for and how they should be run:

The service thus established shall promote and regulate the use of the Federal areas known as national parks, monuments, and reservations . . . by such means and measures as conform to the fundamental purpose of the said parks, monuments, and reservations, which is to conserve the scenery and the natural and historic objects and the wild life therein and to provide for the enjoyment of the same in such manner and by such means as will leave them unimpaired for the enjoyment of future generations.[3]

The law ended the government's near powerlessness to punish wrongdoing by directing the secretary of the interior to set rules and regulations for how to behave in the parks, with violators subject to penalties set by the U.S. Penal Code. The Organic Act thus imposed what Stephen Mather called a "double mandate," telling the Park Service to help park visitors enjoy the parks now but not to detract from the ability of future visitors to do the same. Ever since, the Park Service has been trying to strike a balance between those two goals.

The principal draftsman of that portion of the law was Frederick Law Olmsted Jr. In lieu of the double mandate, he might have simply cut and pasted in the principle laid down by his father in the 1865 Yosemite report: "The first thing to be kept in mind . . . is the preservation and maintenance as exactly as possible of the natural scenery; the restriction, that is to say, within the narrowest limits consistent with the necessary accommodation of visitors, of all artificial constructions and the prevention of all construction markedly inharmonious with the scenery or which would unnecessarily obscure, distort or detract from the dignity of the scenery."[4]

It's unclear, though, whether Rick Olmsted even knew of his father's Yosemite report. Yet Rick was more than just Fred's namesake son. He was the anointed one, who had grown up with many of father's projects and worked closely with the old man on some of the later ones. So even if Rick had never laid eyes on the Yosemite report or heard the tale of its suppression, he was steeped in his father's way of thinking about nature, including the wild kind that goes into national parks. It's no stretch, then, to see the son's dual mandate as a rewording of the father's expression of the same idea, with a present-users-versus-future-generations tension subbing for constraints such as "the narrowest limits consistent with the necessary accommodation of visitors." And it's possible that an interpretation of the filial version as a sort of codicil to the paternal will would

The Olmsteds

have strengthened the protection given to national parks and their natural resources over the years.

Indeed, we know of at least one case in which the Park Service did apply a standard like the one in the senior Olmsted's report. During World War II, the War Production Board cast a covetous eye on the splendid Sitka spruce forests that Olympic National Park in Washington State had been established to protect. Sitka spruce, it so happened, was both useful for manufacturing military planes and in short supply. With encouragement from the timber industry, the War Production Board requested that logging—a practice generally prohibited in national parks—be allowed in Olympic to further the war effort.

Resistance came from Park Service director Newton Drury, who argued that "the virgin forests in the national parks should not be cut unless the trees are absolutely essential to the prosecution of the war, with no alternative, and only as a last resort. Critical necessity rather than convenience should be the governing reason for such sacrifice of an important part of our federal estate."[5] Drury had the Park Service go all out to find alternatives, such as stands of Sitka spruce in Alaska and Canada. When the issue came to a head at a 1943 congressional hearing, the War Production Board backed down; it had discovered that the planes could be made just as well from materials other than wood.

If Drury had rested his case for saving the Olympic spruces on his obligation to future generations, the War Production Board could have argued that unless the United States fought fascism with everything it had, there might not *be* future American generations to enjoy the trees. By using stronger terms that might have come from Frederick Law Olmsted's playbook—"absolutely essential," "no alternative," "last resort"—Drury apparently caused the War Production Board to examine its conscience.

On its own, the present-versus-future language of the Organic Act has not always ensured wise management. Consider what happened after the law's specification of wildlife as one of the assets to be conserved in the parks took hold. The inclusion was long overdue. George Catlin's "nation's park" idea had done nothing for either half of the symbiotic relationship he fantasized about perpetuating. Plains Indians continued to be stripped of their land and moved around like pawns on a game board, and the unchecked slaughter of bison—six million killed in the period 1870–75 alone—brought the species so close to extinction in the wild that Yellowstone National Park was pressed into service as a kind of national ER.

Moreover, to paraphrase another George (Orwell), some animals were less equal than others. For decades after the establishment of Yellowstone and other parks, disfavored species were at risk of being culled or wholly eliminated lest they prey on other, more likable ones. Here, for example, is an acting superintendent of Yosemite National Park responding to a letter from George Grinnell that the superintendent's boss, Stephen Mather, had passed along for comment. "There is no such thing," Grinnell had maintained, "as 'vermin' among the animals comprising the native life within park areas." The superintendent disagreed, arguing for the sacrifice of enough mountain lions "to give reasonable protection to the park deer, which are more desirable."[6]

But as Benjamin Franklin had known, the law of unintended consequences applies to us all, wildlife managers included. Dubious about certain proposals to aid the poor of London, Franklin drew an analogy with the case of New Englanders who wiped out the blackbirds that were eating their corn. The blackbirds had preyed on worms, which proliferated in the birds' absence and destroyed the corn crop anyway. Something similar happened in the American West a couple of centuries later, after a successful campaign to rid Yellowstone of wolves, which had been preying on "more desirable" species, especially elk.

The result, as reported by evolutionary biologist Sean B. Carroll, was that "elk populations irrupted . . . and the larger herds took a heavy toll on the system's trees and plants. The ecosystem was not in its natural state or 'intact' without the wolves." Ecosystem indeed was a concept that took a long time to gain currency. When it did, a movement to reintroduce wolves into Yellowstone sprang up and slowly gained momentum until 1995, when the antiwolf policy was reversed. The animals' reintroduction caused what Carroll calls "cascading effects. Wolves are natural enemies of coyotes, which are smaller *mesopredators* [i.e., midlevel ones]. Coyote populations declined by 39 percent in Yellowstone National Park and in the adjacent Grand Teton National Park. . . . Coyotes in turn prey on young pronghorn antelope. Long-term studies have revealed that [pronghorn] fawn survival rates were four times higher in sites with wolves than without them."[7] Since the reintroduction, the wolf population has increased to almost a hundred in the park and more than five hundred in the greater Yellowstone ecosystem.

Was the Yellowstone wolf cleansing "more desirable" than the status quo? At the time of its imposition, yes—if polled, a majority of park visitors would surely have voted for the policy. Was it right? In hindsight, no. The Park Service's antiwolf crusade upheld one half of the dual mandate (pleasing contemporary visitors to Yellowstone) at the expense of the other half (keeping the park and its resources intact for future generations). Had Rick Olmsted's present-versus-future rule been fortified with his father's "necessary" test for departures from the "dignity of the scenery," the Yellowstone wolves might have been left to fend for themselves.

Frederick Law Olmsted was, among other things, a bureaucrat par excellence (recall his stewardship of the Sanitary Commission), but in ruminating on wild parks he may have overlooked a stage in any young agency's development. As Stephen Mather knew, to grow big and strong it needs a constituency.

The story of how Mather became the first head of the National Park Service is an American classic. On his résumé were stints as a reporter for the *New York Sun* and a distributor of borax, a mineral used as an abrasive in detergents and other products. He helped devise the 20 Mule Team Borax ad campaign, which transformed a nondescript white powder into a colorful commodity redolent of the Old West.

By 1915 Mather was rich and ready for new challenges. One presented itself when he vacationed in the High Sierra that summer: the slipshod management of Yosemite and Sequoia National Parks, which he complained about in a letter to a fellow alumnus of the University of California, Secretary of the Interior Franklin K. Lane. "Dear Steve," Lane shot back, "If you don't like the way the national parks are being run, come on down to Washington and run them yourself."[8] Mather took the bait, signing on as Lane's assistant for national parks but delegating day-by-day administration to a young lawyer named Horace Albright. That left Mather free to concentrate on his specialty: selling a product. Should anyone raise an eyebrow, Mather could point to the Organic Act clause telling the Park Service to promote the parks.

Mather's ambitions jibed with See America First, a railroad campaign to persuade well-off Americans to vacation in their homeland rather than in Europe. At a 1917 conference on the future of the national parks, Oklahoma congressman Scott Ferris called the amount of money spent by American tourists abroad "no less than alarming," especially since the "wonders and beauties" overseas are "only half as grand as nature has generously provided for them at home." Ferris urged his fellow conferees to work with Congress "to keep at least a part of that money at home where it belongs."[9] This philosophy augured well for national parks: rather than resent them for taking land out of circulation, lawmakers could embrace them for their ability to pump tourist dollars into the economy.

To sing the parks' praises, Mather hired—and paid out of his own pocket—Robert Sterling Yard, a former colleague at the *New York Sun*. Yard carried out his assignment so ably that he later wondered if he hadn't overdone it, generating "a tidal wave of newspaper and magazine publicity that in time passed far beyond all control."[10] Resulting from his labors in the remainder of 1916 alone were an issue of *National Geographic* devoted entirely to the parks and a book, *National Parks Portfolio*, combining photographs and text to extol the parks as both sources of national pride and prime vacation spots. When Congress passed a law nixing the kind of financial arrangement Mather and Yard had worked out, Yard left Interior to perform the same function as executive secretary of a new NGO, the National Parks Educational Committee, again with Mather paying his salary.

Yard's handiwork did not go unnoticed by chambers of commerce and entrepreneurs in towns near the parks. As explained by historian Paul S. Sutter, among those capitalizing on Yard's powers of persuasion were "regional boosters, opportunistic politicians, and a variety of commercial interests [that plugged] the parks into an increasingly sophisticated commercial matrix and [distorted] the role of the national parks as educational spaces. They had made marketplaces of nature's temples, and they were advertising the wild for their own gain."[11] At the center of that matrix was

The Olmsteds

the automobile, and traffic jams in Yosemite Valley became commonplace. Conservationists warned that the national parks were in danger of being loved to death.

Partisans of such desirable amenities as paved roads, grand hotels, fire-falls, and manicured viewpoints in national parks were wont to accuse their opponents of elitism. (As noted earlier, a major reason for admitting cars to the parks in the first place had been to refute that charge.) The elitist label stuck to the aristocratic Grinnell, who had practically begged for it in "Animal Life as an Asset of National Parks," an article he cowrote for a 1916 issue of *Science* magazine. In support of their thesis that the parks could be the last bastions for dwindling populations of North American wildlife, the authors reviled "laying out straight roads, constructing artificial lakes, trimming trees, clearing brush, [or] draining marshes" as being in "the worst of bad taste."[12] It's unfortunate that they framed the issue as a matter of taste when their real concern was a far graver one: the survival of imperiled species in the wild.

A rejoinder to the elitist charge came from the ranks of the National Forest Service. While the Park Service applies a double mandate, the Forest Service juggles multiple uses of its land, notably logging, mining, livestock grazing, wildlife management, and recreation. In the 1920s one of the Forest Service employees, Aldo Leopold, proposed a way to put the brakes on his agency's urge to build roads for the convenience of "motor tourists": by designating wilderness areas, in which no development to speak of had already occurred and none to speak of would be allowed in the future. *And if you think my idea favors the rich*, Leopold in effect said, *think again*. He conjured up a posh traveler who relies on "hired guides, large pack trains, and other expensive trimmings," giving onlookers the impression that "this is the sort of thing the wilderness idea seeks to perpetuate." Not so, said Leopold. "It is the other kind of man, the man who can not afford to travel farther, and who must seek his wilderness near home or not at all, whose standard of living is endangered by the impending motorization of every last nook and corner of the continental United States."[13]

Robert Marshall, a contemporary of Leopold's and, like him, a co-founder of the Wilderness Society, met the elitist charge head-on. Governments, Marshall pointed out, commonly support cultural institutions—the symphony, the opera, the theater, museums (and later PBS, NPR, and the National Endowment for the Arts)—that appeal to a relatively small coterie. The thinking is that the arts can enrich communities by appealing to our better nature. Marshall believed that wilderness should be on that list too. As he put it in 1928, "A small share of the American people have an overpowering longing to retire periodically from the encompassing clutch of mechanistic civilization." On their behalf, he asserted "a right to a minor portion of America's vast area for the nourishment of this particular appetite."[14]

Two years earlier Leopold had won approval for the first official American wilderness area, within the Gila National Forest in Arizona. The absence of roads and other forms of development was both what qualified the area to be picked and what its new status would preserve. The decision-maker in that case was the nation's chief forester, who hoped to see more such areas designated in other national forests, as indeed happened. But because subsequent administrators can override their predecessors' decisions, conservationists sought statutory protection for wilderness. Their lobbying culminated in the Wilderness Act of 1964, which immediately designated 9.1 million acres of federal wilderness and ordered managers of national forests, national parks, and national wildlife refuges to review their holdings for other roadless areas deserving of the same treatment. A wilderness area stays in the park, forest, or refuge to which it belongs but is kept in its pristine state, closed to vehicular traffic but open to hiking, backpacking, canoeing, and other forms of low-impact recreation. The law speaks of wilderness as a place where "man . . . is a visitor who does not remain."[15] (Today we would hope that wilderness is also a place where visitors leave their mobile phones turned off—except in case of emergency. How can you have a sublimely wild experience while being pestered by news, phone calls, texts, tweets, and likes?)

In the early years of its operation, the Wilderness Act did not sit well with some national park personnel, who thought it interfered with their prerogatives and called into question their past custodianship of the parks. Eventually, however, skeptics saw that the law could help them withstand pressure to favor the first half of the Organic Act's double mandate (catering to today's visitors) over the second half (leaving the parks unim-

The Olmsteds

paired for tomorrow's). Today more than 80 percent of the total acreage in national parks is managed as wilderness.

The Park Service had inadvertently given the Wilderness Act campaign a boost by carrying out a controversial program. During World War II and the years immediately afterward, the parks had been neglected—so much so that, writing for *Harper's Magazine* in 1953, the historian and conservationist Bernard DeVoto portrayed them as scraping by on a "hot-dog stand budget." DeVoto sarcastically proposed closing Yellowstone, Grand Canyon, Great Smokies, Everglades, and other national parks and holding them "in trust for a more enlightened future," noting that "meanwhile letters from constituents unable to visit Old Faithful . . . and Bright Angel Trail would bring a nationally disgraceful situation to the really serious attention of the Congress which is responsible for it."[16]

Galvanized by this and other, similar critiques, the Park Service rolled out Mission 66, a ten-year program to recondition the parks in time for the agency's golden anniversary in 1966. Heavy on road building, light on benefits to wildlife, Mission 66 struck conservationists as an ill-advised attempt to flood the parks with what historian Richard West Sellars calls "resort-style development."[17] By the time the program ended, Congress had given it a billion dollars of funding. As for the public, annual visits to the national parks more than tripled between 1955 and 1974, from fourteen million to forty-six million, and in national monuments the number climbed from five to seventeen million. (Mission 66 was also good to a certain profession. For the duration, an insider asserted, the Park Service was the "largest single user of landscape architects in the country—possibly in the world.")[18]

A vivid—and far from complimentary—picture of Mission 66 in action can be found in Edward Abbey's environmental classic *Desert Solitaire* (1968). In the mid-1950s, when Abbey reported for duty as a seasonal ranger in Arches National Monument (now Arches National Park) in Utah, his bosses showed him around. As Abbey describes it:

> Arches National Monument remains at this time what the Park Service calls an undeveloped area, although to me it appears quite adequately developed. The roads . . . lead to within easy walking distance of most

of the principal arches, none more than two miles beyond the end of a road. The roads are not paved, true, but are easily passable to any automobile except during or immediately after a rainstorm. The trails are well marked, easy to follow; you'd have to make an effort to get lost. There are three small campgrounds, each with tables, fireplaces, garbage cans and pit toilets. (Bring your own water.)[19]

All of this suited Abbey fine, not least because the monument was attracting few motorized tourists. "They stay away because of the unpaved entrance road, the unflushable toilets in the campgrounds, and the fact that most of them have never even heard of Arches National Monument." Alas, Abbey added, "All this must change. . . . On the very first day [the bosses] had mentioned something about developments, improvements, a sinister Master Plan. . . . I paid little heed and had soon forgotten the whole ridiculous business. But only a few days ago something happened which shook me out of my pleasant apathy."[20]

Abbey's jitters were occasioned by the arrival of workmen from the U.S. Bureau of Public Roads, come to survey the monument's roads as the first step in paving them. He bided his time while the surveyors did their job, including marking routes with wooden stakes pounded into the ground. In a preview of the civil disobedience glorified in his novel *The Monkey Wrench Gang* (1975), Ranger Ed waited until the surveyors left. Then "for about five miles I followed the course of their survey . . . and as I went I pulled up each little wooden stake and threw it away." Abbey had no illusion that his mischief would stop the paving. Still, he said, it "made me feel good."[21]

In a 2009 interview Dayton Duncan, the producer of Ken Burns's national park series for PBS, took issue with those who, like Abbey, demean the visitor who enjoys the parks largely from behind a windshield:

I've stood at viewpoints and watched a busload of people get off, and thought to myself, The most exercise those 50 people are going to have this year is getting off that tour bus and walking the 25 yards into the beautiful scenic view and say, 'Wow, isn't that something,' turn around, and get back on their bus. And that's easy to caricature. But those people, nonetheless, will have been touched by that experience.

And when somebody says, 'They're thinking of building a dam in the Grand Canyon,' they'll say, 'Don't you let them do that!' And they have as legitimate a stake as the person who's going to do the two-week backcountry, hard-core experience where they can be by themselves in nature. It belongs to all of us.[22]

Also keep in mind what Edmund Burke said about the psychological effect of a brush with the sublime: It "produces a sort of swelling and triumph, that is extremely [gratifying] to the human mind; and this swelling is never more perceived, nor operates with more force, than when without danger we are conversant with terrible objects; the mind always claiming to itself some part of the dignity and importance of the things which it contemplates."[23] Who are we to say that tourists who get off their tour buses to be conversant, however briefly, with the "terrible objects" in Yosemite Valley or Yellowstone's Geyser Basin are not assimilating some part of those objects' "dignity and importance"?

Joseph L. Sax's *Mountains without Handrails* (1980), which punches far above its 152-page weight, is a treatise on the Park Service's dual mandate. Profiting from the rediscovery of the senior Olmsted's Yosemite report, Sax seized on one of its central tenets: that wild or mostly wild parks offer relief from the burden of leading a tamed, relentlessly purposeful life. "Engagement with nature," Sax asserts, "provides an opportunity for detachment from the submissiveness, conformity, and mass behavior that dog us in our daily lives; it offers a chance to express distinctiveness and to explore our deeper longings. At the same time, the setting—by exposing us to the awesomeness of the natural world in the context of 'ethical' recreation—moderates the urge to prevail without destroying the vitality that gives rise to it; to face what is wild in us and yet not revert to savagery."[24]

Citing Thoreau's praise of contemplative recreation in *Walden* and "Walking," Sax provides a sketch of the right-minded fugitive from the beaten path: "To be willing to fish or climb without an audience; to be able to draw satisfaction from a walk in the woods, without calling on others for entertainment; to be content with a fishless day, demanding no string of fish to be counted and displayed: These are the characteristics of the individual who has 'refined' wildness without taming it into the personality of the mass man."[25]

Sax is no tree-hugging Scrooge. He sees nothing wrong with providing hotels for park visitors unwilling to camp in tents or with allowing "supportive services" such as stores and gas stations to do business inside "more remote parks." To be excluded, however, are "facilities that are attractions in themselves, lures that have nothing do with facilitating an experience of the natural resources around which the area has been established."[26] Swimming pools and ski resorts are good examples of "attractions in themselves" that Sax would keep out of national parks and monuments because they are widely available elsewhere and irrelevant to the appreciation of great natural wonders.

Sax might also have cited another plus to visiting the parks in an unprogrammed and uncoddled way. Catlin and Olmsted and Hayden reveled in their privileged encounters with "pristine beauty and wildness" (Catlin on the Great Plains), "the greatest glory of nature" (Olmsted on Yosemite), and "a vision . . . worth a lifetime" (Hayden on Yellowstone Lake). They sought what so many other adventurous nineteenth-century Americans did before and after them: a satisfaction of the itch to explore, a stimulating expectation that around the next bend of the river or behind the next boulder or in the saddle of the next pass they might come upon something new, amazing, perhaps challenging or even dangerous. To base land use policies on the assumption that most visitors to national parks no longer want to have, or are capable of having, this kind of excitement may be another form of elitism—the patronizing kind.

We are well into the era when a car is no longer a luxury but a necessity for almost everyone except residents of a city with first-rate public transportation. So what about those Americans who still don't own a car (or at least not one fit to drive hundreds of miles to the nearest national park) and who can't afford a long getaway by bus? In the 1970s the fanfares for the common man sounded by Olmsted, Leopold, and other thinkers resonated in Washington DC. The Interior Department responded with an initiative to benefit city dwellers: a preliminary urban parks study, as contained in a January 1977 report of that name.

The Olmsteds

To set the stage, the report quoted former National Park Service director George Hartzog: "We're about out of the opportunity to set aside wilderness areas. . . . What we need to do is set aside areas close to or in the cities. City people are dying of social pollution, and they need room to move in."[27] When the study got underway in the summer of 1976, Congress had already created three urban parks at the federal level, calling them national recreation areas to distinguish them from traditional national parks: Gateway, serving New York City, and Golden Gate, serving the Bay Area of Northern California, both in 1972; and Cuyahoga, serving Cleveland and Akron, Ohio, in 1974 (since redesignated Cuyahoga Valley National Park). These were big projects that entailed acquiring a lot of expensive land, and Congress wanted a rough idea of how many more candidates for the same treatment might be out there. Hence the Interior Department study.

It brought together field reports covering twenty-eight standard metropolitan statistical areas across the country. Six sites from this pool made the cut as "arguably worthy of becoming federal urban parks: Baltimore's Aberdeen Proving Grounds; New Jersey's Pine Barrens; Wilmington's Green Swamp [in North Carolina]; Portland's Columbia River Gorge [in Oregon and Washington]; Providence's Narragansett Bay Islands; and the Las Vegas Wash." While acknowledging that this list might not be exhaustive, the study report reassured lawmakers that there was "a limited universe of potential Federal park sites [rather than] an endless queue of proposals."[28]

Administrations changed just as the study came out, and it fell by the wayside. In 1978 Congress created another urban park—Santa Monica Mountains National Recreation Area, serving greater Los Angeles—and then no more. Yet with American cities continuing to grow—80 percent of us now live in one, according to the Census Bureau—the democratic park-making ethos that informed Olmsted's work in midtown Manhattan and Yosemite Valley may be due for a revival.

If with Mission 66 the Park Service erred on the side of making things easy for visitors, in recent decades it has exercised more managerial restraint. Take, for example, Canyonlands National Park in Utah, established in 1964 and kept in a near-primitive state ever since. It's a large park—337,598 acres, to be exact—in which roads are few. As the Canyon-lands website warns, no roads directly link the park's far-flung districts, and it can take from two to six hours to drive from one to the next. As a result, "most people find it impractical to visit more than one area in a single trip." Moreover, "there are no lodging or dining facilities in the park."[29]

The parks established by the Alaska National Interest Lands Conservation Act of 1980 reflect a similarly lean approach to accommodating visitors. Denali National Park and Preserve, for example, has only one road, almost all of which is off-limits to automobiles. Rather, visitors park their cars and tour Denali aboard the buses made available for that purpose. For anyone seeking a less supervised and wilder Denali experience, the best option is backpacking.

In 2006 the Park Service codified this stricter interpretation of the dual mandate as part of a thoroughgoing restatement of its policies. The document's Section 9.1.1.2, "Integration of Facilities into the Park Environment," provides that "whenever possible, major park facilities—especially those that can be shared with other entities—should be developed outside park boundaries."[30] Thus management of the national parks may now be truer to the Olmsteds' vision for them than ever before.

At times, Olmsted Senior can seem almost too good for the rest of us mere mortals, even as a physical specimen. In a letter of advice to the principal of a military academy in 1866, Olmsted projected onto the cadets his own prodigious capacity for walking (at least, before his carriage accident): "No boy's education [is] tolerably good, even as preparatory to college or other advanced schools, who could not trot 12 miles in two hours or walk 16 miles in four hours or from twenty to thirty miles in a day without painful fatigue."[31] Later in life, however, Olmsted seems to have lightened up, admitting that "[a] man moving fast cannot enjoy scenery contemplatively."[32]

Then there is Olmsted's lament that his designs were "constantly & everywhere arrested, wrecked, mangled and misused." After his death, the arresting and mangling increased so markedly that one wonders whether he had expected too much from ordinary citizens, who couldn't grasp the master's plans or wanted to tart them up with in-park ball fields, restaurants, and zoos, and too much from public officials, who couldn't say no.

The Olmsteds

In the last quarter of the twentieth century, though, the American environmental movement widened its scope to take in designed landscapes. Since its founding in 1980 the National Association for Olmsted Parks has worked to preserve and restore Olmsted parks and parkways and has sponsored Olmsted research, notably the compilation of his papers into a twelve-volume set published by Johns Hopkins University Press. In 2022, to mark the centennial of Olmsted's birth—which happily comes in same year as the 150th birthday of Yellowstone National Park—the association will coordinate a nationwide celebration of the Olmsted legacy. At the local level, groups like the Central Park Conservancy and the Buffalo Olmsted Parks Conservancy have sought to realign Olmsted designs as closely as possible with his original intent, pushed for the addition of Olmsted parks to the National Register of Historic Places, and helped make up for budget shortfalls by mustering volunteers to work in the field under the supervision of park employees.

Much work remains to be done, however. For an example, look to Audubon Park in New Orleans, designed by Olmsted's stepson, John Charles Olmsted, as a member of the Olmsted firm. As described by Tony Horwitz, Audubon Park has a golf course, a zoo, an aquarium, "a Paracourse FitCircuit with fifteen stations to do exercises, and herds of people on bikes and skateboards." Horwitz admits, "I had a pleasant enough amble [in the park], and the fitness on display was a healthy contrast to the excess of the French Quarter. But I couldn't shake [Frederick Law] Olmsted's voice, and could imagine his dismay that a park linked to his family name now bore so little trace of his aesthetic or social vision."[33]

Even Niagara Falls could still use some rehabilitation. The scene today calls to mind a stretch of the U.S. Interstate Highway System, where just outside a fairly narrow corridor of road-cum-greenery loom the billboards and structures that Lady Bird Johnson's highway beautification program shoved back from the right-of-way, but not far enough. To cite just one example of the trouble with Niagara, the American-side view of an exoskeletal elevator climbing up and down a skyscraper on the Canadian side poses a question first asked by Olmsted Senior in his 1880 Niagara "Notes": *"How, in the long run, is the general experience of visitors affected by measures and courses which are determined with no regard to the influence of the scenery?"*[34]

As of this writing, there are 423 units in the American national park system, of which 63 are national parks. Since 1872 the national park movement has branched out worldwide, for a current total of more than 4,000 parks in over a hundred countries; the U.S. National Park Service has contributed heavily to this trend through the advisory programs of its Office of International Affairs. UNESCO has done its part, too, creating a category of superparks called World Heritage sites, among them anthropological ones such as Machu Picchu, historic ones such as the Great Wall of China and Vatican City, and natural ones such as the Great Barrier Reef, Yosemite, and Yellowstone. The park movement has reached as far as war-racked Afghanistan, which in 2009 established Band-e-Amir National Park to protect—and bring tourists to—a chain of deep-blue lakes in Bamyan Province.

The shade of Olmsted Senior would no doubt take special pleasure in the subset of European national parks once owned by the high and mighty. Gran Paradiso National Park in Italy and Mercantour National Park in France used to be hunting grounds for the dukes of Savoy (later the kings of Italy). Bialowieza in Poland started out as a similar reserve for Polish kings and Russian czars. Such rededications have gone a ways toward curing the malady Olmsted had first noticed in England and then flagged in his Yosemite report: "The enjoyment of the choicest natural scenes in the country and the means of recreation connected with them is . . . a monopoly . . . of a very few, very rich people."[35]

The beauty of the national park idea is that descendants of those dukes, kings, and emperors can still enjoy Gran Paradiso, Mercantour, and Bialowieza. It's just that, thanks in no small part to Frederick Law Olmsted, they must do so on the same terms as everybody else.

NOTES

1. Frederick Law Olmsted, *The Papers of Frederick Law Olmsted* (Baltimore: Johns Hopkins University Press, 1986), 4:203.

INTRODUCTION

1. Frederick Law Olmsted, *Yosemite and the Mariposa Grove: A Preliminary Report, 1865* (Yosemite National Park CA: Yosemite Association, 2009), 11–12.
2. Laura Roper, *FLO: A Biography of Frederick Law Olmsted* (Baltimore: Johns Hopkins University Press, 1973), 301.

1. YOU CAN HAVE THE ARNO

1. Stephen Marcus, *Dickens from Pickwick to Dombey* (New York: W. W. Norton, 1985), 241.
2. Marcus, *Dickens*, 242.
3. Marcus, *Dickens*, 249.
4. Charles Dickens, *American Notes: A Journey* (1842; repr., New York: Fromm International, 1985), 63, 157, 158, 146.
5. Charles Dickens, *Martin Chuzzlewit* (Baltimore: Penguin Classics, 1968), 919.
6. Fanny Trollope, *Domestic Manners of the Americans* (1932; repr., London: Penguin Classics, 1997), 317.
7. Anthony Trollope, *An Autobiography* (1883; repr., Oxford: World's Classics, 1980), 161–62.
8. "There Is Room for All, and Millions More," *American Heritage* 12, no. 3 (April 1961): 112.
9. Trollope, *Domestic Manners*, xxxvi.
10. Hans Huth, "Yosemite: The Story of an Idea," *Sierra Club Bulletin* 33, no. 3 (March 1948).
11. Sydney Smith, "Who Reads an American Book?," *Edinburgh Review* 33 (1820): 69–80, http://www.usgennet.org/usa/topic/preservation/epochs/vol5/pg144.htm.
12. Washington Irving, *The Legend of Sleepy Hollow and Other Stories* (New York: Penguin Classics, 2014), 53.
13. John F. Sears, *Sacred Places: American Tourist Attractions in the Nineteenth Century* (1989; repr., Amherst: University of Massachusetts Press, 1998), 39.

14. George Steiner, *Tolstoy or Dostoevsky: An Essay in the Old Criticism* (Chicago: University of Chicago Press, 1985), 32.

15. Edgar Allan Poe, *Essays and Reviews* (New York: Library of America, 1984), 523, 530.

16. Richard Ruland and Malcolm Bradbury, *From Puritanism to Modernism: A History of American Literature* (New York: Penguin Books, 1992), 73–74.

17. Poe, *Essays and Reviews*, 512, 506.

18. Robert E. Spiller, Willard Thorp, Thomas H. Johnson, Henry Seidel Canby, Richard M. Ludwig, and William M. Gibson, eds., *Literary History of the United States*, vol. 1, *History*, 4th ed. (New York: Macmillan, 1974), 171.

19. Roderick Nash, *Wilderness and the American Mind* (New Haven CT: Yale University Press, 1967), 42.

20. Garry Wills, *Head and Heart: American Christianities* (New York: Penguin, 2007), 34.

21. Nash, *Wilderness*, 23.

22. Nash, *Wilderness*, 81.

23. Huth, "Yosemite."

24. Ralph Waldo Emerson, *Nature and Selected Essays* (New York: Penguin Classics, 1982), 83.

25. Mark Twain, *The Innocents Abroad* (1869; repr., New York: Signet Classics, 1966), 182.

2. LAND OF THE FREE

1. Elizabeth McKinsey, *Niagara Falls: Icon of the American Sublime* (Cambridge: Cambridge University Press, 1985), 35.

2. Dayton Duncan, *The National Parks: America's Best Idea* (New York: Knopf, 2009), 8.

3. Herman Melville, *Moby-Dick* (New York: Library of America, 1991), 610.

4. McKinsey, *Niagara Falls*, 36.

5. Fanny Trollope, *Domestic Manners of the Americans* (1932; repr., London: Penguin Classics, 1997), 295, 298.

6. Charles Dickens, *American Notes: A Journey* (1842; repr., New York: Fromm International, 1985), 200.

7. W. D. Howells, Mark Twain, Nathaniel S. Shaler, et al., *The Niagara Book*, new and rev. ed. (New York: Doubleday, Page, 1901), 290.

8. McKinsey, *Niagara Falls*, 3.

9. Conor Cruise O'Brien, *The Great Melody: A Thematic Biography and Commented Anthology of Edmund Burke* (London: Minerva, 1993), 39.

10. Edmund Burke, *On Taste; On the Sublime and Beautiful; Reflections on the French Revolution; A Letter to a Noble Lord* (New York: Collier & Son, 1909), 36.

11. Burke, *On Taste*, 58.

12. Quoted in Richard H. Gassan, *The Birth of American Tourism: New York, the Hudson Valley, and American Culture, 1790–1830* (Amherst: University of Massachusetts Press, 2008), 101.

13. Marjorie Hope Nicholson, *Mountain Gloom and Mountain Glory: The Development of the Aesthetics of the Infinite* (Seattle: University of Washington Press, 1997), 150.

14. Nicholson, *Mountain Gloom*, 34.

15. Nicholson, *Mountain Gloom*, 346.

16. Francis Parkman, *The Oregon Trail* (New York: Dodd, Mead, 1964), 232.

17. Henry Wadsworth Longfellow, "A Psalm of Life," Poetry Foundation, accessed March 13, 2021, https://www.poetryfoundation.org/poems/44644/a-psalm-of-life.

18. Walt Whitman, *Leaves of Grass and Selected Prose*, ed. Sculley Bradley (New York: Holt, Rinehart & Winston, 1949), 494.

19. Whitman, *Leaves of Grass*, 540.

20. Nicholson, *Mountain Gloom*, 3.

3. THE COUNTEREXAMPLE

1. Richard H. Gassan, *The Birth of American Tourism: New York, the Hudson Valley, and American Culture, 1790–1830* (Amherst: University of Massachusetts Press, 2008), 3, 103.

2. Pierre Berton, *A Picture Book of Niagara Falls* (Toronto: McClelland & Stewart, 1993), 11.

3. Gordon Donaldson, *Niagara! The Eternal Circus* (Toronto: Doubleday Canada, 1979), 122.

4. Robert E. Spiller et al., *Literary History of the United States*, 4th ed. (New York: Macmillan, 1974), 732.

5. Alfred Runte, "Beyond the Spectacular: The Niagara Falls Preservation Campaign," *New York Historical Society Quarterly* 37 (January 1973): 34.

6. Francis R. Kowsky, *The Best Planned City in the World: Olmsted, Vaux, and the Buffalo Park System* (Amherst MA: Library of American Landscape History, 2013), 157.

7. Pierre Berton, *Niagara: A History of the Falls* (New York: Kodansha International, 1997), 130.

8. Hans Huth, *Nature and the American: Three Centuries of Changing Attitudes*, new ed. (Lincoln: University of Nebraska Press, 1990), 172.

9. Donaldson, *Niagara!*, 153.

10. Donaldson, *Niagara!*, 152.

11. Donaldson, *Niagara!*, 153.

12. John F. Sears, *Sacred Places: American Tourist Attractions in the Nineteenth Century* (1989; repr., Amherst: University of Massachusetts Press, 1998), 30.

13. Berton, *Niagara*, 130.

14. Quoted in Elizabeth McKinsey, *Niagara Falls: Icon of the American Sublime* (Cambridge: Cambridge University Press, 1985), 133.

15. Mark Twain, *The Signet Classic Book of Mark Twain's Short Stories*, ed. Justin Kaplan (New York: Signet Classics, 1985), 24.

16. Berton, *Niagara*, 131.

17. Berton, *Niagara*, 36.

18. W. D. Howells, Mark Twain, Nathaniel S. Shaler, et al., *The Niagara Book*, new and rev. ed. (New York: Doubleday, Page, 1901), 259–60.

19. Howells, Twain, Shaler, et al., *Niagara Book*, 252–53.

20. Quoted in Berton, *Niagara*, 88.

21. Berton, *Niagara*, 132.

22. Alfred Runte, *National Parks: The American Experience*, 3rd ed. (Lincoln: University of Nebraska Press, 1997), 1.

4. AN IDEA IN EMBRYO

1. George Catlin, *Letters and Notes on the Manners, Customs, and Condition of the North American Indians* (1842; repr., New York: Dover, 1973), 1:261–62.

2. Catlin, *Letters and Notes*, 1:262.

3. Henry David Thoreau, "Chesuncook," *Atlantic Monthly* 2, no. 10 (August 1858): 317.

4. Bradford Torrey and Francis H. Allen, eds., *The Journal of Henry David Thoreau* (Boston: Houghton Mifflin, 1906), 8:220–21.

5. Henry David Thoreau, "Walking," in Perry Miller, *Major Writers of America* (New York: Harcourt, Brace & World, 1962), 1:628.

6. Frederick Law Olmsted Jr. and Theodora Kimball, eds., *Frederick Law Olmsted: Landscape Architect, 1822–1903* (1922; repr., New York: Benjamin Blom, 1970), 2:5.

7. Olmsted and Kimball, *Frederick Law Olmsted*, 2:7.

8. Quoted in John F. Sears, *Sacred Places: American Tourist Attractions in the Nineteenth Century* (1989; repr., Amherst: University of Massachusetts Press, 1998), 116.

9. Benita Eisler, *The Red Man's Bones: George Catlin, Artist and Showman* (New York: W. W. Norton, 2013), 11.

10. Eisler, *Red Man's Bones*, 15.

11. Catlin, *Letters and Notes*, 1:18–19.

12. Catlin, *Letters and Notes*, 1:203.

13. Catlin, *Letters and Notes*, 1:60.

14. Eisler, *Red Man's Bones*, 136.

15. Catlin, *Letters and Notes*, 1:94–95; 2:257.

16. John C. Ewers, *Indian Life on the Upper Missouri* (Norman: University of Oklahoma Press, 1988), 193.

17. Eisler, *Red Man's Bones*, 281.

18. Catlin, *Letters and Notes*, 2:241.

19. Catlin, *Letters and Notes*, 1:262.

20. Jacques Barzun, *From Dawn to Decadence: 500 Years of Western Cultural Life, 1500 to the Present* (New York: HarperCollins, 2000), 50.

21. Brenda Wineapple, *White Heat: The Friendship of Emily Dickinson and Thomas Wentworth Higginson* (New York: Knopf, 2008), 96.

22. Henry David Thoreau, *A Week on the Concord and Merrimack Rivers* (1849; repr., New York: Library of America, 1985), 12.

23. Thoreau, *Week on the Concord*, 201–2.

24. Donald Worster, *A Passion for Nature: The Life of John Muir* (New York: Oxford University Press, 2008), 213.

25. Joseph Wood Krutch, ed., *Great American Nature Writing* (New York: William Sloane, 1950), 106.

26. Josiah D. Whitney, *The Yosemite Book: A Description of the Yosemite Valley and the Adjacent Region of the Sierra Nevada, and of the Big Trees of California* (New York: Julius Bien, 1869), 73.

27. See, for example, Jedediah Purdy, "Environmentalism's Racist History," *New Yorker*, August 13, 2015, https://www.newyorker.com/news/news-desk/environmentalisms-racist-history.

28. Olmsted and Kimball, *Frederick Law Olmsted*, 2:14.

5. THE LANDSCAPE READER

1. Walt Whitman, *Leaves of Grass and Selected Prose*, ed. Sculley Bradley (New York: Holt, Rinehart & Winston, 1949),

2. Witold Rybczynski, *A Clearing in the Distance: Frederick Law Olmsted and America in the 19th Century* (New York: Touchstone, 2000), 34.

3. Frederick Law Olmsted Jr. and Theodora Kimball, eds., *Frederick Law Olmsted: Landscape Architect, 1822–1903* (1922; repr., New York: Benjamin Blom, 1970), 1:46.

4. Olmsted and Kimball, *Frederick Law Olmsted*, 1:46.

5. Frederick Law Olmsted, *The Papers of Frederick Law Olmsted* (Baltimore: Johns Hopkins University Press, 1986), 2:3.

6. Olmsted, *Papers*, 2:6.

7. Charles Beveridge, ed., *Frederick Law Olmsted: Writings on Landscape, Culture, and Society* (New York: Library of America, 2015), 42–43.

8. Laura Roper, *FLO: A Biography of Frederick Law Olmsted* (Baltimore: Johns Hopkins University Press, 1973), 71.

9. Lee Hall, *Olmsted's America: An "Unpractical Man" and His Vision of Civilization* (Boston: Bullfinch, 1995), 32.

10. Olmsted, *Papers*, 2:8.

11. Beveridge, *Frederick Law Olmsted*, 88–89.

12. Edmund Wilson, *Patriotic Gore: Studies in the Literature of the American Civil War* (1962; repr., Boston: Northeastern University Press, 1984), 222.

13. Roper, *FLO*, 89.

14. Beveridge, *Frederick Law Olmsted*, 56.

15. Beveridge, *Frederick Law Olmsted*, 90.

16. Roper, *FLO*, 88.

17. Roper, *FLO*, 93.

18. Beveridge, *Frederick Law Olmsted*, 86.

19. Rybczynski, *Clearing in the Distance*, 130.

20. Olmsted, *Papers*, 2:27, 29.

21. Leo Tolstoy, *War and Peace*, trans. Anthony Briggs (London: Penguin Classics, 2007), 417.

22. Sara Norton and M. A. DeWolfe Howe, *Letters of Charles Eliot Norton, with Biographical Comment* (Boston: Houghton Mifflin, 1913), 1:211.

23. Olmsted and Kimball, *Frederick Law Olmsted*, 2:36.

24. Roper, *FLO*, 130.

25. Roper, *FLO*, 262.

26. Olmsted and Kimball, *Frederick Law Olmsted*, 2:24.

27. Olmsted and Kimball, *Frederick Law Olmsted*, 2:25.

28. Quoted in Beveridge, *Frederick Law Olmsted*, 488–89.

29. Olmsted and Kimball, *Frederick Law Olmsted*, 2:39–40.

30. Rybczynski, *Clearing in the Distance*, 19.

31. Roper, *FLO*, 133.

32. Ethan Carr, *Wilderness by Design: Landscape Architecture and the National Park Service* (Lincoln: University of Nebraska Press, 1998), 19.

33. Beveridge, *Frederick Law Olmsted*, 757.

34. Rybczynski, *Clearing in the Distance*, 167.

35. Hall, *Olmsted's America*, 61–62.

36. Rybczynski, *Clearing in the Distance*, 169–70.

37. Rybczynski, *Clearing in the Distance*, 177.

38. Beveridge, *Frederick Law Olmsted*, 478.

39. Tony Horwitz, *Spying on the South: An Odyssey across the American Divide* (New York: Penguin, 2019), 401.

40. Quoted in Justin Martin, *Genius of Place: The Life of Frederick Law Olmsted* (Boston: Da Capo, 2012), 157.

41. Roper, *FLO*, 146.

42. Roper, *FLO*, 154.

43. Roper, *FLO*, 154.

44. Olmsted, *Papers*, 3:36–37.

45. Beveridge, *Frederick Law Olmsted*, 162.

46. Roper, *FLO*, 176.

47. Allen C. Guelzo, *Fateful Lighting: A New History of the Civil War & Reconstruction* (New York: Oxford University Press, 2013), 414.

48. Roper, *FLO*, 197.

49. Roy Morris Jr., *The Better Angel: Walt Whitman in the Civil War* (New York: Oxford University Press, 2000), 110.

50. Martin, *Genius of Place*, 212.

51. Beveridge, *Frederick Law Olmsted*, 221.

52. Roper, *FLO*, 213.

53. Beveridge, *Frederick Law Olmsted*, 181.

54. Olmsted and Kimball, *Frederick Law Olmsted*, 2:73–74.

55. Roper, *FLO*, 231.

56. Charles E. Beveridge and Paul Rocheleau, *Frederick Law Olmsted: Designing the American Landscape* (New York: Rizzoli, 1995), 26.

6. HOW TO SELL A PARK BILL

1. Kevin Starr, *Americans and the California Dream, 1850–1915* (New York: Oxford University Press, 1973), 101.

2. Hans Huth, "Yosemite: The Story of an Idea," *Sierra Club Bulletin* 33, no. 3 (March 1948).

3. John F. Sears, *Sacred Places: American Tourist Attractions in the Nineteenth Century* (1989; repr., Amherst: University of Massachusetts Press, 1998), 124.

4. Huth "Yosemite."

5. Weston J. Naef, *Era of Exploration: The Rise of Landscape Photography in the American West, 1860–1885* (Buffalo NY: Albright-Knox Art Gallery, 1975), 79.

6. Quoted in Naef, *Era of Exploration*, 82.

7. Quoted in Sears, *Sacred Places*, 134.

8. Quoted in Sears, *Sacred Places*, 128.

9. Huth, "Yosemite" (emphasis mine).

10. Huth, "Yosemite."

11. Robert Denning, "A Fragile Machine: California Senator John Conness," *California History* 85, no. 4 (2008): 29.

12. Albert D. Richardson, *Beyond the Mississippi: From the Great River to the Great Ocean, Life and Adventure on the Prairies, Mountains, and Pacific Coast* (Hartford CT: American, 1867), 443.

13. This and subsequent excerpts from the Senate floor debate are from Cong. Globe, 38th Cong., 1st sess. (1864), 2300–2301.

14. Allen C. Guelzo, *Fateful Lighting: A New History of the Civil War & Reconstruction* (New York: Oxford University Press, 2013), 289.

15. Quoted in Guelzo, *Fateful Lightning*, 289.

16. Ulysses S. Grant, *Memoirs and Selected Letters* (New York: Library of America, 1990), 774.

17. Joseph H. Engbeck Jr., *The Enduring Giants*, 3rd ed. (Sacramento: California Department of Parks and Recreation, 1988), 76.

18. Engbeck, *Enduring Giants*, 77.

19. Engbeck, *Enduring Giants*, 77.

20. Francis Farquhar, *History of the Sierra Nevada* (Berkeley: University of California Press, 1969), 85.

21. Engbeck, *Enduring Giants*, 78.

22. Engbeck, *Enduring Giants*, 78.

23. Quoted in Huth, "Yosemite."

24. Farquhar, *History of the Sierra Nevada*, 85.

25. Quoted in Huth, "Yosemite."

26. Josiah D. Whitney, *The Yosemite Book: A Description of the Yosemite Valley and the Adjacent Region of the Sierra Nevada, and of the Big Trees of California* (New York: Julius Bien, 1869), https://www/yosemite.ca.us/library/the_yosemite_book/chapter _1.html.

27. Huth, "Yosemite."

28. Alfred Runte, *Yosemite: The Embattled Wilderness* (Lincoln: University of Nebraska Press, 1990), 3.

29. William M. Stewart, *Reminiscences of Senator William M. Stewart of Nevada*, ed. George Rothwell Brown (New York: Neale, 1908), 191.

7. IN PRAISE OF DILIGENT INDOLENCE

1. Samuel Bowles, *Our New West: Records of Travel between the Mississippi River and the Pacific Ocean* (Boulder CO: University Libraries, n.d.), 425.

2. Frederick Law Olmsted, *The Papers of Frederick Law Olmsted* (Baltimore: Johns Hopkins University Press, 1986), 5:23.

3. Olmsted, *Papers*, 5:4.

4. Laura Roper, *FLO: A Biography of Frederick Law Olmsted* (Baltimore: Johns Hopkins University Press, 1973), 235.

5. Bowles, *Our New West*, 425.

6. Roper, *FLO*, 242–43.

7. Roper, *FLO*, 247.

8. Witold Rybczynski, *A Clearing in the Distance: Frederick Law Olmsted and America in the 19th Century* (New York: Touchstone, 2000), 231.

9. Olmsted, *Papers*, 3:7.

10. Rybczynski, *Clearing in the Distance*, 234.

11. Rybczynski, *Clearing in the Distance*, 236.

12. Charles Beveridge, ed., *Frederick Law Olmsted: Writings on Landscape, Culture, and Society* (New York: Library of America, 2015), 712.

13. Beveridge, *Frederick Law Olmsted*, 483.

14. Rybsczynski, *Clearing in the Distance*, 242.

15. Samuel Bowles, *Across the Continent: A Summer's Journey to the Rocky Mountains, the Mormons, and the Pacific States, with Speaker Colfax* (Springfield MA: Samuel Bowles, 1865), iii.

16. George S. Merriam, *The Life and Times of Samuel Bowles* (1885; repr., St. Clair Shores MI: Scholarly Press, 1970), 2, 15.

17. John Keats, letter of February 19, 1818, to John Hamilton Reynolds, http://www.john -keats.com/briefe/190218.htm.

18. Frederick Law Olmsted, *Yosemite and the Mariposa Grove: A Preliminary Report, 1865* (Yosemite National Park CA: Yosemite Association, 2009), 1.

19. Olmsted, *Yosemite and the Mariposa Grove*, 2–3.

20. Olmsted, *Yosemite and the Mariposa Grove*, 9.

21. Olmsted, *Papers*, 6:61.

22. "The Yosemite Valley and the Mariposa Big Trees: A Preliminary Report (1865) by Frederick Law Olmsted, with an Introductory Note by Laura Wood Roper," *Landscape Architecture* 43, no. 1 (October 1952): 17.

23. Olmsted, *Yosemite and the Mariposa Grove*, 11.

24. Olmsted, *Yosemite and the Mariposa Grove*, 11–13.

25. Olmsted, *Yosemite and the Mariposa Grove*, 17.

26. Olmsted, *Yosemite and the Mariposa Grove*, 18.

27. Olmsted, *Yosemite and the Mariposa Grove*, 24.

28. Olmsted, *Yosemite and the Mariposa Grove*, 16.

29. Olmsted, *Yosemite and the Mariposa Grove*, 16.

30. Ralph Waldo Emerson, "Thoreau," *Atlantic Monthly* 58 (August 1862), https://www.theatlantic.com/magazine/archive/1862/08/thoreau/306418/.

31. Olmsted, *Yosemite and the Mariposa Grove*, 7–8.

32. André Gide, *The Counterfeiters with Journal of "The Counterfeiters,"* trans. Dorothy Bussy (New York: Vintage, 1973), 171.

33. Olmsted, *Yosemite and the Mariposa Grove*, 6.

34. Albert D. Richardson, *Beyond the Mississippi: From the Great River to the Great Ocean, Life and Adventure on the Prairies, Mountains, and Pacific Coast* (Hartford CT: American, 1867), 431.

35. Richardson, *Beyond the Mississippi*, 420.

36. Olmsted, *Yosemite and the Mariposa Grove*, 4.

37. Olmsted, *Yosemite and the Mariposa Grove*, 7.

38. Olmsted, *Yosemite and the Mariposa Grove*, 5, 8–9.

39. Olmsted, *Papers*, 8:153.

40. "Theodore Roosevelt Quotes," National Park Service, last updated April 10, 2015, https://www.nps.gov/thro/learn/historyculture/theodore-roosevelt-quotes.htm.

41. Josiah D. Whitney, *The Yosemite Guide-Book* (Cambridge MA: Welch, Bigelow, 1869), 21.

42. Bowles, *Across the Continent*, 430.

43. Francis Farquhar, *History of the Sierra Nevada* (Berkeley: University of California Press, 1969), 138.

44. Olmsted, *Yosemite and the Mariposa Grove*, 3.

8. THE NERVOUS PROMOTER

1. Quoted in George S. Merriam, *The Life and Times of Samuel Bowles* (1885; repr., St. Clair Shores MI: Scholarly Press, 1970), 1:100.

2. Quoted in Merriam, *Life and Times*, 1:179.

3. Quoted in Merriam, *Life and Times*, 1:222.

4. Samuel Bowles, *Our New West: Records of Travel between the Mississippi River and the Pacific Ocean* (Boulder CO: University Libraries, n.d.), 156–57.

5. Perry Miller, ed., *Major Writers of America* (New York: Harcourt, Brace & World, 1962), 2:39, 44.

6. Merriam, *Life and Times*, 2:79.

7. Samuel Bowles, *Across the Continent: A Summer's Journey to the Rocky Mountains, the Mormons, and the Pacific States, with Speaker Colfax* (Springfield MA: Samuel Bowles, 1865), 230–31.

8. Bowles, *Across the Continent*, 231.

9. Bowles, *Across the Continent*, iv.

10. Quoted in Aubrey L. Haines, *Yellowstone National Park: Its Exploration and Establishment* (Washington DC: U.S. Department of the Interior, 1974), 33.

11. Merriam, *Life and Times*, 2:80.

12. Bowles, *Our New West*, 385.

13. Merriam, *Life and Times*, 2:427.

14. Thomas H. Johnson, *Emily Dickinson: An Interpretive Biography* (New York: Atheneum, 1976), 254.

15. Johnson, *Emily Dickinson*, 254.

16. Quoted in Merriam, *Life and Times*, 2:449.

17. Frederick Law Olmsted, *The Papers of Frederick Law Olmsted* (Baltimore: Johns Hopkins University Press, 1986), 5:36; Witold Rybczynski, *A Clearing in the Distance: Frederick Law Olmsted and America in the 19th Century* (New York: Touchstone, 2000), 260.

18. Frederick Law Olmsted Jr. and Theodora Kimball, eds., *Frederick Law Olmsted: Landscape Architect, 1822–1903* (1922; repr., New York: Benjamin Blom, 1970), 2:80.

19. Bowles, *Across the Continent*, 310–11.

9. CONTESTED GROUND

1. Samuel Bowles, *Our New West: Records of Travel between the Mississippi River and the Pacific Ocean* (Boulder CO: University Libraries, n.d.), 384–85.

2. Hans Huth, "Yosemite: The Story of an Idea," *Sierra Club Bulletin* 33, no. 3 (March 1948).

3. Alfred Runte, *Yosemite: The Embattled Wilderness* (Lincoln: University of Nebraska Press, 1990), 18.

4. Runte, *Yosemite*, 23.

5. Runte, *Yosemite*, 24.

6. *New York Evening Post*, June 18, 1868, 2.

7. *New York Evening Post*, June 18, 1868, 2.

8. *New York Evening Post*, June 18, 1868, 2.

9. Runte, *Yosemite*, 24–25.

10. Runte, *Yosemite*, 25–26.

11. Hutchings v. Low, 82 U.S. 77 (1872). Subsequent excerpts are from this case.

12. Francis Farquhar, *History of the Sierra Nevada* (Berkeley: University of California Press, 1969), 124–26.

13. Richard West Sellars, *Preserving Nature in the National Parks* (New Haven CT: Yale University Press, 1997), 18.

14. Runte, *Yosemite*, 52.

15. Alfred Runte, *National Parks: The American Experience*, 3rd ed. (Lincoln: University of Nebraska Press, 1997), 164.

16. Runte, *Yosemite*, 42.

17. Douglas H. Strong, *Dreamers & Defenders: American Conservationists* (Lincoln: University of Nebraska Press, 1997), 91.

18. Ashburner v. California, 103 U.S. 575, 579, 578 (1880).

19. H. Duane Hampton, *How the U.S. Cavalry Saved Our National Parks* (Bloomington: Indiana University Press, 2017), 140–41.

20. Roderick Nash, *Wilderness and the American Mind* (New Haven CT: Yale University Press, 1967), 131.

21. Charles Beveridge, ed., *Frederick Law Olmsted: Writings on Landscape, Culture, and Society* (New York: Library of America, 2015), 673–75.

22. Hampton, *How the U.S. Cavalry*, 141.

23. Runte, *Yosemite*, 55.

24. Quoted in Richard J. Orsi, *Sunset Limited: The Southern Pacific Railroad and the Development of the American West, 1850–1930* (Berkeley: University of California Press, 2005), 352.

25. John Muir, *The Yosemite* (New York: Century, 1912), https://yosemite.ca.us/john_muir_writings/the_yosemite/chapter_16.html.

10. WHIFFS OF SULFUR

1. Hiram Martin Chittenden, *The Yellowstone Park* (1895; repr., Norman: University of Oklahoma Press, 1964), 7.

2. Chittenden, *Yellowstone Park*, 49.

3. Quoted in Merrill J. Mattes, "Behind the Legend of Colter's Hell: The Early Exploration of Yellowstone National Park," *Mississippi Valley Historical Review* 36, no. 2 (September 1949): 266.

4. George Black, *Empire of Shadows: The Epic Story of Yellowstone* (New York: St. Martin's, 2012), 77.

5. Albert Matthews, "The Word Park in the United States," *Publications of the Colonial Society of Massachusetts* 8 (1906): 373–99.

6. Aubrey L. Haines, *Yellowstone National Park: Its Exploration and Establishment* (Washington DC: U.S. Department of the Interior, 1974), 26. The next few pages rely mainly on this source.

7. Haines, *Yellowstone National Park*, 29.

8. Haines, *Yellowstone National Park*, 33, 45.

9. Haines, *Yellowstone National Park*, 47.

10. Haines, *Yellowstone National Park*, 165.

11. Haines, *Yellowstone National Park*, 56.

12. Haines, *Yellowstone National Park*, 54.

13. Haines, *Yellowstone National Park*, 63.

14. Quoted in Aubrey L. Haines, *The Yellowstone Story: A History of Our First National Park* (Yellowstone National Park WY: Yellowstone Library and Museum Association, 1977), 1:108.

15. Lee H. Whittlesey, ed., *Lost in the Yellowstone: "Thirty-Seven Days of Peril" and a Handwritten Account of Being Lost*, 2nd ed. (Salt Lake City: University of Utah Press, 2015), 4. The next several paragraphs rely mainly on this source.

16. Quoted in Whittlesey, *Lost*, 4–5.

17. Whittlesey, *Lost*, 5–6.

18. Whittlesey, *Lost*, 8.

19. Whittlesey, *Lost*, 10.

20. Whittlesey, *Lost*, 11–12.

21. Whittlesey, *Lost*, 18.

22. Whittlesey, *Lost*, 21.

23. Nathaniel Pitt Langford, *The Discovery of Yellowstone Park: Journal of the Washburn Expedition to the Yellowstone and Firehole Rivers in the Year 1870* (1905; repr., Lincoln: University of Nebraska Press, 1972), 47.

24. Haines, *Yellowstone Story*, 1:129.

25. Whittlesey, *Lost*, 32.

26. Whittlesey, *Lost*, 46–48.

27. Haines, *Yellowstone Story*, 1:132.

28. Whittlesey, *Lost*, 53–54.

29. Whittlesey, *Lost*, 58.

30. Marlene Deane Merrill, ed., *Yellowstone and the Great West: Journals, Letters, and Images from the 1871 Hayden Expedition* (Lincoln: University of Nebraska Press, 1999), 172.

31. Whittlesey, *Lost*, 60.

32. Nathaniel Langford, "The Wonders of the Yellowstone," *Scribner's Monthly* 2, no. 1–2 (May–June 1871), 10.

33. Langford, *Discovery of Yellowstone Park*, 117–18.

34. John Clayton, *Wonderlandscape: Yellowstone National Park and the Evolution of an American Cultural Icon* (New York: Pegasus, 2017), 90.

35. Langford, "Wonders of the Yellowstone," 128.

36. Matthews, "Word Park," 399.

37. Haines, *Yellowstone Story*, 1:135.

38. Paul Schullery and Lee Whittlesey, *Myth and History in the Creation of Yellowstone National Park* (Lincoln: University of Nebraska Press, 2003), 59.

39. Langford, *Discovery of Yellowstone Park*, 118.

40. Quoted in Haines, *Yellowstone National Park*, 85.

41. Haines, *Yellowstone National Park*, 86.

42. Mike Foster, *Strange Genius: The Life of Ferdinand Vandeveer Hayden* (Niwot CO: Roberts Rinehart, 1994), 205.

11. THE MAN WHO PICKED UP STONES

1. Mike Foster, *Strange Genius: The Life of Ferdinand Vandeveer Hayden* (Niwot CO: Roberts Rinehart, 1994), 11.

2. James G. Cassidy, *Ferdinand V. Hayden: Entrepreneur of Science* (Lincoln: University of Nebraska Press, 2000), 36.

3. Foster, *Strange Genius*, 39.

4. Mark Twain, *Roughing It* (1872; repr., New York: Penguin Classics, 1981), 337; Samuel Bowles, *Across the Continent: A Summer's Journey to the Rocky Mountains, the Mormons, and the Pacific States, with Speaker Colfax* (Springfield MA: Samuel Bowles, 1865), 335.

5. Foster, *Strange Genius*, 63.

6. Foster, *Strange Genius*, 65–66.

7. Foster, *Strange Genius*, 75.

8. Foster, *Strange Genius*, 81.

9. Foster, *Strange Genius*, 82.

10. Foster, *Strange Genius*, 86.

11. William H. Goetzmann, *Exploration and Empire: The Explorer and the Scientist in the Winning of the American West* (New York: W. W. Norton, 1978), 493

12. Foster, *Strange Genius*, 117.

13. Cassidy, *Ferdinand V. Hayden*, 77.

14. Foster, *Strange Genius*, 156.

15. Foster, *Strange Genius*, 166.

16. Goetzmann, *Exploration and Empire*, 498.

17. William Henry Jackson, *Time Exposure: The Autobiography of William Henry Jackson* (1940; repr., Albuquerque: University of New Mexico Press, 1986), 26.

18. Weston J. Naef, *Era of Exploration: The Rise of Landscape Photography in the American West, 1860–1885* (Buffalo NY: Albright-Knox Art Gallery, 1975), 220.

19. Naef, *Era of Exploration*, 220.

20. Foster, *Strange Genius*, 169.

21. Jackson, *Time Exposure*, 236.

22. Naef, *Era of Exploration*, 221.

23. Jackson, *Time Exposure*, 186.

24. F. V. Hayden, *Preliminary Report of the United States Geological Survey of Montana and Portions of Adjacent Territories, Being a Fifth Annual Report of Progress* (Washington DC: Government Printing Office, 1872), 162.

25. George Black, *Empire of Shadows: The Epic Story of Yellowstone* (New York: St. Martin's, 2012), 344.

26. Alfred Runte, *Trains of Discovery: Western Railroads and the National Parks*, 4th ed. (Lanham MD: Roberts Rinehart, 1998), 18.

27. Hayden, *Preliminary Report*, 3.

28. Marlene Deane Merrill, ed., *Yellowstone and the Great West: Journals, Letters, and Images from the 1871 Hayden Expedition* (Lincoln: University of Nebraska Press, 1999), 63.

29. Jackson, *Time Exposure*, 197.

30. Hayden, *Preliminary Report*, 90.

31. Merrill, *Yellowstone and the Great West*, 27.

32. Hayden, *Preliminary Report*, 158.

33. Hayden, *Preliminary Report*, 18, 79, 81.

34. Hayden, *Preliminary Report*, 96, 115, 65.

35. Hayden, *Preliminary Report*, 123.

36. Aubrey L. Haines, *Yellowstone National Park: Its Exploration and Establishment* (Washington DC: U.S. Department of the Interior, 1974), 106.

37. Goetzmann, *Exploration and Empire*, 511.

38. Haines, *Yellowstone National Park*, 104–5.

39. Haines, *Yellowstone National Park*, 103.

40. Merrill, *Yellowstone and the Great West*, 180.

12. SAVING GRAVEL

1. M. John Lubetkin, *Jay Cooke's Gamble: The Northern Pacific Railroad, the Sioux, and the Panic of 1873* (Norman: University of Oklahoma Press, 2006), 58.

2. Aubrey L. Haines, *The Yellowstone Story: A History of Our First National Park* (Yellowstone National Park WY: Yellowstone Library and Museum Association, 1977), 1:350.

3. Haines, *Yellowstone Story*, 1:155.

4. Aubrey L. Haines, *Yellowstone National Park: Its Exploration and Establishment* (Washington DC: U.S. Department of the Interior, 1974), 110.

5. Nathaniel Pitt Langford, *The Discovery of Yellowstone Park: Journal of the Washburn Expedition to the Yellowstone and Firehole Rivers in the Year 1870* (1905; repr., Lincoln: University of Nebraska Press, 1972), xlvii–xlviii.

6. Hiram Martin Chittenden, *The Yellowstone Park* (1895; repr., Norman: University of Oklahoma Press, 1964), 82.

7. Robert Hughes, *American Visions: The Epic History of Art in America* (New York: Knopf, 1997), 200.

8. William Henry Jackson, *Time Exposure: The Autobiography of William Henry Jackson* (1940; repr., Albuquerque: University of New Mexico Press, 1986), 200.

9. Jackson, *Time Exposure*, 196.

10. F. V. Hayden, *Preliminary Report of the United States Geological Survey of Montana and Portions of Adjacent Territories, Being a Fifth Annual Report of Progress* (Washington DC: Government Printing Office, 1872), 163.

11. Haines, *Yellowstone National Park*, 118–19.

12. Haines, *Yellowstone National Park*, 119.

13. Quoted in Haines, *Yellowstone National Park*, 122.

14. Haines, *Yellowstone National Park*, 124.

15. Hayden, *Preliminary Report*, 164–65.

16. Quoted in Chris J. Magoc, *Yellowstone: The Creation and Selling of an American Landscape, 1870–1903* (Albuquerque: University of New Mexico Press, 1999), 35, 19.

17. Hayden, *Preliminary Report*, 162.

18. Quoted in Haines, *Yellowstone National Park*, 128.

19. Magoc, *Yellowstone*, 167.

20. Quoted in M. John Lubetkin, *Jay Cooke's Gamble: The Northern Pacific Railroad, the Sioux, and the Panic of 1873* (Norman: University of Oklahoma Press, 2006), 144

21. Quoted in Lubetkin, *Jay Cooke's Gamble*, 277.

22. Quoted in Lubetkin, *Jay Cooke's Gamble*, 275.

23. Quoted in T. J. Stiles, *Custer's Trials: A Life on the Frontier of a New America* (New York: Knopf, 2015), 402–3.

24. Jackson, *Time Exposure*, 222.

25. Lubetkin, *Jay Cooke's Gamble*, 285.

26. William H. Goetzmann, *Exploration and Empire: The Explorer and the Scientist in the Winning of the American West* (New York: W. W. Norton, 1978), 519–20.

27. James G. Cassidy, *Ferdinand V. Hayden: Entrepreneur of Science* (Lincoln: University of Nebraska Press, 2000), 189, 192.

28. Marlene Deane Merrill, ed., *Yellowstone and the Great West: Journals, Letters, and Images from the 1871 Hayden Expedition* (Lincoln: University of Nebraska Press, 1999), 206.

29. Donald Worster, *A River Running West: The Life of John Wesley Powell* (Oxford University Press, 2001), 365.

30. Mike Foster, *Strange Genius: The Life of Ferdinand Vandeveer Hayden* (Niwot CO: Roberts Rinehart, 1994), 314–15.

31. Worster, *River Running West*, 365.

13. A SHAKY START

1. Aubrey L. Haines, *The Yellowstone Story: A History of Our First National Park* (Yellowstone National Park WY: Yellowstone Library and Museum Association, 1977), 1:179.

2. Elliott West, *The Last Indian War: The Nez Perce Story* (Oxford University Press, 2009), 87, 90.

3. West, *Last Indian War*, 155.

4. West, *Last Indian War*, 291, 223.

5. Nathaniel Pitt Langford, *The Discovery of Yellowstone Park: Journal of the Washburn Expedition to the Yellowstone and Firehole Rivers in the Year 1870* (1905; repr., Lincoln: University of Nebraska Press, 1972), xlix.

6. Haines, *Yellowstone Story*, 2:106.

7. H. Duane Hampton, *How the U.S. Cavalry Saved Our National Parks* (Bloomington: Indiana University Press, 2017), 40–41.

8. Haines, *Yellowstone Story*, 1:322–23.

9. John Taliaferro, *Grinnell: America's Environmental Pioneer and His Relentless Drive to Save the West* (New York: Liveright, 2019), 116.

10. Quoted in Taliaferro, *Grinnell*, 117, 119.

11. Chris J. Magoc, *Yellowstone: The Creation and Selling of an American Landscape, 1870–1903* (Albuquerque: University of New Mexico Press, 1999), 64, 65.

12. Magoc, *Yellowstone*, 78, 63.

13. Magoc, *Yellowstone*, 60–61.

14. Haines, *Yellowstone Story*, 2:257.

15. Haines, *Yellowstone Story*, 2:347.

16. Hampton, *How the U.S. Cavalry*, 167.

17. Hampton, *How the U.S. Cavalry*, 183–84, 190.

18. Brian C. Kalt, "The Perfect Crime," *Georgetown Law Review* 93, no. 675 (2005): 677.

19. Kalt, "Perfect Crime," 677.

20. Kalt, "Perfect Crime," 678.

14. CLEANING MEN

1. Quoted in Pierre Berton, *Niagara: A History of the Falls* (New York: Kodansha International, 1997), 135.

2. Mariana Griswold Van Rensselaer, *Henry Hobson Richardson and His Works* (New York: Dover, 1969), 27.

3. Francis R. Kowsky, *The Best Planned City in the World: Olmsted, Vaux, and the Buffalo Park System* (Amherst MA: Library of American Landscape History, 2013), 160.

4. Elizabeth McKinsey, *Niagara Falls: Icon of the American Sublime* (Cambridge: Cambridge University Press, 1985), 263.

5. Quoted in Kowsky, *Best Planned City*, 162.

6. Kowsky, *Best Planned City*, 163.

7. Berton, *Niagara*, 137.

8. Charles Beveridge, ed., *Frederick Law Olmsted: Writings on Landscape, Culture, and Society* (New York: Library of America, 2015), 565.

9. Chris J. Magoc, *Yellowstone: The Creation and Selling of an American Landscape, 1870–1903* (Albuquerque: University of New Mexico Press, 1999), 83.

10. *The Distinctive Charms of Niagara Scenery: Frederick Law Olmsted and the Niagara Reservation* (Niagara Falls NY: Buscaglia-Castellani Art Gallery of Niagara University, 1985), 22.

11. Frederick Law Olmsted, *The Papers of Frederick Law Olmsted* (Baltimore: Johns Hopkins University Press, 1986), 7:473.

12. Olmsted, *Papers*, 7:473.

13. Olmsted, *Papers*, 7:471–72.

14. Justin Martin, *Genius of Place: The Life of Frederick Law Olmsted* (Boston: Da Capo, 2012), 348.

15. Berton, *Niagara*, 140.

16. Laura Roper, *FLO: A Biography of Frederick Law Olmsted* (Baltimore: Johns Hopkins University Press, 1973), 381.

17. Berton, *Niagara*, 141.

18. Van Rensselaer, *Henry Hobson Richardson*, 38; Kowsky, *Best Planned City*, 164.

19. *Distinctive Charms*, 13.

20. Quoted in Kowsky, *Best Planned City*, 167.

21. Martin, *Genius of Place*, 349.

22. Roper, *FLO*, 396.

23. Berton, *Niagara*, 146.

24. Berton, *Niagara*, 148.

25. Berton, *Niagara*, 149.

26. Kowsky, *Best Planned City*, 169.

27. *Distinctive Charms*, 23.

28. Kowsky, *Best Planned City*, 170.

29. *Distinctive Charms*, 7.

30. Kowsky, *Best Planned City*, 170.

31. Witold Rybczynski, *A Clearing in the Distance: Frederick Law Olmsted and America in the 19th Century* (New York: Touchstone, 2000), 374.

32. Kowsky, *Best Planned City*, 153.

33. W. D. Howells, Mark Twain, Nathaniel S. Shaler, et al., *The Niagara Book*, new and rev. ed. (New York: Doubleday, Page, 1901), 264–65.

34. *Distinctive Charms*, 14.

15. GOING OUT WITH TWO BANGS

1. Frederick Law Olmsted, *The Papers of Frederick Law Olmsted* (Baltimore: Johns Hopkins University Press, 1986), 7:6.

2. Laura Roper, *FLO: A Biography of Frederick Law Olmsted* (Baltimore: Johns Hopkins University Press, 1973), 331, 351.

3. Charles Beveridge, ed., *Frederick Law Olmsted: Writings on Landscape, Culture, and Society* (New York: Library of America, 2015), 584–85.

4. Roper, *FLO*, 435.

5. Roper, *FLO*, 384.

6. John F. Sears, *Sacred Places: American Tourist Attractions in the Nineteenth Century* (1989; repr., Amherst: University of Massachusetts Press, 1998), 229.

7. Witold Rybczynski, *A Clearing in the Distance: Frederick Law Olmsted and America in the 19th Century* (New York: Touchstone, 2000), 385.

8. Rybczynski, *Clearing in the Distance*, 355.

9. Beveridge, *Frederick Law Olmsted*, 701.

10. Rybczynski, *Clearing in the Distance*, 391–92.

11. Roper, *FLO*, 447.

12. William Cronon, ed., *Uncommon Ground: Toward Reinventing Nature* (New York: Norton, 1995), 485.

13. Quoted in Roper, *FLO*, 418.

14. Beveridge, *Frederick Law Olmsted*, 653, 667.

15. Roper, *FLO*, 418.

16. Gifford Pinchot, *Breaking New Ground* (1947; repr., Washington DC: Island Press, 1998), 49.

17. Char Miller, *Gifford Pinchot and the Making of Modern Environmentalism* (Washington DC: Island Press, 2001), 113–14.

18. Roper, *FLO*, 454.

19. Olmsted, *Papers*, 9:49–50.

20. Roper, *FLO*, 420.

21. Roper, *FLO*, 467.

16. THE OLMSTEDS

1. Quoted in Alfred Runte, *National Parks: The American Experience*, 3rd ed. (Lincoln: University of Nebraska Press, 1997), 65–66.

2. An Act for the Preservation of American Antiquities, 16 U.S.C. 431–33, 34 Stat. 225 (1906).

3. An Act to Establish a National Park Service, 39 Stat. 535 (1916).

4. Frederick Law Olmsted, *Yosemite and the Mariposa Grove: A Preliminary Report, 1865* (Yosemite National Park CA: Yosemite Association, 2009), 21.

5. Joseph L. Sax, *Mountains without Handrails: Reflections on the National Parks* (Ann Arbor: University of Michigan Press, 1980), 65.

6. Alfred Runte, *Yosemite: The Embattled Wilderness* (Lincoln: University of Nebraska Press, 1990), 130.

7. Sean B. Carroll, *The Serengeti Rules: The Quest to Discover How Life Works and Why It Matters* (Princeton NJ: Princeton University Press, 2016), 178, 182.

8. Runte, *National Parks*, 101.

9. Runte, *National Parks*, 104–5.

10. Paul S. Sutter, *Driven Wild: How the Fight against Automobiles Launched the Modern Wilderness Movement* (Seattle: University of Washington Press, 2002), 102.

11. Sutter, *Driven Wild*, 111.

12. Runte, *Yosemite*, 110.

13. Sutter, *Driven Wild*, 47.

14. Sutter, *Driven Wild*, 208.

15. An Act to Establish a National Wilderness Preservation System, 13 U.S.C. (1964).

16. Bernard DeVoto, "Let's Close the National Parks," *Harper's Magazine* 207 (October 1953): 49–52.

17. Richard West Sellars, *Preserving Nature in the National Parks* (New Haven CT: Yale University Press, 1997), 46.

18. Sellars, *Preserving Nature*, 184.

19. Edward Abbey, *Desert Solitaire: A Season in the Wilderness* (1968; repr., New York: Ballantine, 1971), 10–11.

20. Abbey, *Desert Solitaire*, 48–49.

21. Abbey, *Desert Solitaire*, 67.

22. Samuel Hughes, "Hymn to the Parks," *Pennsylvania Gazette* 108, no. 1 (September–October 2009): 41.

23. Edmund Burke, *On Taste; On the Sublime and Beautiful; Reflections on the French Revolution; A Letter to a Noble Lord* (New York: Collier & Son, 1909), 46.

24. Sax, *Mountains without Handrails*, 42.

25. Sax, *Mountains without Handrails*, 45.

26. Sax, *Mountains without Handrails*, 88.

27. U.S. Department of the Interior (DOI), "A Preliminary Urban Parks Study," January 1977, 2.

28. DOI, "Preliminary Urban Parks Study," 12–13.

29. "Canyonlands," National Park Service, last updated January 14, 2021, http://www .nps.gov/cany/index.htm.

30. National Park Service, DOI, *Management Policies 2006: The Guide to Managing the National Park System*, August 31, 2006, https://www.nps.gov/policy/mp/policies .html.

31. Charles Beveridge, ed., *Frederick Law Olmsted: Writings on Landscape, Culture, and Society* (New York: Library of America, 2015), 403.

32. Tony Horwitz, *Spying on the South: An Odyssey across the American Divide* (New York: Penguin, 2019), 152.

33. Horwitz, *Spying on the South*, 152–53.

34. Beveridge, *Frederick Law Olmsted*, 564.

35. Olmsted, *Yosemite and the Mariposa Grove*, 17–18.

INDEX

Page numbers with f *indicate photos.*

Abbey, Edward, 209, 210
Across the Continent (Bowles), 93, 94
Adirondacks innovation, 192
Ahwahneechee tribe, 61, 112
Alaska National Interest Lands Conservation Act, 201, 214
Albright, Horace, F9, xvi, 130–33, 205
Allen, George, 146, 149
American mores or institutions, 3–4
American Notes (Dickens), 2
American scenery, 10, 22
Antiquities Act, 200, 201
antiwolf policy, 204, 205
Ashburner v. California, 109
The Asylum, or Alonzo and Melissa (Mitchell), 8
At Home and Abroad (Taylor), 6
Audubon Park, 215

backpacking, 208, 214
Baird, Spencer, 134, 136, 137, 138, 141, 144
Barlow, John, 145, 150
Barnum, Phineas T., 71, 72
Bellows, Henry Whitney, 54, 57, 63, 76, 78, 192
Bierstadt, Albert, 65, 66
Biltmore Estate, 189, 191, 194–95
bison/buffalo, 117, 170, 173, 175, 203–4; Catlin on, 27–28, 31, 34–35

Blaine, James G., 134
Blondin (Jean François Gravelet), 24–25
Bowles, Samuel, F5, xix, 17, 76, 80–81, 91–99, 191
Brace, Charles Loring, 41, 42, 43, 159, 190, 192
Breaking New Ground (Pinchot), 195
Bridger, Jim, 116, 117, 118, 138

campfire myth, F11, 94, 115, 120, 121, 130–32
Canadian Rockies, xvi, 199
Carpenter, Robert Emmett, 172, 173
Catlin, George, xiii; death of, 34; early life of, 30–31; and fondness for Indians, 31–32, 34; and Henry David Thoreau, 28; marriage of, 31; "nation's park idea" of, 203–4; paintings by, 32–34; and vision of refuge for Indians, 27, 30
Central Park, xiv, xvii, 46, 48–52
Chase, Salmon P., 121, 122
Chicago World's Fair, 191, 193. *See also* World's Columbian Exposition
Chittenden, Hiram Martin, 116, 131, 153
Church, Frederic, 180, 182
city parks, 6, 29, 37, 41, 193
Civil War, 54, 62, 91, 140
Clagett, William H., 152, 153, 156
Clark, William, 8, 31, 115, 144

Cole, Thomas, 9–10
Colfax, Schuyler, 80, 81, 94, 96
concessions in parks, 107–8, 160, 165, 168, 170, 171
Conness, John, F4, xiii, 65–74, 132, 164
Cook, Charlie, F9, 120–23, 130, 133–34
Cooke, Jay, 122, 134, 151–52, 158–60
Crystal Palace Exhibition, 70, 71, 72

Dana, Charles A., 75
De Lacy, Walter Washington, 119, 122
Delano, Columbus, 144, 149, 155
Desert Solitaire (Abbey), 209–10
Dickens, Charles, 1–4, 14, 33, 39
Doane, Gustavus, 122, 126, 134, 145
Domestic Manners of the Americans (Trollope), 3, 4, 21
Dorsheimer, William, 179, 181, 184, 185
Downing, Andrew Jackson, 29–30, 37, 41, 47, 49–51, 192
Drake, Joseph Rodman, 6, 7, 8
Dred Scott decision, 92
Drury, Newton, 203
Duncan, Dayton, 210–11
Dunnell, Mark H., 155, 156

Elliott, Charles William, 162–63
Elliott, Henry Wood, 145, 149, 154
Everts, Truman C., 122, 123, 125–29

federal land, 66, 73, 78, 105, 171, 200–201
Field, Stephen J., 105
firefall at Yosemite Valley, 107, 207
Folsom, David E., 120, 121, 122, 132
forest fires, 169–70
Foster, Lafayette Sabine, 68, 69
Franklin, Benjamin, 204

Gardner, James T., 102, 161, 181, 182
geysers, 116, 118–21, 136, 142, 148, 182
Goat Island, 179–80

Gore, Sir St. George, 117, 118
Grand Canyon, 88, 127, 146, 153–54, 209, 211
Greeley, Horace, 62, 64, 67, 71, 72
Green, Andrew Haswell, 53, 98, 185, 187–88
Greensward Plan, 50, 51, 53, 98, 189
Grinnell, George Bird, 170, 204

Haines, Aubrey, 127, 132, 151, 156, 174
Halleck, Fitz-Greene, 7, 8
Hanford, W. H., 71, 72
Harrison, Jonathan Baxter, 184, 185, 186
Hatch, Rufus, 170, 171, 172
Hayden, Ferdinand, xiv, xv; and Alvred Nettleton, 144, 152; death of, 164; early life of, 135; education of, 135–36; explorations undertaken by, 136–50; and Ferdinand Meek, 136, 139; and fossils, 138; and Henry Elliott, 145, 154; illness of, 163–64; and James Gardner, 161; and Jim Bridger, 118; and John Powell, 162, 163; lobbying by, 144; and Mark Dunnell, 155, 156; as a naturalist, 138–40; park mapping by, 160–61; as a prime mover, F6; as a professor, 140–41; reports prepared by, 142, 146, 149; retirement of, 164; and Spencer Baird, 136; surveys done by, 137, 144, 161; and Thomas Moran, 142, 144–45, 154; at U.S. Geological Survey, 141; and Washburn-Langford Expedition, 134; and William Jackson, 142–43
Hedges, Cornelius, 120, 130, 131, 132, 133
Hetch Hetchy Valley, 113, 114
Higginson, Thomas Wentworth, 35, 36
Holmes, Oliver Wendell, 65
hot springs, 116, 118–19, 124–25, 146–48
Howard, Oliver Otis, 166, 167
Howells, William Dean, 24, 25, 188
Hudson River, 9, 20, 50
Hutchings, James M., 63, 101–6, 108–9, 156
Hutchings v. Low, 105

Indians, xiii, 3, 23; Bowles's disdain for, 92; vision of a refuge for, 27, 30; and Yellowstone country, 115. *See also* Catlin, George

The Innocents Abroad (Twain), 10

international copyright law, 3

Irving, Washington, 5, 7, 46, 47

Jackson, William H., 142, 143, 154, 161

James, Henry, 23, 179, 180, 181

Jefferson, Thomas, xiv, 13, 14

Johnson, Robert Underwood, 109–10

A Journey in the Back Country in the Winter of 1853–54 (Olmsted), 45

A Journey in the Seaboard Slave States (Olmsted), 45

A Journey through Texas (Olmsted), 45

Kalt, Brian C., 176, 177

Kelley, William Darrah "Judge," 151, 152

Kelley-to-Nettleton-to-Hayden initiative, 152–53

Kimball, Theodora, 29

King, Clarence, 102, 163–64, 181

King, Thomas Starr, 62, 78, 135

Kuppens, Francis Xavier, 119, 120

Lacey, John F., 173, 174

Lacey Act, 174

Lamon, James C., 101–4, 106, 156

land use, 201, 212

Langford, Nathaniel, F11, 121–22, 125–26, 128–34, 152–53, 168–69

Leaves of Grass (Whitman), 8, 10

Leopold, Aldo, 207, 208

Lotus-Eating (Curtis), 10

Mammoth Cave, 6, 8

Mammoth Hot Springs, F10, 148, 156

Mariposa Battalion, 61, 63

Mariposa Estate, xvii, 75–79, 94, 99

Mariposa Grove, xvii, 66, 78, 84, 86, 106

Marshall, Robert, 207, 208

Mather, Stephen, 204, 205, 206

Meagher, Thomas, 119, 120

Meek, Fielding B., 136, 139

Melville, Herman, 8, 13

Merced River, 36, 61, 65, 79

The Metallic Wealth of the United States (Whitney), 88

military rule, 173, 174, 175

Mills, William H., 111, 112, 113

miners, 28, 70, 71, 78

Mission 66, 209, 213–14

Moran, Thomas, 130, 142, 144–45, 148–51, 153–54, 162

Mother of the Forest, 71, 73

Mountain Gloom and Morning Glory (Nicholson), 16

mountain men, 61, 117

mountainous sublimity, 16–17

Mountains without Handrails (Sax), 210–11

Mount Rainier, 199, 200

Mowat, Oliver, 180, 183, 185, 186

Mr. Midshipman Easy (Marryat), 4

Muir, John, 36, 108–14

National Association for Olmsted Parks, 215

national monuments, 200, 201, 209

national park movement. *See* park movement

national parks, xiii–xiv; and city dwellers, 51, 212–13; European, 216; idea for, xiv, 19, 29, 34, 35, 115; and road-building in, 209–10; wilderness management in, 207–9

National Park Service: and antiwolf policy, 204, 205; contributions of, 216; creation of, 174–75; dual mandate, 211, 214; first leader of, 205; Mammoth Hot Springs, F10, 148, 156; and Mission 66, 209, 213–14; and Nathaniel Langford, F11; and See America First campaign, 206

National Parks Organic Act, 201, 202, 203
Natural Bridge, 13, 14
natural wonders, 17, 19, 26, 96, 113, 212
Nettleton, Alvred Bayard, 144, 152
New World, 8, 9, 10, 19, 199
Nez Perce, 165–68
The Niagara Book (Howells), 25
Niagara Falls, 8; as American icon of sub-
    lime, 14; businesses attracted to, 20–21;
    as a counterexample, 26; dare-devils at,
    21; and Erie Canal, 20; and Goat Island,
    179–80; government ownership of,
    186; mills around, 21–22; and Niagara
    Reservation, 186–87; painting about,
    25–26; ratings of, 23; recreational users
    at, 19–20; rehabilitation of, 215; and
    scenery preservation petition, 181–84;
    shops around, 22–23; sorry state of, 86;
    tightrope walkers at, 24–25; and tour-
    ists, 16, 20, 22–24; views about, 14–15
Niagara Falls Association, 184, 185
nontreaty Indians, 165, 166
Norris, Philetus W., 169
Northern Pacific Railroad, 121–22, 158–
    60, 165, 170, 172–73
Norton, Charles Eliot, 46, 48, 183–85, 192
Notions of the Americans (Cooper), 5

Old Faithful, F7, 129, 209
Old World, 5, 7, 35, 138
Olmsted, Frederick Law, xiii–xiv; and
    Andrew Green, 53; and appointment to
    state commission, 79–80; and appre-
    ciation of nature, 85–86; and Biltmore
    report, 195; books written by, 45; buggy
    accident of, 53; and Calvert Vaux, 49,
    51, 179–80, 186–87; and camping trip
    with family, 78; as a cape-wearing
    dandy, F2; and Carl Schenck, 197; as
    CEO, 52; and Charles Dana, 75; and
    Charles Norton, 183–85; death of, 196;

early life of, 39–40; frail health of, 196;
    and Gifford Pinchot, 195–97; and Goat
    Island, 179–80; in Great Britain, 41–43;
    and Henry Richardson, 179–80; and
    his brother, 39, 40, 41; and his father,
    40, 42; in his later years, F8; landscap-
    ing projects undertaken by, 189–97;
    as leader of Yosemite Commission,
    xvii–xix; long walks taken by, 39; and
    Mariposa Estate, 75–77; marriage of,
    49; and move to New York, 97–98;
    and Niagara Falls Association, 184;
    and Olmsted legacy, 215–16; and
    park movement, 37–38, 44; as park
    superintendent, 46–49; presence of, in
    Chicago, 193–94; and Prospect Park,
    179; reputation of, xiv; and Richard
    Hunt, 194; and Robert Johnson, 110;
    and Samuel Bowles, 17, 76, 80–81,
    94–99, 191; and Sanitary Commission,
    54–59, 75–76; and scenery preserva-
    tion petition, 181–84; sons of, 191;
    and southerners, 43–45; and William
    Dorsheimer, 179; at Yale College, F1.
    See also Yosemite Valley
Olmsted, Rick, 196, 202, 205
The Oregon Trail (Parkman), 17
Organic Act. *See* National Parks Organic
    Act
Our New West (Bowles), 95, 101
An Overland Journey (Greeley), 64

park movement, xiii, 37–38, 44, 195, 199, 216
parks: city, 6, 29, 37, 41, 193; description
    of, 29; open-to-all, 47; public, xviii, 29,
    41, 47; urban, xiii, 20, 189, 212, 213. *See
    also* national parks
Peale, Albert C., 145, 146
*A Philosophical Enquiry into the Origin of
    Our Ideas of the Sublime and Beautiful*
    (Burke), 15, 18

Pinchot, Gifford, 195–97
poaching, 165, 168–70, 173
Poe, Edgar Allan, 6, 7
Poker Joe, 167
Powell, John Wesley, 162, 163
Preliminary Report of the United States
    Geological Survey of Montana and
    Portions of Adjacent Territories; being
    a Fifth Annual Report of Progress
    (Hayden), 143–50
Prospect Park, 23, 179
public land, 101–2, 104, 105, 108, 156
public parks, xviii, 29, 41, 47

Raymond, Israel Ward, 66–68, 89, 90,
    101, 152
recreation areas, 201, 213
Report of Progress of the Exploration in
    Wyoming and Idaho for the Year 1878
    (Hayden), 162
Richardson, Albert, 86, 87
Richardson, Henry Hobson, 179, 180, 192
Roper, Laura Wood, 47, 82, 103, 191
Roughing It (Twain), 64

Sax, Joseph L., 211, 212
Scenes of Wonder and Curiosity in Califor-
    nia (Hutchings), 64
Schoolcraft, Henry Rowe, 137
See America First campaign, 206
sequoias, 69, 86, 87
Sierra Nevada, 61–63, 101, 108, 111, 199
Sitting Bull, 159, 167, 168
slavery issue, 3, 43, 44, 45
Southern Pacific R.R. Co., 111, 112, 113
Special Report of the New York State Survey
    on the Preservation of the Scenery of
    Niagara Falls, 181
squatters, 93, 101, 148
Sundry Civil Appropriation Act, 172, 173
The Switzerland of America (Bowles), 95

Taylor, Bayard, 6, 8
Thoreau, Henry David, 27, 28, 35–36
tightrope walkers, 24–25
Time Exposure (Jackson), 143
tourists: charges levied on, 23–24; and
    Niagara Falls, 16, 20, 22
transcontinental railroad, 18, 64, 66, 74,
    104, 151
Travels through Part of the United States and
    Canada in 1818 and 1819 (Duncan), 16
Trollope, Fanny, 3, 4, 14, 15, 21
Twain, Mark, 10, 23, 64, 65, 136, 158
Tweed Ring, 189, 190

Ulrich, Rudolph, 193
Union Pacific Railroad, 141, 151
Union soldiers, 54, 55
urban parks, xiii, 20, 189, 212, 213
U.S. Army Corps of Engineers, 153, 182
U.S. Forest Service, 195, 201
U.S. Sanitary Commission, 54–59, 62, 76

Vanderbilt, George Washington, 194, 195
Vaux, Calvert, 49, 51, 97–98, 179–80,
    186–87, 192
Vest, George, 171, 172, 174
Viele, Egbert, 47, 50, 52

Walden (Thoreau), 35, 36, 211
Walks and Talks of an American Farmer in
    England (Olmsted), 41, 42
War Production Board, 203
Washburn, Henry Dana, 121–23, 125–26,
    131–34
Washburn-Langford Expedition, 121, 123,
    129, 132–34, 145
Watkins, Carleton E., 64, 65
Weed, Charles Leander, 63, 64
A Week on the Concord and Merrimack
    Rivers (Thoreau), 35
The White Hills (King), 62

Whitman, Walt, 8, 18, 56, 81
Whitney, Josiah, xviii, xix, 36–38, 87–89, 102, 111
Wilderness Act, 208, 209
Wilderness and the American Mind (Nash), 9
wilderness park, 93, 94, 96, 101, 197
wildlife, 87, 168, 170, 175–76, 201, 203–4
wild parks, 27, 28, 205, 211
Williams, George H., 104, 105
World's Columbian Exposition, 189

Yard, Robert Sterling, 206–7
Yellowstone country, xiv, 115, 116, 118, 143, 149
Yellowstone expeditions, 120–22, 142, 143
Yellowstone Lake, 132, 146, 147, 148, 152, 212
Yellowstone National Park, xiii, xiv, xviii; annual appropriation for, 169; and anti-wolf policy, 204, 205; campfire myth of, F11, 94, 115, 120, 121, 130–32; concessions at, 160, 165, 168, 170, 171; early visitors to, 115–20; federal ownership of, 158–59; first car allowed into, 174; as the first national park, 115, 130; first superintendent for, 128, 168; and forest fires, 169–70; hot springs and geysers in, 116–19, 147; and Lacey Act, 173–74; legislative history of, 154–57; military rule of, 173, 174, 175; poaching at, 165, 168–70, 173; and self-sustainability issue, 165–66, 169; specimens collected from, 153; and territorial system issues, 176–77; thermal features of, 117, 118, 119, 147; wildlife protection at, 175
Yellowstone River, 115, 117, 118, 127, 146
Yellow Wolf, 175
Yosemite and the Mariposa Grove: A Preliminary Report, 1865 (Olmsted), xvii–xix, 36, 86
Yosemite Act, 106, 157
Yosemite Park bill, 65–66, 68–70, 78, 151
Yosemite Park Commission, xvii, 81, 98, 102, 107, 109–11
Yosemite Valley: becomes national park, xvii–xviii, 73, 200; bifurcated status of, 112–13; building a railroad into, 111–12; concessionaires' issues at, 107–8; description of, 86; and foliage issues, 107; and George Williams, 104, 105; hands-off approach for, 84–85; hotel built in, 108; and James Hutchings, 101–6; and John Muir, 36–37; management of, 82–90; and private speculation, 103, 105; publicity about, 63–66; report on, xvii–xix, 81–82, 104, 110, 187–88, 202–3; and Schuyler Colfax, 80; sheep grazing in, 108, 109, 110; squatters in, 93, 101, 148; "sublimity" of, 17; survey of, 102; and Thomas King, 62–63; views about, 79. *See also* Yosemite Park bill

Zumwalt, Daniel K., 112